EVALUATION RESEARCH METHODS:
A Basic Guide

SAGE FOCUS EDITIONS

Evaluation Research Methods:
A Basic Guide

edited by
Leonard Rutman

 **SAGE PUBLICATIONS**   Beverly Hills   London

For information address:

SAGE PUBLICATIONS, INC.
275 South Beverly Drive
Beverly Hills, California 90212

SAGE PUBLICATIONS LTD
28 Banner Street
London EC1Y 8QE, England

Printed in the United States of America

Library of Congress Cataloging in Publication Data

Main entry under title:

Evaluation research methods.

   (Sage focus editions ; v. 3)
   1. Evaluation research (Social action programs)
—Addresses, essays, lectures.
I. Rutman, Leonard. II. Series.
H62.E85   300'.1'8   77-17264
ISBN 0-8039-0907-1
ISBN 0-8039-0908-X pbk.

FIRST PRINTING

CONTENTS

ACKNOWLEDGMENTS

Welfare Grants Division of National Health and Welfare funded the Evaluation Research Training Institute at Carleton University, Ottawa. Each of the contributors to this book conducted a training session and prepared articles which covered the content of the session. Special thanks to Welfare Grants Division for supporting the project and making this book possible.

I am grateful to Tom Cook who reviewed the draft manuscript thoroughly and made valuable suggestions for improving the book. Jeff Greenberg and Marty Abrams provided useful assistance on specific chapters. The preparation of this book entailed close collaboration with the authors. I wish to thank them for their excellent cooperation in the writing of their chapters. Finally, I wish to acknowledge the secretarial work of Reta Affleck, Beverley Goold, and Doreen Hallam.

INTRODUCTION

The sociopolitical context within which evaluation research is planned and conducted poses numerous constraints on undertaking rigorous scientific research to measure program effectiveness. Various groups often have an interest in the program under study, including legislators, funding bodies, administrators, practitioners, clients, and the general public. Among these groups there may well be different interests in the evaluative study, especially if the results are expected to influence decisions about the termination, continuation, or expansion of programs. It is within such a context that the focus of the evaluation is defined, the variables for inclusion in the study are identified, the design is determined, and the findings considered for utilization.

Numerous issues other than the technical ones of research design and data collection instruments confront the evaluator. It is first necessary to make some sense out of the program which is to be evaluated. Inevitably, the evaluator inherits the problems of the budgeting, planning, and management processes. The program is often poorly articulated. The goals and expected effects are generally vague and stated in a rhetorical manner. Causal assumptions linking the program to the goals and effects are usually questionable, because they are either not explicit or not plausible. These issues of program evaluability must be dealt with and resolved to ensure the conduct of an appropriate evaluation that can be used for program planning and development. This requires collaboration with program administrators and personnel.

The people with whom the evaluator must collaborate, administrators and staff, are often hesitant about having an evaluation of their program. The administrator naturally fears the shortcomings which the study could reveal. In addition, there is a concern over the disruption that the research may have on the provision of service and the burden that it will place on the staff. Since it is the administrator, not the evaluator, who usually controls the operation of the program, cooperation is required to properly conduct the evaluation. Agreements must be secured about program implementation and modifications which are required by the evaluation. Administrative support is necessary to ensure that the program is implemented in the prescribed manner, that the program does not change direction during the experimental period, and that the staff fulfill their obligations to the research (e.g., recording).

Program staff have their own fears about the evaluation. Having a strong service orientation, the staff often have little understanding about the technical requirements of research or little appreciation of the benefits which could accrue from the study. Instead, they are anxious about having their practice scrutinized under the microscope of the researcher, despite assurances that the evaluation is concerned with methods of intervention and not with the work of individual practitioners. Evaluation studies can easily be sabotaged and undermined by practitioners if these issues are not adequately resolved.

There are also numerous legal and ethical constraints. The issues which get studied and the research designs used are often limited by legal requirements of statutory programs which establish the rights and requirements for certain services, including the basic entitlements. Ethical arguments also influence the design of evaluation studies, especially in regard to withholding a service from some people considered "worthy" or "needy." Legal and ethical factors operate as constraints even in instances where there is ample reason to question the value of a program.

Throughout this book, these issues are raised and the tasks in planning an evaluative study are examined with these constraints kept in mind. Technical competence in basic research methodology is obviously necessary, but not sufficient for planning and conducting evaluation research. A research design and data collection procedures which meet scientific standards may be used inappropriately to test programs which are not evaluable. The study may include irrelevant questions and miss important ones. It may be impossible or impractical to implement the proposed study in the "real world" because of the legal, ethical, and administrative constraints.

The chapters identify the practical problems which must be addressed by the evaluator in carrying out the various tasks in planning an evaluation design. Since evaluation research relies on the techniques and procedures of basic research methodology, these are dealt with in the book. It is impossible, however, to give detailed attention to basic social research methodology in a book on evaluation research. There are numerous research texts available which can provide the interested reader with a more extensive discussion of these issues. This book emphasizes the conceptual and methodological issues which are more peculiar to the conduct of evaluations which attempt to determine and account for the effectiveness of programs.

The articles have been written in a prescriptive manner, providing specific direction for planning an evaluation study. Admittedly, in a relatively new discipline such as evaluation research, there are different points of view on what constitutes the important issues and on the appropriateness of solutions. There is the need to debate contentious issues in order to advance the state of the art. This book, however, does not serve as a forum for this debate. Instead, it aims to provide concrete directions for use in planning evaluation studies.

Illustrations from evaluations across a variety of health, education, and social programs have been used extensively. These illustrations should aid the reader in understanding the conceptual and method-ological issues. In addition, they serve as examples on the feasibility of undertaking certain tasks and resolving specific issues.

The chapters in this book focus on major steps in planning an evaluation study. For each step, numerous tasks are identified and discussed. This is a conceptually useful framework for organizing the content of the book. The reader should recognize, however, that in practice the evaluator does not simply move from one step to the next. For example, although the topic on the utilization of findings is dealt with in the latter part of the book, in practice this issue is dealt with in the initial stages. At the very beginning, attention is paid to involving decision makers, planning for the dissemination of the report, and considering other ways of increasing the likelihood that the findings will be utilized. Similarly, data analysis issues are considered in the earlier steps of developing data collection instruments and the research design. In other words, the resolution of particular tasks must be viewed in relation to the whole endeavor.

An edited book has the benefit of including contributions by leading specialists in the field. To take full advantage of such writings, it is important to assure some integration of the pieces. To a large extent this was accomplished by providing the authors clear directions about the content that they were expected to cover in their chapter. Further integration is provided through the first chapter, "Planning an Evaluation Study," which provides an overview of the topics covered in the book. In addition, a brief preface to each chapter provides important linkages.

Carleton University   —*Leonard Rutman*

This chapter discusses the implications of the proposed definition of evaluation research, making explicit its underlying orientation. The evaluation study is expected to critically and rigorously examine the program's operation and account for the outcomes (goals and other effects, whether intended or unintended). The evaluator's role is seen, first and foremost, as a social scientist rather than as a technician. Therefore, while the evaluator attempts to accommodate the information needs of decision makers, an attempt should be made to include the concerns of others interested in the program as well as issues which have practical or theoretical significance. In many instances, this will produce a study which examines the program's potentially negative effects or challenges its fundamental assumptions. It may be difficult to include questions in the evaluation which are not of immediate and practical concern to those who fund the study or administer the program. Nevertheless, the evaluator is encouraged to push for the inclusion of critical questions and not to simply provide technical services. If an evaluator does so, the evaluation can serve as the basis of accountability to a wider audience.

The growing interest in evaluation research is related to the contribution it is expected to make toward improved planning, better management, and greater accountability. While there are many types of studies which can be used for the purposes of planning and management, effectiveness evaluations are usually required as the basis for accountability. Yet such studies make stringent assumptions about preconditions: (1) that the program is clearly articulated; (2) that the goals and effects are clearly specified: and (3) that the causal assumptions appear plausible. This chapter spells out the nature of these preconditions and their rationale.

The initial challenge confronting the evaluator is to determine whether the program adequately meets the preconditions for effective-

ness evaluations. In so doing, the evaluator can avoid doing inappropriate effectiveness studies of programs which are not evaluable. Two procedures are suggested for determining program evaluability: an evaluability assessment and formative research. These procedures are briefly summarized here but are the focus for the following two chapters. This chapter also provides an overview of the rest of the book by identifying the tasks and issues in planning an evaluation study to measure program effectiveness.

1

PLANNING AN EVALUATION STUDY

Leonard Rutman

In the past several years, there has been a growing interest in evaluation research. Much of the impetus for doing evaluation studies has come from organizations which hold social programs accountable for their performance. In these instances, evaluation research is expected to provide data on the "value for money" to supplement the long-standing concern with financial accountability. This growing interest in evaluation research appears to have been spurred by the skepticism about social programs which has resulted, at least to some extent, from the numerous reports that have shown the ineffectiveness of many large-scale interventions and the practice of different professions. Viewed from a somewhat different perspective, however, evaluation research is becoming increasingly accepted as a useful input for planning and policy-making. In this regard, it is felt that some of the impediments to rational decision-making can be, at least in part, overcome through the conduct and use of evaluation research.

There are varying viewpoints about the nature of evaluation research and the purposes which such studies are expected to serve. While there is general agreement over the more technical issues of research methodology, there are differences over the sociopolitical questions, such as: evaluation for what? and evaluation for whom? The author's own viewpoint on these questions will be made explicit in the discussion which attempts to provide definitional clarity to the term and in the elaboration of the issues and tasks entailed in the process of planning and conducting evaluation research, and considering the findings for use in social planning or policy-making.

DEFINING EVALUATION RESEARCH

The definition used by the author is: "Evaluation research is, first and foremost, a process of applying scientific procedures to accumulate reliable and valid evidence on the manner and extent to which specified activities produce particular effects or outcomes."[1] Attention will now be focused on the components of this definition to reveal the perspective taken toward the methodology and purposes of evaluation research.

USE OF SCIENTIFIC PROCEDURES

The first part of the definition emphasizes the importance of scientific procedures to collect reliable and valid evidence. There is general agreement among writers that evaluation research is expected to adhere as closely as possible to currently accepted standards of research methodology. There are inevitably some constraints which necessitate compromises in the "ideal" design and data collection procedures, including, among others: cost, administrative factors, legal requirements, and ethical considerations. Emphasis is nevertheless placed on approaching the highest practical degree of scientific adequacy. It is in the context of such constraints that attention is paid to maximizing the rigor in dealing with such basic methodological issues as reliability and validity, sampling, randomization, research design, and data analysis.

FOCUS ON PROCESS AND OUTCOMES

An important component of the proposed definition is that attention is paid to the manner and extent to which the specified activities produce the measured results. Too often evaluation research focuses solely on outcomes. From such studies, it is impossible to account for the results and similar efforts cannot be replicated elsewhere if the results are positive and avoided if the results are negative. If evaluation research is to shed light on factors that succeed or fail to produce measured results, then special attention must be paid to the program components and processes and not solely to outcomes. The implication of placing emphasis on the program's process is that a major task in the planning of an evaluation study entails the conceptualization of the program in operational terms so that it can be monitored, not only to provide a description of the program's operation and thereby determine whether it was implemented in the intended manner, but in addition, to make inferences about the outcomes on the basis of program attributes.

NOT RESTRICTING OUTCOMES TO GOALS

Most definitions of evaluation research mention that programs are measured against their stated goals. Inherent in these definitions is the notion that there is some goal which has a value attached to it and the task of evaluative research is, therefore, to first identify and then determine the program's degree of success in attaining the goal. Following this perspective, evaluation researchers often limit their attention to only those outcomes which fall under the stated goals. This places restrictions on the scope of the research because such an approach can miss latent goals (i.e., those which are not formally stated), unintended consequences, as well as other anticipated effects.

Indicating that the outcomes studied in an evaluation should not be restricted to stated goals is not meant to underplay the importance of identifying, operationalizing, and measuring accomplishment of program goals. Special attention needs to be focused on the goals to ensure their inclusion in the evaluation. In addition, however, other possible consequences should be identified and included in the research. These additional outcomes could be derived from other related research, logic, or hunches drawn from experience with particular programs.

CONSIDERING INFORMATION NEEDS OF DECISION MAKERS

Included in many definitions of evaluation research is some statement about the ultimate purpose for which the study is conducted—i.e., to assist decision makers in their efforts at program development and policy-making. Such a viewpoint is reflected in a definition proposed by Alkin: "Evaluation is the process of ascertaining the decision areas of concern, selecting appropriate information, and collecting and analyzing information in order to report summary data useful to decision makers in selecting among alternatives."[2]

The dilemma which arises is the extent to which the questions examined in an evaluative study are restricted to the information needs of decision makers. Certainly attempts should be made to identify the main concerns of decision makers for possible inclusion in the research. In addition, however, the researcher may wish to pursue questions of a theoretical nature, shed light on issues where it is unlikely that short-term policy change will be undertaken, and challenge fundamental assumptions underlying the program which is being evaluated. Merely because data on such issues may not be of immediate importance or even wanted by decision makers should not preclude the possibility of pursuing them in the evaluation, particularly if the researcher takes a critical posture as a social scientist vis-à-vis the program being evaluated rather than as a technician whose work is totally constrained by the wishes of decision makers.

In summary, the proposed definition of evaluation research, like most other definitions, places major emphasis on the use of generally accepted scientific procedures to collect reliable and valid data. This definition stressed that evaluations should focus on program processes, and not merely on effects or outcomes. To broaden the range of questions posed in an evaluation study, the proposed definition does not place restrictions on considering consequences of a program which fall outside the formally stated goals. Similarly, the questions pursued by the evaluation research need not be constrained by the information needs of decision makers.

PRECONDITIONS FOR TESTING PROGRAMS

Evaluation research is normally viewed as a procedure for testing the effectiveness and efficiency of particular programs. Such a perspective, however, assumes the existence of an evaluable program which meets certain preconditions: (1) a clearly articulated program; (2) clearly specified goals and/or effects; and (3) a rationale linking the program to the goals and/or effects. These preconditions should normally be developed through program planning and management. Yet it is rare to find programs which adequately meet these preconditions. It is suggested that evaluation researchers address these issues and refuse to be coopted in testing programs for their effectiveness and efficiency when they are not evaluable. The premature testing of programs which are not evaluable is likely to produce irrelevant studies which have little use for program planning, management, or as a basis of accountability.

This section will elaborate the reasons for insisting on the presence of these preconditions prior to testing programs. A major implication arising from this discussion is the need to determine if a program is evaluable. In those instances where these preconditions are missing or inadequately developed, the evaluative researchers must collaborate with planners and managers in the process of articulating the program, specifying the goals and other effects, and analyzing the assumed causal assumptions. In the following section there will be a discussion of some approaches which can be undertaken to develop an evaluable program.

A CLEARLY ARTICULATED PROGRAM

Program labels such as community health centers, new careers, Headstart, or multiservice centers are so vague and/or include such a wide variety of approaches that there is no common or uniform meaning to these terms. It is essential to be sure that everyone refers to the same thing when applying a label to a particular program. Unless there is some reasonably coherent and accurate definition of the program, it is not possible to attribute the measured results to a clearly recognized intervention. Instead, conclusions can only be drawn about relatively undefined inputs. In these instances, there is no direction for replicating programs with any assurance that the same "thing" is being reproduced. Also, it is difficult to determine whether the program which is evaluated differs in a major way from other similar services. The articulation of a program can reveal the nature of the service, at least in terms of an "ideal" description.

Even if a program is clearly defined, there is no assurance that it is implemented in the prescribed manner. However, an articulated program can be conceptualized in measurable terms and ultimately data could be collected on the program's operation. From such data, the program's actual implementation could be determined. There are numerous benefits which can be realized. Such monitoring often reveals problems in the conduct of a program. In addition, having data on the program's actual operation can assist researchers to avoid attributing effects to a program which never really took place, which operated at a low level of competence, or which was implemented in such a different manner that it hardly represents the type of program which is supposedly being tested. Thus, it is possible to determine whether the results were confounded by having a poorly administered program and not due to something inherent about the program itself. The articulation and monitoring of a program's operation also provide a basis for attributing the measured results to attributes of the program. In this regard, the ideal is to determine whether particular components of a program are effective, including the extent to which a particular style or manner of implementation influences the outcomes. If this was effectively pursued, then there would be some direction provided for future research in which program attributes are purposefully varied or manipulated to determine outcomes. Moreover, the likelihood of using the findings is greater when data are available on specific program components rather than on complex global programs.

CLEARLY SPECIFIED GOALS AND/OR EFFECTS

Programs are generally expected to meet certain needs or to solve particular problems. It is common for them to state their mission according to goals. In addition, there may be implicit goals which the program pursues but which are not formally stated. Although it is assumed that planners and managers have paid attention to goal specification, it is rare to find programs where this has been properly undertaken. Instead, it is common to find goals which are: vaguely stated in global or long-range terms, contradictory, or unrelated to the program's activities. Since goals serve as the criteria of program success, they must be clearly specified for the purpose of developing measures. If goal specification has not been adequately handled through the planning and management processes, then the evaluative researcher must assume the responsibility for undertaking the necessary collaborative activities to assure the clear specification of goals.

Planners, managers, and evaluators can benefit from the process of goal specification. Goals provide a basis for determining what particular aspect of an overall problem is given priority; reflecting the accepted diagnosis or causal explanation of the social problems; identifying the ideological bias upon which the program is based; and sorting out conflicting or competing goals. Moreover, clearly specified goals provide the basis for holding programs accountable.

The process of goal specification provides some assurance that crucial variables have been identified and will be included in the evaluation. The failure to go through this process presents a potential danger of not including important variables in the research, simply because there was no effort to identify program goals.

The above comments reflect a goal-oriented approach to evaluation research. Yet there are other viewpoints, particularly by those who prefer a systems approach[3] and by proponents of goal-free evaluation.[4] The arguments which are posed against goal-oriented research include, among others: (1) the explicit service goal is only one goal of a program and there are other important goals that are concerned with survival (e.g., acquisition and maintenance of necessary resources, the coordination of activities, and the adaptation to internal and environmental demands) which should serve as criteria of effectiveness; (2) there is great difficulty in specifying the "real" goals from those goal statements which represent political rhetoric, provide justification for funding requests, mobilize support from among different constituencies, and legitimate the program; (3) goals are forever changing, either because the mandate allows an innovative program to "wing it" or because there is adaptation and change in response to internal and environmental demands; and (4) the exclusive focus on goals means that side-effects are ignored in the evaluation.

All of the above-mentioned arguments against goal-oriented research raise valid issues and difficulties. However, these points do not necessarily lead to the conclusion that the identification and specification of goals for the purpose of evaluation should be abandoned. Rather, a major implication which arises is that an exclusive focus on formally stated goals is by itself inadequate. The task of the evaluator is therefore to also identify latent goals as well as anticipated effects (which are either intended and/or unintended) for inclusion in the evaluation. This requires the evaluator to identify the claims of various parties who have gone on record as saying that the program produces particular effects (negative or positive). The dilemma in casting the net so widely in identifying a complete set of possible outcomes is that this can raise unrealistic expectations for the evaluation study. In general, under constraints of time and resources, the more questions that are asked in a study, the lower the quality of the answers to any question. Therefore, a process of setting priorities is necessary to determine the most crucial questions for inclusion in the evaluation.

LINKING RATIONALE

Programs assume, either implicitly or explicitly, a rationale suggesting the reasons why the program is expected to reach the stated goals or produce the identified effects. The justification for identifying this linking rationale is to determine whether a program is evaluable. First, some programs state goals toward which there is no actual effort directed. In these situations, programs are held accountable for goals which are merely stated but not actually pursued, with the predictable results of being ineffective vis-à-vis those goals. Thus, the first task is to determine whether there is any link between program efforts and outcomes.

Second, even if there appears to be some activity directed toward the specified goals and/or effects, an analysis of the problem condition which the program aims to resolve may reveal that the program constitutes an inappropriate or inadequate response. This is particularly evident in the evaluations of programs which assume that the cause of

major social problems is the pathology of individuals.[5] In these instances, the programs appear to be based on either inadequate or
erroneous explanations of the problems which they address. A somewhat related issue concerning the linking rationale is whether the
program (such as manpower training) has made inflated promises in the
form of long-range or ultimate goals (e.g., reducing unemployment)
when it can realistically only accomplish more immediate goals (e.g.,
the attainment of vocational skills). Thus, programs should not assume
that the accomplishment of immediate and modest goals will necessarily lead to the attainment of ultimate goals. The evaluation study must
therefore include the immediate goals in the research and attempts to
test propositions about the connection (i.e., validity assumptions) between immediate, intermediate, and ultimate goals. Otherwise, the
danger is that the evaluation may measure unachievable goals or expected results while failing to include those which are in reach of the
program.

The focus on the linking rationale should reveal whether the program is evaluable. It is necessary to determine whether the rationale
connecting the program to the goals or expected outcomes is sufficiently sound to merit an evaluation. Where the testing for program effectiveness and efficiency is premature, it may be apparent that it is first
necessary to modify the program or change the goals and expected
results.

In summary, the preconditions for evaluating the effectiveness and
efficiency of programs include: (1) a clearly articulated program; (2)
clearly specified goals and expected effects; and (3) a rationale linking
the program to the goals and expected effects. If these preconditions
are absent and the program is nevertheless evaluated, then it is likely
that the study will be inappropriate and largely irrelevant for the
purposes of planning, budgeting, and managing programs. In these
instances, there may be doubts and questions about what took place
when the program was implemented. Data may be collected on goals or
expected effects which are so vague that the data have little meaning.
Finally, there may be a failure to recognize the weakness of the
rationale linking the program to the goals and expected effects so that
the pitfalls of the evaluation could have been avoided through prior
analysis.

DEVELOPING EVALUABLE MODELS

The previous discussion provided the rationale for insisting on the
presence of the preconditions for an evaluable program before studying

its effectiveness and efficiency. At this point, an attempt will be made to identify procedures for determining the evaluability of a program and for developing an evaluable program model. First, there will be some discussion of an evaluability assessment involving the examination of program documents and discussions between the evaluation researcher and program personnel. Second, to supplement the evaluability assessment, formative research will be presented as a strategy of collecting data about the program's operation as a means of further identifying and elaborating each of the preconditions. The evaluability assessment and formative research should produce the necessary groundwork for the more detailed and formal planning of an evaluation study.

EVALUABILITY ASSESSMENT

Wholey and colleagues at the Urban Institute in Washington have done extensive work on developing procedures for an evaluability assessment.[6] The main thrust of an evaluability assessment is an analysis of the decision-making system to be served by an evaluation study and clarifying the questions to be answered. This involves a sequential series of steps which bound and define the program from two perspectives, that of the user and that of the evaluator.

The first step entails the identification of the primary intended users of the planned evaluation and from their point of view, determining what activities and objectives constitute the program. The second step involves collecting information on the intended program activities, goals, objectives, and the assumed causal relationships. Such information is located in documents and through interviews with program managers and other users of the information. The third step includes a synthesis of the information which has been collected, resulting in the development of a "rhetorical program model" which is a flow model or models depicting intended resource inputs, intended program activities, intended impacts, and the assumed causal links. In the fourth step, an attempt is made to determine the extent to which the program, as represented by the rhetorical model, is sufficiently unambiguous that evaluation is feasible and potentially useful. Two criteria are applied: (1) Have the intended users of evaluation agreed on a set of measures of program activities and program objectives? (2) Have the intended users of the evaluation agreed on a set of plausible, testable assumptions linking program activities to program outcomes and impacts? The product of this step is an evaluable program model or models depicting only those program activities and objectives for which there exists agreed-upon measures of success and testable causal relationships. The fifth step involves the feedback of the results of the analysis to the program managers/intended users and the identification of program components and objectives that are amenable to evaluation.

FORMATIVE RESEARCH

Whereas the evaluability assessments address the preconditions for evaluation research through an examination of documents and collaboration with the intended users (i.e., managers and policy makers), formative research pursues the same concerns by collecting data on the program's operation. In situations where the preconditions for evaluation research are absent or inadequately developed, there are several reasons for supplementing the evaluability assessment with formative research. First, even if the evaluability assessment may produce the best effort of management or policy makers to conceptualize the program, its goals and outcomes, and the causal assumptions or linking rationale, formative research can be used to verify their understanding. In so doing, there is a check on the accuracy of the intended users' perceptions. Second, the evaluability assessment is likely to reveal difficulties that managers face in actually conceptualizing these preconditions. Formative research documents what takes place when the program is operating and can therefore inform management about the program's operation and some of its consequences, thereby providing some basis for shifting or changing the program as well as revising the goals and expected outcomes. Such data therefore can contribute toward the development of an evaluable program. Third, the discussion on the nature of evaluation research emphasized the point that evaluation research need not be restricted to measuring only those outcomes which fall under the formally stated goals. Formative research can discover latent goals and side-effects which may not have been identified in the evaluability assessment.

Formative research relies upon available information on the program and uses a variety of data-gathering procedures to describe the program's operation, to identify the effects produced by the program, and to determine the nature of the problem(s) being addressed. Attention can be paid to the influence of the context and constraints of the program on its operation and impacts. Finally, formative research can be undertaken to observe the effects of different means of implementing the program in order to modify and develop the program.[7]

In summary, both the evaluability assessment and formative research aim to determine the evaluability of a program. Whereas the evaluability assessment addresses the preconditions for evaluation research through examination of documents and discussions with the intended users, formative research focuses on the same concerns by examining the operation of the program. The results of both the evaluability assessment and formative research represent efforts which contribute toward the planning of the evaluation research which is ultimately concerned with program effectiveness and efficiency.

PLANNING THE FORMAL
EVALUATION STUDY: AN OVERVIEW

To provide an overview of the considerations in planning an evaluation study, various steps can be identified with particular tasks. Although the delineation of such steps is useful for drawing conceptual distinctions and for organizing the discussion of numerous relevant issues, this does not imply that the planning of an evaluation entails a linear progression from one discrete step to another. In fact, since the resolution of critical issues at any one stage will often have important implications for the others, it is always necessary to keep in mind the requirements of the whole endeavor whenever particular tasks are considered.

In this discussion, it is assumed that the program is essentially evaluable. While there may still be a need to clarify and elaborate the program, goals and/or effects, and linking rationale, these preconditions should be sufficiently well-developed to enable the preparation of a study concerned with program effectiveness and efficiency. If the preconditions are absent or inadequately developed, these shortcomings become apparent when the task of specifying variables is undertaken.

DETERMINING PURPOSES OF THE EVALUATION

For any particular program, there are usually different parties who have varying interests in the program and the research which evaluates it. An initial task in the planning of an evaluation design is the identification of the varying purposes, overt and covert, of the different parties who are involved with the program and its evaluation. The pursuit of this task may be somewhat precarious, since the various parties are asked to clarify their purposes and, in addition, to reveal hidden agendas. Yet it is necessary to confront the question of purpose so that none of the parties enters the evaluative study blindly.

The overt purposes for conducting evaluation research usually center around the need for data to hold programs accountable and to inform decision-making in planning and management. As the specific nature of these purposes is clarified, then the evaluation can be planned to produce the needed information.

There are, however, numerous covert purposes for undertaking evaluative research. Suchman has termed studies guided by hidden motivations "pseudoevaluations." Included in his list of such misuses of evaluation are: (1) "eyewash"—a deliberate focus on the surface appearance of a program to make it look good; (2) "whitewash"—an attempt to cover up program failures during the investigation; (3) "submarine"—the political use of research to destroy a program; (4) "posture"—evaluation research as a ritual having little substance (often undertaken only because it was a condition for funding); (5) "postponement"—using evaluation to postpone needed action.[8] While these covert purposes are generally attributed to the funding organizations and program administrators, the evaluative researcher can also share these unacknowledged reasons for conducting the evaluative research.

The evaluator needs to find out who initiated the study and for what purpose. He should identify the groups who support and oppose the evaluation, including the motives for their position. The researcher should also explore the intended and/or potential use of the evaluation study. These questions are pursued in order to provide the evaluative researcher an understanding of the context within which the research will be conducted. If on the basis of this understanding the evaluator decides that he or she wishes to conduct the study, he is less likely to be used as a pawn in the pursuit of covert purposes held by funding bodies or program administrators. Moreover, he will be in a better position to anticipate problems in the planning and conduct of the research, and in the efforts to utilize the findings.

Similarly, program administrators have a legitimate reason for inquiring about the researcher's motives for conducting the study. In addition to questioning the researcher about his technical skills and orientation to evaluation research, administrators can determine the researcher's familiarity with the substantive area which is being investigated. While such an exchange between the administrator and researcher may entail a certain amount of tension, it does provide the opportunity for both to decide whether their purposes are sufficiently compatible to warrant collaboration.

Where insufficient attention is paid to the various purposes held by different parties, there is a greater chance that the study will be irrelevant and that the research effort will be detrimentally affected. Even in situations where there is essential agreement on purpose, there are bound to be numerous differences over various aspects of the evaluative study. However, agreement over the purpose of the research would presumably minimize the number of these differences and make the resolution somewhat easier. Moreover, it provides some degree of assurance that the research will address the agreed-upon purposes for the evaluation.

SPECIFICATION OF VARIABLES

As already indicated, an evaluability assessment and formative research are useful for identifying pertinent variables and their presumed causal linkages. It is rare, however, to find instances where such pre-evaluation planning occurs. Instead, researchers usually tend to launch immediately into preparing a design aimed at testing programs for their effectiveness and, in so doing, implicitly assume that the preconditions are present and adequately developed. In such situations, attention paid to articulating variables in the manner suggested in this section should reveal these shortcomings. For programs which adequately meet the preconditions, this section will provide guidelines and a framework for further specifying relevant variables.

(1) Articulating the program: To articulate the program, the question posed is: What are the components of the program? The task of articulating programs requires that the components or specific elements be identified and operationalized. For example, a legal aid clinic could include such component activities as providing: legal advice; referral to relevant agencies; consumer education; and representation at court. Each of these would then be further elaborated—for example, referral could include: suggesting places where the client can go; sending a letter of introduction; phoning on behalf of the client and making arrangements for a visit; or actually accompanying the client to the place of referral. Having specified referral in these terms, it is then possible to gather data and determine the nature of the referral process which takes place in practice and the consequences (e.g., satisfaction or receipt of service) from each type of referral.

This emphasis on articulating program components reflects a preferred strategy for evaluation research which is commonly called component testing. This involves efforts to determine the effectiveness of particular program components or activities and differs from project evaluations, which attempt to determine the effectiveness of a cluster of program activities which fall under the rubric of a project. For example, in examining Headstart, component testing would attempt to determine the outcomes for such program activities as particular approaches to developing linguistic skills, or special nutritional programs. Project evaluations would be concerned with drawing global conclusions about specific projects that encompass numerous program components. This can be expanded to national program evaluations which draw conclusions about numerous projects belonging to a national program (such as Headstart). Component testing is a means of evaluating a specific project or national programs since the focus is on activities which cut across projects. There is greater generalizability from component testing, and it is more within the reach of current research methodology than is project evaluation, or studies of complex national programs.

(2) Specifying goals and/or effects: The ultimate aim of evaluation research is to determine the consequences of program interventions. If goals are stated and the resulting effects are in this direction, then the program is considered more or less successful. The goals accepted for the evaluation are usually those which are stated by program administrators. However, since there are different groups who have an interest in the program and whose goals may differ, the acceptance of one group's goals for inclusion in the evaluation may be at the expense of excluding the goals of another group. Therefore, there is a dilemma as to whose goals are to be included in the evaluation. This is related to another issue which has already been indicated: There are expected outcomes of a program which do not represent goals. The dilemma of deciding whose goals to include is therefore resolved by the identification of all pertinent effects, including goals stated by different groups. The difficult task is then to delimit the study to the most important ones.

The first task is the identification of formally stated program goals as well as latent goals and other expected effects or outcomes. There are various approaches for pursuing these tasks. First, a search can be made of documents such as budget requests, minutes of policy-making groups, briefs, and available publications. Second, interviews can be conducted with the various groups interested in the program. Third, theory can be drawn upon to identify possible consequences. Fourth, research which has been conducted on issues relevant to the program or evaluations of similar programs can be examined to identify outcomes for inclusion in the design.

Having identified the goals and/or effects, the task is to ensure that they are specific. Too often goals are stated in such vague and global terms as improving social functioning, rehabilitation of offenders, or community betterment. Instead, efforts should be made to state clear and concrete goals, such as holding a job, increased earnings, or improved grades in school. The point being made is that the subsequent task of developing reliable and valid measures is made easier if goals and/or effects are clearly specified.

(3) **Specifying antecedent variables**: In addition to articulating the program, data must be collected on the antecedent variables—those factors that are independent of the program but constitute the context and constraints within which the program operates. To identify antecedent variables, the question posed is: What are the characteristics of the clients (individuals, families, or communities), workers, organizations, and policies which are the focus of change and/or constitute the context within which change is expected to occur? In deciding what specific information should be collected, there are guidelines which can be used. First, what information is needed for purely descriptive purposes to provide a background understanding of the project—participants, personnel, policy, organizational characteristics and community context? Second, what factors are likely to influence outcomes—e.g., social class of the clients, experience of the workers, organizational climate? Third, what is the nature of the problem which brings clients to the service (e.g., alcoholism, unemployment, child abuse, criminal behavior)? These data are useful not only to describe the program's focus, but in addition, they serve as a baseline measure to determine whether the problem was resolved. In other words, having collected such data before involvement with the program and at a subsequent follow-up, change in these problem areas can be determined.

(4) **Specifying intervening variables**: There are often factors which have an important influence in facilitating or impeding goal accomplishment. These are referred to as intervening variables and, in identifying them, it is necessary to ask: After the implementation of the program, what are the factors that may facilitate or impede goal accomplishment? It is important to identify intervening variables because by understanding their influence, it is possible to maximize the program's benefit. This can be illustrated with reference to training provided to staff of penal institutions. The training may attempt to sensitize the staff to problems of inmates (e.g., alcohol or drugs) and provide suggestions for dealing with them. The training may be successful in that the staff learned the necessary skills. Yet the effects of the training can be facilitated or impeded by organizational climate—i.e., where the

organization is supportive, the lessons learned can be applied and perhaps the benefits realized. If the effects of intervening variables can be determined, then planning can include consideration of those factors which facilitate goal accomplishment. Intervening variables can be identified through an examination of the theoretical link between the program and goals, from an analysis of related research, and from hunches expressed by different groups which have some knowledge of or interest in the program.

Having specified the relevant variables, it is necessary to identify the linkages among the antecedent variables, the program, the intervening variables, and the goals and/or effects. In the process, an impact model is developed which makes explicit the causal assumptions and which provides the basis for questioning their plausibility. Is the program effort being directed at the stated goals and/or expected effects? This question grounds the more academic exercise of conceptualizing the impact model to reality. If nothing is being done to pursue certain goals or expected effects, then why should the program be held accountable for their accomplishment? Yet goals are often stated even though the program does not appear to be doing anything to pursue them. If an evaluation still measures the program in terms of such rhetorical goals, then negative results are predictable. Where it is discovered that there are goals for which no program effort is being directed, then two alternatives are open: Either those goals should be dropped or the program modified so as to pursue them.

Once the nature of the effort directed at the goals and/or effects is identified, the next question is: What is the basis for stating that the program can potentially accomplish the stated goals? It is useful to raise this concern because it is common to have evaluations of programs which are relatively puny interventions yet expected to accomplish ambitious results. The answer to this question lies in the analysis of the appropriateness of the rationale and assumptions underlying the program. In so doing, reliance is placed on available theory and research as well as hunches drawn from experience in the field.

This section on specifying variables included steps which provide guidelines for identifying variables for possible inclusion in the evaluation design. The decision about which variables should actually be included is facilitated by drawing linkages among the variables, revealing the rationale underlying these linkages, and ascertaining the soundness or plausibility of the rationale. Thus, this stage produces a model of the program which includes all of the variables for which measures must be developed.

DEVELOPMENT OF MEASURES

The previous discussion dealt with guidelines and procedures for identifying and specifying variables for inclusion in the evaluation study. The focus now shifts from the earlier discussion on "what to measure" to "how to measure." In this section, attention will be paid to: (1) the selection of indicators for the specified variables; (2) issues of reliability; and, (3) validity. Each of these concerns is sufficiently complex to warrant a more detailed discussion than is possible in this chapter. Nevertheless, an attempt will be made to at least identify and clarify the pertinent issues.

(1) Indicators. Even for relatively specific variables whose meaning is generally understood, there are alternative indicators which can be chosen for the purpose of measurement. For example, social class can be determined according to such indicators as income level, occupation, a combination of occupation and education, the respondents' perceptions of their own class position, or relationship to the means of production. Each of these indicators reflects differences in ideological perspectives and theoretical positions. Nevertheless, researchers must select indicators which are most relevant to the purposes of the evaluation and the characteristics of the program.

(2) Reliability. In considering reliability, the concern is how much of the variation in the measured phenomenon is due to inconsistencies in measurement, rather than in the phenomenon being measured. Can the measure be depended upon to secure consistent and stable results? These questions are important because there are numerous factors which result in random error—i.e., differences in results obtained at different times appear to follow no logically consistent pattern. Among the sources of unreliability are: (1) respondent's or subject's mood, fatigue, or motivation which affect his or her responses; (2) observer's measurement, which can be influenced by the same factors affecting the subject's responses; (3) the conditions under which the measurement is made, which may produce responses which do not reflect the "true" score; (4) problems with the measurement instrument, such as poorly worded questions in an interview; and (5) processing problems such as simple coding or mechanical errors.[9]

The dilemma in determining the reliability of an instrument centers around the problem of actual change. A measure which produces different results upon repetition may indicate that change has taken place and not that the measure is unreliable. This is especially problematic for phenomena that are highly variable. The assumption which is made in determining reliability is that the characteristic being measured is stable and that there is a "true" value or score about which the data fluctuate because of chance errors.

Researchers must address the above-mentioned sources of unreliability in the planning of an evaluation study. Wherever possible, available tests can be used which have a known degree of reliability. Where new tests or instruments are developed, checks can be made on their stability and consistency. Caution can be taken in administering the tests to provide a conducive setting and to avoid fatigue or other factors which could affect the respondents and observers. The sources of unreliability stemming from the processing of data require close attention through supervision and cross-checks.

(3) Validity. Validity refers to the degree to which the instrument succeeds in measuring what it purports to measure. With validity, there is concern with the "meaning" of the measure which in turn is determined by the "purpose" for which the measure was designed. While reliability is a necessary condition for validity, it is not sufficient to ensure validity. In contrast to reliability, which concerns itself with random error, validity reflects those errors which are systematic or constant. Such errors are a form of "bias" and slant the results in a particular direction, rather than at random.

To clarify the term, a brief description of some of the different types of validity will be provided along with suitable illustrations. Face validity, a commonly used criteria, is justified on the grounds that it is an apparently obvious (on the face of it) way of measuring the phenomenon of interest. For example, an arithmetic test which deals with numerical and quantitative concepts is justified as valid because on the face of it there is a measurement of arithmetic skills.

Content validity concerns the extent to which a test encompasses a reasonable sample of the totality of responses or behaviors which characterize the variable of interest. In testing children's speaking skills, for example, the following elements can be rated: overall expressive ability, grammatical errors, rhythm and intonation, enunciation, time of production, and number of words produced. If there is agreement that these measured responses adequately represent speaking skills, then the instrument can be considered to have content validity.

Criterion validity subsumes concurrent and predictive validity. Concurrent validity concerns itself with the extent to which the scores or responses from one measure correlate with a generally accepted and accurate standard. For example, different intelligence tests can be used in an evaluation. New tests to measure intelligence, which were designed for the research, could be shown to have criterion validity if they correlated highly with an established valid test.

A measure is considered to have predictive validity if it can accurately predict something that takes place in the future. Vocational aptitude tests could be considered to have predictive validity if they accurately predicted how well people would do in the vocations for which success is predicted.

ADDRESSING DESIGN CONSIDERATIONS

Evaluation research should be designed to allow dependable inferences about the "causal" relationship of the program to the measured effects. Research designs which approximate systematic experiments virtually rule out the error of attributing to the program an effect which is actually produced by some uncontrollable variables. This section will identify and briefly elaborate threats to internal validity—i.e., plausible interpretations of program effects—which must be ruled out if these effects are attributable to the program. The elements of an experimental design will be described, showing how threats to internal validity are safeguarded. This section will end with a discussion of external validity—i.e., the generalizability of findings across times, settings, and persons.

(1) Internal validity: Confidence in the causal inference that the program produced the measured effects is enhanced when plausible alternative explanations have been ruled out. These plausible alternative explanations are the threats to internal validity. In his article "Reforms as Experiments," Donald T. Campbell identified the following threats to internal validity:

(a) history: events, other than the program, occurring during the experimental time period which could account for the effects

(b) maturation: changes that occur naturally with the passage of time

(c) instability: unreliability of measures, fluctuations in sampling, autonomous instability of measures

(d) testing: the effect of taking a test upon the scores of a second testing

(e) instrumentation: changes in the measurement instrument or persons doing the measurement which may produce effects on the measured scores or results

(f) regression artifacts: pseudo-shifts occurring when persons or treatment units have been selected on the basis of their extreme scores

(g) selection: biases resulting from differential recruitment of comparison groups, affecting the results

(h) experimental mortality: the differential loss of respondents from the comparison groups

(i) selection-maturation interaction: selection biases resulting in differential rates of "maturation" or autonomous change.[10]

To illustrate the notion of threats to internal validity, the implications of selection and experimental mortality will be discussed. For example, if children who participated in some experimental projects belonged to parents who voluntarily enrolled them in an experiment, then one could argue that the measured results are due to such factors as the support and motivation of the parents or the higher scholastic aptitude of the children in the experimental group. Experimental mortality or attrition refers to the loss of subjects from the experiment, for whatever reason. This creates the problem of bias because those who drop out of the experiment are almost certainly different on a variety of characteristics from those who continue as participants.

While alternative explanations for the measured results can never be entirely eliminated, the onus is on the researcher to assemble enough logical and/or statistical evidence to show that the alternative explanations are less plausible than the main one—namely, the program. In reference to the above example, it would be necessary to determine whether the experimental and control groups did differ on such variables as support and motivation of the parents or the scholastic aptitude of the children.

In those instances where there are recognized differences between experimental and control groups, researchers often use an analysis of covariance to adjust the outcome scores for any initial difference, such as scholastic aptitude. However, Cook and Campbell find fault with this common practice, saying that in most practical situations it is the case that

> there is no way of equating non-equivalent groups via statistical procedures unless measurement is error-free. While these adjustments will reduce pretest group differences, they will not eliminate them. Consequently, any adjusted post-test differences in a covariance analysis will reflect an unknown combination of possible treatment effects and pre-test differences that have not been adjusted away.[11]

A similar line of logic is used in considering each of the threats to internal validity. Experiments include safeguards to the problems of internal validity and are, therefore, proposed as the preferred design for program evaluation. In those situations where it is both feasible and relevant to the type of information desired, a controlled experiment represents the "ideal" design for drawing inferences about the causal relationship of the program to the measured effects.

(2) **Experimental design:** An experimental design involves the establishment of experimental and control groups through random assignment. "Before" measures are taken for both groups. The experimental group is exposed to the program under study, while the control group is not. At a determined follow-up period, "after" measures are taken for both groups.

Random assignment to experimental and control groups is the essential feature of true experiments because it provides the best available assurance that the two groups are alike on both measured and unmeasured (or unknown) variables, so that the observed differences following the program can be attributed to the program with some confidence and a specific degree of precision.[12] There are numerous legal, ethical, political, and administrative constraints which often prohibit or make difficult random assignment.[13] In these situations, there are quasi-experimental designs which may be substituted.[14]

In those situations where it is both administratively feasible and relevant to the type of information desired, the model of a controlled experiment represents the ideal design for evaluative studies. Moreover, researchers should recognize the implications of any compromise in the ideal design and establish procedures for addressing threats to internal validity which arise from such compromises.

(3) **External validity.** A major concern of evaluative studies is the generalizability of findings across times, settings, and persons. Threats to external validity are those factors which limit or restrict the generalizability of the findings. Threats to external validity include:

(a) interaction of treatments: respondents experience more than one treatment

(b) interaction of testing and treatment: the pre-testing of respondents might condition the reception of the program being evaluated

(c) interaction of selection and treatment: the generalizability of the findings is restricted to the peculiar characteristics of the groups in the program—e.g., middle-class volunteers

(d) interaction of testing and setting: the generalizability of the findings to other settings[15]

There are numerous ways in which to increase external validity. Efforts to increase the heterogeneity of the subjects involved in an experimental program allow for greater generalizability about the types of people for whom the program is relevant. Attempts should be made to minimize the experimental flavor of the program and the resulting reactivity to novel projects. In this regard, the experimental project should be undertaken in a context which resembles the natural condition to which the results will be generalized. Replications at different times with different people and across settings (e.g., types of organizations or locations) also increase external validity.

Whereas an experimental design safeguards threats to internal validity, this is not necessarily the case with respect to external validity. In fact, the necessary controls for true experiments may decrease external validity. Since the main concern must be to establish the causal relationship between the program and the measured results, internal validity is given general primacy over external validity. The optimal design, however, is one having internal and external validity.

UTILIZATION OF FINDINGS

A major disappointment in the field of evaluation research is general recognition of the low utilization of findings. Researchers tend to cite the organizational and professional resistances to change as well as the "political" considerations which seem to dominate planning and policy-making. Administrators and policy makers express dissatisfaction with poor research methodology, irrelevant and inappropriate studies, the lack of comparable studies, the noncumulative body of evidence, and the lack of clear direction or recommendations emanating from the research. Other explanations for the low utilization of findings center on the interaction between researchers and policy makers or administrators—e.g., poor communication, lack of involvement in the planning and conduct of the study, poor timing of the report and inadequate dissemination. All of these factors, as well as others, deserve close attention to improve the likelihood of utilization.

A major factor which appears to be related to the nonutilization of findings is the separation of planning, management, and evaluation as processes. This is reflected in organizational structures where there are separate units or divisions that have responsibilities for these functions. To at least some extent, the failure to integrate evaluation research into the planning and management activities contributes to the conduct of inappropriate research (i.e., prematurely testing programs which are not evaluable). Such studies are therefore unlikely to be utilized for program changes. The evaluability assessment and formative research which entails the collaboration of researchers, planners, and managers, and the subsequent cooperation in the planning and conduct of the formal study, should result in more appropriate, relevant, and useful evaluations.

There is growing recognition that findings are more likely to be utilized if key decision makers are involved in the planning of the study, in discussing the findings, and in considering how the results of the research can be used to improve their programs. The planning of an evaluation requires the development of collaborative relationships which should facilitate the conduct of a relevant study and increase the likelihood that the findings will be utilized.

The planning of an evaluation should also focus on specific strategies which the researchers can use in the role of a change agent. This would contain a dissemination approach which includes published material, more direct forms of communication (e.g., conferences, workshops, etc.), and active efforts aimed at mounting replications.

CONCLUSION

This chapter has attempted to introduce the reader to the nature of evaluation research and to provide an overview of the tasks entailed in planning an evaluation study. The danger in undertaking such an ambitious task is that there is often insufficient attention paid to complex issues. The notes to this chapter can provide the interested reader greater detail. Hopefully, this chapter will be useful for organizing the relevant issues and providing some guidelines for resolving them.

NOTES

1. Leonard Rutman and Joe Hudson, "Evaluating Human Services: A Process Approach," *Social Work Processes* (eds.) Beulah R. Compton and Burt Galaway. Homewood: The Dorsey Press, 1974, p. 410.

2. Robert C. Alkin, "Evaluation Theory Development," *Evaluating Action Programs: Readings in Social Action and Evaluation* (ed.) Carol H. Weiss. Boston: Allyn & Bacon, 1972, p. 107.

3. Amitai Etzioni, "Two Approaches to Organizational Analysis: A Critique and Suggestion," *Administrative Science Quarterly* 5, 1960, pp. 257-277, and Herbert Schulberg and Frank Baker, "Program Evaluation Models and the Implementation of Findings," *Readings in Evaluation Research* (ed.) Francis G. Caro. New York: Russell Sage Foundation, 1971, pp. 72-80.

4. Susan Salasin, "Exploring Goal-Free Evaluation: An Interview with Michael Scriven," *Evaluation* 2, 1, 1974, pp. 9-16.

5. See, for example, Walter C. Bailey, "Correctional Outcome: An Evaluation of 100 Reports," *Journal of Criminal Law, Criminology and Police Science* 57, 2, June 1966, pp. 153-160; N. Caplan and S. D. Nelson, "On Being Useful: The Nature and Consequences of Psychological Research on Social Problems,"

American Psychologist 28, 1973, pp. 199-211; and Robert Martinson, "What Works? Questions and Answers about Prison Reform," *The Public Interest*, No. 35, Spring 1974, pp. 22-54.

6. Joseph S. Wholey et al., "Evaluation: When Is It Really Needed?" *Evaluation*, 2, 2, 1975, pp. 89-94.

7. See, Leonard Rutman, "Evaluating Explorations and Demonstrations for Planning in Criminal Justice," *Criminal Justice Research* (ed.) Emilio Viano. Lexington, Mass.: D. C. Heath and Company, 1976, pp. 235-246.

8. Edward Suchman, "Action for What? A Critique of Evaluative Research," in *Evaluating Action Programs* (ed.) Carol H. Weiss. Boston: Allyn & Bacon, 1972, p. 81.

9. Edward Suchman, *Evaluative Research*. New York: Russell Sage Foundation, 1967, pp. 118-119.

10. Donald T. Campbell, "Reforms as Experiments," *American Psychologist,* 24, 4, 1969, pp. 409-429. For a more recent discussion which includes an expanded list of threats to internal validity, see Thomas D. Cook and Donald T. Campbell, "The Design and Conduct of Quasi-Experiments and True Experiments in Field Settings," *Handbook of Industrial and Organizational Psychology* (ed.) Marvin D. Dunnette. Chicago: Rand McNally, 1976, pp. 223-326.

11. Thomas D. Cook and Donald T. Campbell, "The Design and Conduct of Quasi-Experiments and True Experiments in Field Settings," p. 251.

12. For an excellent book on the use of experiments for evaluating programs, see Henry W. Riecken and Robert F. Boruch, *Social Experimentation*. New York: Academic Press, 1974.

13. The commonly used arguments against randomized experiments are described and countered in Robert F. Boruch, "On Common Contentions About Randomized Field Experiments," *Experimental Testing of Public Policy* (eds.) R. F. Boruch and Henry W. Riecken. Boulder, Colorado: Westview Press, 1974, pp. 107-145.

14. D. T. Campbell and J. C. Stanley, *Experimental and Quasi-Experimental Design for Research*. Chicago: Rand McNally, 1966; and Thomas D. Cook and Donald T. Campbell, "The Design and Conduct of Quasi-Experiments and True Experiments in Field Settings."

15. Ibid.

In the previous chapter, the following preconditions of an evaluable program were elaborated: (1) clearly articulated program; (2) clearly specified goals and effects; and (3) plausible causal assumptions that link the program to the goals and effects. In Chapter 2, the evaluability assessment is presented as a means of determining which program components can be appropriately evaluated for their effectiveness.

The evaluability assessment is a procedure entailing the analysis of documents and conduct of interviews to depict a model of the program. Specific direction is provided to move from the initial "rhetorical" model of the program to an "evaluable" model. The evaluable model includes the program components as well as the goals and effects which are measurable and where the causal linkages are plausible.

The evaluability assessment provides some assurance that relevant variables are surfaced for inclusion in the evaluation. It also enables the evaluator to avoid undertaking inappropriate evaluations where the preconditions are absent. The evaluability assessment serves as an excellent opportunity for developing collaborative relationships with administrators and program staff. Such collaboration can familiarize the evaluator with the organizational context of the program, the purposes of the research, the likely uses of the evaluation, the goals of the service, and the attributes of the program. It provides greater assurance that the important concerns of program personnel will be included in the evaluation. Finally, this collaborative process can facilitate cooperation in the conduct of the research and increase the likelihood that the findings will be utilized.

2

EVALUABILITY ASSESSMENT

Joseph S. Wholey

Evaluation compares a program or set of programs, as defined by management or policy makers, with reality: the activities and effects actually occurring. The first evaluation design task, analysis of the decision-making system and clarification of the questions to be answered, is carried out to define the program to be evaluated in terms that agree with the manager's or policy maker's intentions. This task is crucial to evaluation design because it provides the criteria for deciding how much and what types of information to seek in the evaluation. At a minimum, the following factors should be specified.

- The users of the information to be obtained and its believed uses.

- The amount, type, and level of detail of information that particular users will need if they are to take actions different from those that they would probably take without the information.

AUTHOR'S NOTE: An expanded version of this chapter is in Joseph S. Wholey, *Evaluating Government Performance.* Washington: The Urban Institute, 1977 (in draft). The material in this chapter is drawn primarily from Richard E. Schmidt et al., *The Market for Evaluation Services in the Department of Health, Education, and Welfare.* The Urban Institute, May 1975; Pamela Horst et al., "Program Management and the Federal Evaluator," *Public Administration Review,* July/ August 1974, pp. 300-308; Pamela Horst et al., *Evaluation Planning at the National Institute of Mental Health.* Washington: The Urban Institute, July 1974; and Joseph S. Wholey et al., "Evaluation: When Is It Really Needed?" *Evaluation* 2, 2, 1975, pp. 89-93.

- The expected impact that would result from testing each of the causal assumptions underlying the program.

- The criteria to estimate information value when it is obtained and used.

This set of information provides the guidance required by evaluation planners in their design work. The concept of expected value of information is crucial to evaluation planning. Evaluation information can be very expensive but has the characteristic of diminishing marginal returns. In deciding which information to buy, the evaluation planner must be able to explicitly consider, and trade off, confidence and expected impact within constraints set by the use to which the evaluation will be put. Estimation of information cost and value is the mechanism for tying the evaluation design steps together. It organizes the information developed in such a way that evaluation design decisions can be made.

Evaluators throughout government are given budgets to evaluate the performance of public programs. They are confronted with many options on ways to approach the evaluation function and, in most large organizations, with an insatiable desire for information on program activities, outcomes, impacts, environments, organizational arrangements, etc. The evaluators are also confronted with a chronic problem—utilization of their studies. One of the major causes of the low use of evaluation studies is that most social programs are not sufficiently well-defined to lead to agreement among management and/or policy makers as to success criteria. The lack of agreement is manifested in the form of criticism, after the fact, of the findings of evaluation studies. Analysis of the decision-making system before the initiation of a study is a method of screening programs to determine in which programs and in which parts of programs there exists sufficient definition to make evaluation likely to be useful. Analysis of the decision-making system is most useful to evaluators seeking close links with program managers or policy makers and least useful to those evaluators who view their function as independent research. Such collaboration does not mean that the evaluator simply serves as a technician on behalf of program managers. Rather, in this collaborative process, there is the opportunity for the evaluator to carry out an analytical function by raising relevant questions, searching for clarification of the program and its goals, identifying potential side effects which merit study, and assisting the manager to view the program more critically.

CONDUCTING THE EVALUABILITY ASSESSMENT

Conducting the evaluability assessment involves a sequential series of steps which bound and refine the program from two perspectives, that of the user (intended audience for the evaluation) and that of the evaluator. Each has something of value to bring to the assessment. The steps are:

- Bounding the problem/program: Determining what federal state, or local activities and what objectives constitute the program— what is the unit that is to be analyzed?

- Collection of program information: Gathering information that defines the program's objectives, activities, and underlying assumptions.

- Modeling: Development of a model that describes the program and the interrelationships of activities and objectives, from the point of view of the intended user of the evaluation information.

- Analysis: Determining to what extent the program definition, as represented by the model, is sufficiently unambiguous that evaluation is likely to be useful. This step also includes the identification of potential evaluation studies.

- Presentation to management/intended user: Feedback of the results of the assessment to representatives of management/intended user and determination of next steps that should be taken.

BOUNDING THE PROBLEM/PROGRAM

The first step is to identify the primary intended users of the planned evaluation and to determine what constitutes the program or object of evaluation (from the point of view of the intended users of the evaluation) in order to define the unit to be analyzed.

Virtually all agencies have a number of activities that are directly related to the legislative program, such as research, evaluation, information systems, technical assistance. Are all of these activities one program, or is each activity an independent program? Many of these activities may be analogous to overhead in a commercial venture. There is no formula for deciding what is a program and what is part of a program. Essentially, the evaluation designer must attempt to determine which of the activities within a manager's purview are justified because of the existence of the legislative program and which have an independent life of their own. For example, research is often a difficult activity in which to determine relationships to programs. Does the research have its own objectives, broader than the program under analysis? Is it a necessary component of the program? Many programs begin with a research component focused on obtaining information for subsequent improvement of the program. The research becomes extended to broader questions beyond the scope of the program. Whether research is part of a program or is independent, it is probably preferable, initially, to include rather than exclude research activities.

The bounding exercise should also include an examination of which management and policy levels are to be included in defining the program to be evaluated. When program objectives are to be examined, it is logical to ask whose objectives they are. In many instances, potential users may also include groups with varying abilities to have impact on the program: other administrators, legislators, public interest groups, professional groups, the general public, etc. It may be a question of what feedback loop you are designing your evaluations for or of what loop the findings may be picked up in.

COLLECTION OF PROGRAM INFORMATION

Having decided roughly the boundaries of the program to be evaluated, it is necessary to collect information defining the program (program activities, objectives, and unanswered questions) from documents and from the point of view of the intended users of the evaluation. Logical sources of information would include (a) legislation, hearings, forward plans, budget justifications, internal division or branch work plans, program guidelines and regulations, reporting systems and past evaluations; and (b) interviews with (representatives of) program and agency management (and possibly others at different management levels, depending on the intended audience for the evaluations). The information to be collected would be objectives, activity descriptions, and any statements describing assumed causal links between activities and objectives. In most programs, there will be a set of objectives related in some hierarchical order or on some time-phased basis. The evaluator should try to get objective statements defined as precisely as possible in terms that are measurable. In getting this information, the evaluator is trying to develop a sense of how well the program manager or other intended user has defined his own objectives and information needs. He is not attempting to question objectives at this stage, however. If a manager defines an objective and has no idea how it might be measured, the fact should be noted for future analysis.

As an organizing device for defining the manager's/user's concept of the program in terms useful for subsequent communication between evaluator and manager/user, we have successfully used formats similar

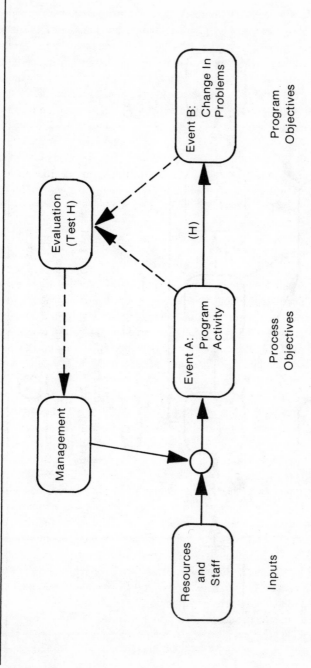

Figure 1: SIMPLIFIED PROGRAM MODEL

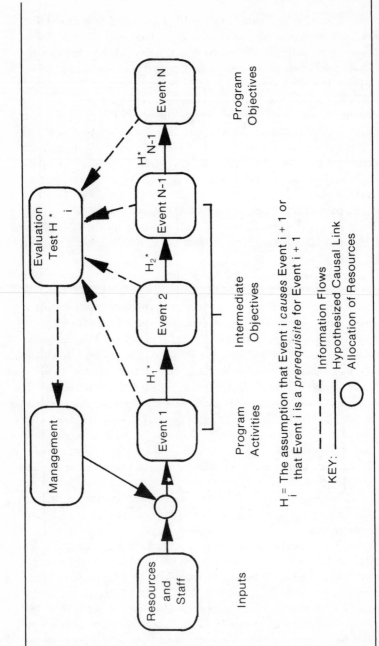

H_i = The assumption that Event i *causes* Event i + 1 or
that Event i is a *prerequisite* for Event i + 1

KEY: ---- Information Flows
        —— Hypothesized Causal Link
        ◯   Allocation of Resources

Figure 2: TYPICAL PROGRAM MODEL

to those illustrated in Figure 1. Figure 1 is a simplified flow model that shows staff and resources allocated by management to accomplish certain program activities (Event A), which are assumed to be prerequisites for, or to result in, some desired change in a well-defined problem (Event B). The solid arrow linking the events represents the assumed causal link that might be tested through evaluation.

Almost as one would do in constructing a PERT chart for the program, the evaluator works with program documentation and program managers or other intended users to define a series of intermediate objectives so that there are plausible causal links from resource inputs through a chain of intended results culminating in achievement of program objectives (see Figure 2). Evaluation studies could then test the assumptions that one event leads to another.

These flow models are developed first on the basis of the legislation and program descriptions, then for each relevant management level or other intended user.

During this part of the evaluation design process, the evaluator must obtain enough time from (representatives of) agency and program managers (or other intended users) to assure himself that he has a comprehensive description and understands the relationships of the component parts of the program. Reliance strictly on documentation (legislation, plans, etc.) will limit the ability of the evaluator to understand the manager's or policy maker's concept of the program.

We use the term "user surveys" to designate either interviews with program or agency management (for those evaluations primarily intended to meet information needs of agency managers) or interviews with samples of those who might use evaluations which are intended to serve a broader audience (e.g., policy makers or managers at state or local level)—these interviews being conducted to help the evaluation planner to become clearer (more specific) on (a) the primary users of the information to be obtained, (b) users' priority information needs, and (c) their degree of satisfaction with existing information sources and prior evaluations.

Figure 3 is a sample guide for the user surveys that ought, if at all possible, to be conducted at this point in the evaluation design process. The interviews are free-form. The flow model is used to record information and to guide the interviewer to fill holes in his knowledge of the manager's view of the program and its objectives; in particular, the manager's definition of events, how he would measure each event, whether he accepts measures currently in use, his assumptions linking events.

In many cases, evaluators will find it impossible to conduct user surveys—instead having to be content with discussions with representatives of intended users (e.g., staff assistants) or even with "informed guesses" as to users' information needs. In such cases, the key point is to acknowledge the gap, and the lessened likelihood that the evaluation will prove to be relevant and useful.

MODELING

The next state of analysis is to develop a model that graphically represents the important intended relationships among program activi-

FIGURE 3

Guide for a User Survey[a]

User surveys conducted to obtain the following kinds of information from representatives of program and agency management or other intended users of evaluation information:

1. What are the objectives of the program?
2. What would you consider acceptable evidence of achievement of program objectives?[b]
3. What mechanisms exist (policies, guidelines, staff activities, etc.) to achieve the above objectives?[c]
4. Why will Event A lead to Event B?[c]
5. What does Congress/OMB expect of the agency/program in terms of performance? Are they consistent from year to year?
6. What do you perceive as the most serious difficulty facing the program in terms of meeting its objectives?
7. What performance information do you need on the job?
8. If you had the above information, what would you do with it?
9. Have you seen the program's present information systems? Is it adequate for your needs?
10. How do you get the information you need to do your job? How satisfied are you with this information?
11. What do you consider to be the most important thing that you must accomplish in the next year? What information do you think you need? How will you get it?
12. What are the most important issues or questions that you believe an evaluation of the program should answer?

a. Richard E. Schmidt et al. The Market for Evaluation Services in the Department of Health, Education, and Welfare. Washington: The Urban Institute, May 1975. "The protocols were not itemized in detail because we wanted to avoid inhibiting respondents by an overdetermined question-and-answer period approach. The protocols, then, were designed mostly as reminders of major topics an;did not result in extremely structured standardized interviews."
b. Yields measures.
c. Yields intermediate objectives or causal assumptions linking events.

ties and objectives as cited in the program documentation and interviews. Methods other than modeling can be and have been used to perform this function, but flow models appear to be a satisfactory and informative method for communicating quickly and effectively the component parts and relationships of program activities and objectives.

An important characteristic of this program model, the "rhetorical program model," is that it captures all of the activities and their objectives, while avoiding the temptation to insert what might appear to be missing or "necessary" objectives or activities. The rhetorical model should represent the program that has been defined by the manager, policy maker, or other intended user and defined in legislation, internal plans, and program justifications. There is no rigid predefined model format used to convey this description of the program.

Figure 4 is a rhetorical model of the NIMH Community Mental Health Center program.[1]

The Community Mental Health Center Program of the National Institute of Mental Health provides funds to several hundred projects across the country, each of which is supposed to create a community mental health center in a specific geographic area. Each center attempts to do such things as provide psychiatric and psychological counseling, provide short-term care at the community level (e.g., halfway houses), help people discharged from mental institutions become reintegrated into the community, and so on.

The two major inputs to the national program are federal staff and the federal funds (several hundred million dollars a year). One of the major activities of the division that runs the community mental health centers program is to administer the grants. The assumption is that by federal regulations, guidelines, technical assistance, and so forth, it is possible to develop operating community mental health centers. It is further assumed these mental health centers becoming operational will result in a whole range of desired outputs and impacts. The six program objectives are identified in Figure 4.

The reduction of inappropriate use of mental hospitals was a major rationale for the establishment of CMHCs, and this is the goal which is most directly concerned with the effects of the program on clients. The goals of increased quality of service would presumably contribute to the reduction of inappropriate use of mental hospitals and in turn lead to the goal of developing a science of community mental health. The remaining objective is the development of economically viable CMHCs which could continue to operate without federal support through state and local funding, fees, and third-party reimbursements.

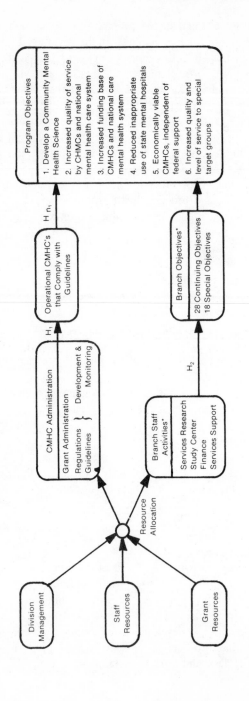

Figure 4: COMMUNITY MENTAL HEALTH CENTRES RHETORICAL PROGRAM MODEL

ANALYSIS

From the evaluator's perspective, two tests should be applied to the rhetorical model: (1) are the objectives stated in measurable terms; and (2) are the assumed causal relationships testable?

Here "measurable" means that there exists agreement on the part of management/intended users as to what would constitute or signal success.[2] Acceptable measures may be objective or subjective. There are really two parts to the question of measurability: (1) the indicator of achievement and (2) the means of verification. It is a standard part of program evaluation methodology that both indicators and means of verification be developed as part of any evaluation. The key question is who should develop the measures of success. The assessment process discussed here rests on the belief that ambiguous objectives should not be rendered unambiguous by an evaluator; that, we believe, is a management or policy question. The analysis of objectives for measurability is not, then, a test of the evaluator's ingenuity in defining measures. It is, rather, a test to determine whether the manager or policy maker has defined what he or she wants the program to accomplish and what evidence is needed to determine this. Lacking such measures, the objective is eliminated from the model, classified temporarily as "unmeasurable" (meaning only that no agreement exists at that moment on what evidence would signal success). The examination should include all objectives, not just the program "impact" objectives. This would certainly include the "process" objectives associated with staff research, technical assistance, or other administrative activities.

The second part of the analysis concerns the assumed causal relationships linking activities to process objectives and process to program objectives. Ideally, these assumptions could be isolated through appropriate tests to provide feedback to a manager or policy maker, indicating that an observed effect was attributable to a particular set of activities and to no other variables. Practically, however, we must settle for substantially less in virtually all federal programs. An assumption is considered "testable" if there exist test comparisons that the manager/intended user would consider adequate indication that observed effects were attributable to program activities.

Taken together, the manager or policy maker's definition of measurable objectives and testable assumptions constitutes his best statement of the evidence he needs to determine whether the program is or is not effective. It is important to note that we are seeking the user's definition, not the evaluator's. When more than one level of management is involved, it is likely that more than one set of definitions will emerge, but in many cases, none will be acceptable. When there is no definition (users do not know and cannot construct any adequate tests of their assumptions), the assumptions (links on the model between activities and objectives) are eliminated from the rhetorical model.

After eliminating from the model any objectives that are not currently measurable and any linking assumptions that are not currently testable, a second "evaluable" program model is developed reflecting the remaining measurable activities, measurable objectives, and testable assumptions. The evaluable model is a subset of the rhetorical model, retaining measurable objectives and plausible, testable assumptions, and representing that portion of the program which is ready for useful evaluation. (Figure 5 is an evaluable model of the NIMH Community Mental Health Centers program.)[3]

The evaluator now has an adequate basis for examining the program's potential for useful evaluations and the manager's need for evaluation. From the evaluator's perspective, the evaluable program model represents a device to focus attention on the required information, screening out not only the unanswerable questions at which evaluations are commonly directed, but also screening out issues or questions concerning which no action would result even were an answer to be forthcoming. It is a step away from the research orientation of many evaluation organizations.

The next stage of evaluation design defines the information that can be collected about the program represented by the evaluable program model. As opposed to the normal situation in which an evaluator finds himself, he would have relatively firm agreement on the success criteria and underlying logic of the program to be evaluated. He can proceed to define an information package that he can produce and deliver to the manager. This package will include evaluations which correspond to the information requirements of the manager as long as the objectives are measurable and the causal assumptions are plausible. Evaluators who act as critical analysts rather than simple technicians can propose questions for inclusion in the evaluation (e.g., side effects) which the manager may not have otherwise considered.

It is possible that, after analysis of the rhetorical program model, both the evaluable program design and the information that can be collected will be extremely simple—in some cases, trivial. In itself, this fact may be important feedback to the manager or policy maker. As shown in Figure 5, the only objective which remained after the analysis was the development of economically viable CMHCs independent of federal support. Of all the national objectives, this was the only one for which measures of success had been determined.

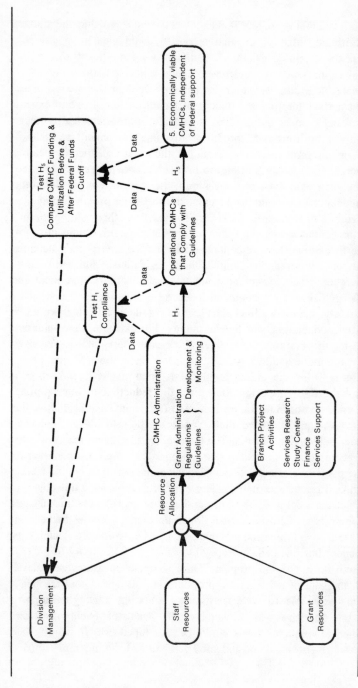

Figure 5: COMMUNITY MENTAL HEALTH CENTRES EVALUABLE PROGRAM MODEL

The examination of the process objectives showed that the staff of the National Institute of Mental Health could identify measurable criteria to determine whether a community mental health center met federal regulations and guidelines. This objective was therefore left in the evaluable model. However, for some of the branch's process objectives, such as "improve the quality of technical assistance and expand the capability of the branches to provide appropriate assistance to responsible authorities," "promote ongoing improvement to technology," or "promote improved planning," there was no apparent measure of success (or a clear relationship between branch objectives and program objectives). These objectives were therefore deleted in the evaluable model of the Community Mental Health Center program.

Figure 5 also presents the types of evaluations that could appropriately be conducted on the Community Mental Health Center Program. In the first evaluation, we could test whether the federal grant administration activities—sending out money, regulations, and guidelines—produce operating community mental health centers that meet the federal guidelines. We could do a second evaluation to test whether community mental health centers that meet federal guidelines would be financially viable without federal money. For example, the evaluation might require that in some number of the cases the evaluator take away the federal money and see whether the centers continued to operate.

Missing from the evaluable model is what might have been considered the most important objective—the reduction of inappropriate use of mental hospitals. Unless it were known that CMHCs did have this impact, it might be argued, there would be little justification for having economically viable CMHCs. The evaluability assessment has concluded that, at this time, it would not be appropriate to conduct an evaluation of the program's effectiveness in reducing inappropriate use of mental hospitals since no acceptable measures of progress toward this objective have yet been defined. The onus is therefore on the program manager and analysts to identify and develop appropriate measures if the manager needs such evaluation information. In other words, the evaluability assessment has revealed the type of work which is necessary to increase the evaluability of the program. Once adequate measures were developed, the goal of reducing inappropriate use of mental hospitals might become amenable to an effectiveness evaluation. Having determined that the objective was measurable, the evaluator could investigate whether a research design could be developed which would yield relatively unequivocal and unbiased estimates of the program's impact.

PRESENTATION TO MANAGEMENT/INTENDED USER

Up to this point, (representatives of) the manager/intended user will have contributed their time to an assessment of the program. The information derived is now given to them in a form that is useful for determination of next steps in the evaluation design process. The information needed is:

- the rhetorical model—an accurate descriptive model of the program reflecting both interviews and documentation;

- the evaluable model—the evaluator's assessment of the program that is being managed and can usefully be evaluated given the current level of agreement on measures and comparison;

- explanation of the analytical process that led to the evaluable model; and

- information that could be collected in relation to performance as defined in the evaluable model.

The evaluator's presentation to management should be aimed at the following:

- obtaining agreement or further clarification of the program design. There may well be differences of opinion or judgment concerning the measurability of specific objectives of the underlying program logic. The presentation affords the program manager or policy maker the opportunity to clarify any objectives or questions of design logic.

- determining the user's need for the information that can be collected. During the presentation, the evaluator will define the type of information he can produce. It is the user's judgment as to whether or not that information is needed. The evaluator can and should suggest ways in which the information might be of use, but only in rare instances will the evaluator actually use the information. The manager is positioned to use it and must make the final decision. There will often be more than one manager concerned with use. The fact that a branch or division manager sees no utility does not preclude an agency manager from assuming the position of major user.

- determining to what extent the manager perceives the need to modify his program design. Whether the findings of the evaluability assessment indicate the need to redesign the program will depend upon the manager's objectives. If he intends to accomplish objectives that are implausible given his current design, he will change the design or give up the objectives, depending on the constraints on his action authority.

IMPLICATIONS—WHAT DO WE DO NEXT?

Certainly at least one part of an evaluator's job is to provide information about programs to the managers of those programs. In theory, at least, this feedback process is supposed to result in better decisions, resulting in turn in more effective programs. The findings from the evaluability assessment will focus the attention of the evaluator on information that can be collected about the activities and objectives for which agreement already exists concerning success measures. The evaluation planning base is a well defined program.

The evaluator must still concern himself with the utility of the information. The last task prior to evaluation design would then be to define—with representatives of the program manager or other intended users—the intended uses of the information that can be gathered by evaluation studies of the program. Although, again in theory, the place to begin such a definition of utility is in the decision process, we have found only rare situations in which a program manager could explicate his decision process in a way that facilitated evaluation. The process of defining intended use with the program manager can help the manager clarify the criteria that he himself might use to initiate actions. Even imprecise definitions of use will let the evaluator know how accurate the information needs to be, thereby at least partially establishing the scope of the study.

NOTES

1. Pamela Horst et al. *Evaluation Planning at the National Institute of Mental Health.* Washington: The Urban Institute, July 1974. This report provides examples of the evaluability assessment approach and discusses the results of applying this approach in one federal agency. It also provides additional examples of rhetorical and evaluable program models.

2. Richard E. Schmidt et al., unpublished manuscript. "Regardless of how abstractly stated is the objective, if the managers have defined measures of success, then the objective is measurable. Note that in many cases, separate measures may not have been defined, but the objective either contains a built-in measure [reduce infant mortality] or is sufficiently clear that adequate measures and instruments can be easily defined [client satisfaction, for example]."

3. Horst et al., *Evaluation Planning.* See note 1.

The evaluability assessment described in Chapter 2 depicts a model of the program from an analysis of documents and through interviews. The dilemma is that this may not produce a complete and accurate depiction of what actually occurs in the field. Formative research can be conducted to identify the program's operation, the problems which it addresses, and the effects which it appears to produce. Used in this way, formative research provides some verification of the findings in the evaluability assessment.

Formative research can also be used to facilitate program development. Besides focusing on the program's operation, its effects, and causal assumptions, data are collected on the context and constraints which may influence the program. The feedback of such information is expected to contribute to program development.

Formative research is not presented as a particular methodology but relies on commonly accepted research methods to shed light on the nature of the program and the factors which influence its operation. This yields an opportunity to determine whether a program meets the preconditions for an effectiveness evaluation and to increase the evaluability of programs.

3

FORMATIVE RESEARCH AND PROGRAM EVALUABILITY

Leonard Rutman

To some extent, the growing interest in evaluation research stems from decision makers who expect to use the findings of evaluation research to contribute to program development, policy-making, budget submissions, and management. However, a major impetus for the conduct of evaluation research has been the concern of accountability. Such research is expected to produce data on "the value for money" spent on public programs. In this context, evaluation research is generally interpreted as the use of research procedures for determining the "success" of a program in reaching its stated goals or producing expected effects.

Evaluations of program effectiveness assume the presence of certain preconditions: (1) the program is clearly articulated; (2) the goals and/or expected effects are clearly specified; and (3) the causal assumptions linking the program to the goals and/or effects are plausible. In those instances where the preconditions are absent or inadequately developed, effectiveness evaluations are premature and, if conducted, these studies are likely to be irrelevant and relatively useless for drawing inferences about program effectiveness. Where the program is poorly articulated, it is difficult to know precisely what was evaluated. Vaguely stated goals and/or effects are not easily measurable and do not provide adequate criteria for determining whether a program produced

59

the expected outcomes. Finally, programs are often evaluated when prior analysis would have revealed that the causal assumptions are not plausible and that there is little likelihood of the program producing the expected outcomes.

Despite the logic of not prematurely evaluating programs for their effectiveness when the preconditions do not justify it, such research is nevertheless commonly conducted when programs are not evaluable.[1] To a large extent, this reflects the overwhelming concern of accountability as the basis for conducting evaluation studies. Programs are often held accountable for goals which are inflated promises to solve major social problems. Evaluators then undertake complex and costly studies to determine whether "rhetorical" goals are met. Yet programs which are not evaluable require greater attention paid the necessary preconditions before being tested for their effectiveness.

The preconditions for evaluable programs should normally be arrived at through program planning and development. However, finding programs that adequately meet these preconditions is rare. Evaluation researchers should therefore address these preconditions and refuse to be coopted into testing programs for their effectiveness when they are not evaluable.

Wholey and colleagues at the Urban Institute in Washington have developed and tested an evaluability assessment procedure. As described in the previous chapter, this procedure entails the examination of program documents as well as interviewers with managers and/or other personnel. Evaluable program components (i.e., particular activities directed at specific outcomes) are identified through this procedure.

Formative research assists in determining program evaluability by monitoring the actual operation of the program. There are several benefits which accrue from the conduct of formative research to determine program evaluability. First, it is possible to check the accuracy of the program model which emerges from the evaluability assessment. Second, there is an opportunity to surface information which did not arise from the program documents and interviews, especially the identification of unintended effects. Third, where there is some uncertainty or lack of clarity about the program, formative research can be used to articulate it, identify effects, and shed light on the problem being addressed.

Aside from simply determining whether a program adequately meets the preconditions for an effectiveness evaluation, formative research can be used to actually increase the evaluability of a program. In contrast to effectiveness evaluations which sit in judgment of programs, formative research is in their service. It is by identifying the factors which appear to influence the program's operation and its outcomes that formative research contributes to increasing program evaluability.

DETERMINING PROGRAM EVALUABILITY

Formative research pays attention to the same preconditions which are the focal concerns of the evaluability assessment—i.e., the program, goals and/or effects, and causal assumptions. However, the conduct of an evaluability assessment provides direction in undertaking formative research. Since the evaluability assessment depicts a model of the program, including components which can be appropriately evaluated, formative research can be used to verify the model as well as to identify other concerns which would provide a more detailed and complete understanding of the program.

This discussion will identify the type of information which formative research collects to determine the evaluability of a program. We will provide the rationale for collecting such information and identify some general approaches for obtaining these data.

PROGRAM ACTIVITIES

Program labels often do not provide a clear understanding of the activities that are actually implemented. For example, as pointed out earlier, there is no uniform meaning attached to such programs as Headstart, New Careers, community health centers, legal aid clinics, and so on. The evaluability assessment should have at least identified major activities which fall under a particular program. In reference to Headstart, program activities could include nutritional supplements, linguistic training, reading exercises, and counseling. A neighborhood information center might provide information, referrals, advocacy, conseling, and community organization.

The concern of formative research is to verify the presence of these activities and to describe the manner in which the activities are actually implemented. For example, the monitoring of referral activities could reveal implementation of the following practices:

(1) the client is simply told how to reach the relevant agency;

(2) the staff telephones the agency and makes an appointment for the client;

(3) the client is accompanied by the staff to the agency; and

(4) a letter of referral is sent on behalf of the client.

In other words, through data collection on the actual operation of the program, it is possible to shed light on the activities that are implemented.

Wilkins' research on legal aid illustrates the description of a program's activities.[2] Several concerns about the program were studied, including:

(1) whether legal aid lawyers tend to exercise selection to higher courts to raise their payments;

(2) if the program promotes the acceptance of a large number of clients to offset the reduced remuneration;

(3) whether legal aid clients accepted by a firm are handed over to junior lawyers; and

(4) if cases fall disproportionately into the hands of solo practitioners rather than firms.

The answers to these questions would obviously clarify issues related to the conduct of the program.

The major purpose for monitoring the program's operation is to determine whether there are uniform activities that are implemented in a systematic manner. In addition, where there is a prescribed or expected manner for the program to conduct its activities, the actual operation can then be compared to the prescribed "ideal." If there are major differences, then difficulties in the administration of the program are revealed. It is thus possible to avoid undertaking a costly and complex evaluation of a program which is not being implemented in the intended manner. Attention can then be paid to changing the program's operation rather than to evaluating its effectiveness.

This concern over determining whether a program was actually implemented as intended is the major focus of "process evaluation." Standards of "good" practice are defined and attempts are made to determine if they have been applied. In the field of medical care, for example, judgments are based on considerations such as the appropriateness, completeness and redundancy of information obtained through clinical history, physical examination, and diagnostic tests; justification of diagnosis and therapy; technical competence in the process of diagnostic and therapeutic procedures, including surgery; evidence of comparative management in health and illness; coordination and continuity of care; acceptability of care to recipient, and so on. This approach requires that a great deal of attention be given to specifying the relevant dimensions, values, and standards to be used in assessment.

The estimates of quality that one obtains are less stable and less final than those that derive from measurements of outcomes. They may, however, be more relevant to the question at hand: whether medicine is properly practiced.[3]

A variety of approaches has been used to monitor program activities. Field staff can be interviewed about their practice or asked to record their work in a log. Such information is often available in administrative forms or files which practitioners are expected to complete. Another procedure is to observe the actual operation of the program, directly or through audio visual aids. Finally, clients can be asked about the nature of the service provided to them.

EFFECTS

Formative research attempts to identify effects of the program. This is in contrast to effectiveness evaluations which aim to determine whether the program produced the measured effects. The emphasis in formative research is on discovery, while effectiveness evaluations are essentially concerned with verification.

The usual practice in developing an evaluation research design is to identify program goals through an examination of documents and perhaps interviews with program personnel. Measures are then developed for these goals. However, there are limitations and shortcomings in this approach. These will be elaborated in order to provide a rationale for using formative research to *identify* program effects.

The goals of a program are often vague, and measurable criteria cannot be easily developed. Examples of such goals are improved mental health, better social functioning, successful rehabilitation, or community integration. Robert Mager's work on goal analysis is a useful exercise for operationalizing "fuzzy" goals into performance indicators.[4]

Even if program goals are specific and measurable, formative research can be justified prior to the conduct of an effectiveness evaluation. This is to avoid a tunnel-vision approach which restricts evaluation studies to manifest goals. There is also the need to identify latent goals—i.e., desired ends of a program which are not publicly stated. For example, the manifest goals of parole are to rehabilitate ex-offenders and protect the public. Yet there are possible latent goals of parole: e.g., (1) reducing the disparity in sentencing behavior of judges by giving longer parole to persons who receive a heavier sentence for similar crimes; (2) to control behavior in the prison by using parole

as a reward; and (3) easing the high expense of institutional confinement.[5] Data could be collected to answer these questions. Whether or
not it is possible to infer that these constitute latent goals of the
program is a moot point. The important thing is the identification of
relevant outcomes for inclusion in an evaluation study.

Formative research can also be used to identify side effects of a
program, whether intended or unintended. This is the central thrust of
goal-free evaluation, an approach which Michael Scriven has popu-
larized.[6] Since evaluation with respect to goals is unduly restrictive in
the effects examined, goal-free evaluation looks for *actual* effects. In
such a process, there is much greater assurance of identifying the widest
range of possible outcomes for inclusion in the evaluation. In fact,
many interesting evaluations have paid attention to potential negative
effects of a program. Evaluations of the negative income tax experiments have measured such concerns as withdrawal from the labor
market and family breakdown. Studies of bilingual education have
focused on the extent to which there is a sacrifice in the child's native
language in learning a foreign one.

Unintended effects can be identified through various means. Available literature and other research often provide clues. Trained observers
can note the effects of the program. However, the most common
procedure is to follow up clients of the program and ask them about its
effects. For example, people who completed a manpower training
program could be called and asked about the effects of the program—
e.g., whether work was obtained, types of jobs taken, the use of their
training in the job, income earned, and so on. In these interviews,
questions can also be raised about intervening factors that influenced
them (e.g., other programs). Efforts can be made to determine which
people are most likely to be affected by the program and why some
people drop out more than others. A host of similar concerns can also
be pursued.

CAUSAL ASSUMPTIONS

Programs make assumptions, either implicit or explicit, about the
cause of the problem being addressed. For example, the rising cost of
health care services is recognized as a major problem requiring attention. While there is little argument over the need to control cost, there
are various solutions being proposed. Each makes different causal
assumptions. If the problem is seen as over-demand by patients for
health care services, then deterrent fees are advocated. On the other
hand, utilization rates have been shown to be determined by the
availability of physicians and the rationing process which they exercise.

With this view, the proposed policy is to limit the supply of physicians and to somehow control the rationing process.

It is now widely recognized that many evaluation studies attempt to determine whether a puny intervention is effective in solving complex and long-standing problems. The predictable finding of these studies is that the programs have failed to produce the expected results. It is beyond the scope of formative research to examine and explain the etiology of major problems which programs address. Nevertheless, to avoid the conduct of evaluations where the causal assumptions are highly questionable, some attention can be focused on the problem which the program aims to solve.

In this regard, it is important to identify the population which the program serves, and thus demographic data are required—e.g., age, sex, marital status, race, ethnicity, nature of employment, geographic location, and other descriptive information. Specific and detailed information should be collected about the needs or problems which the program addresses. For a job training program, there would presumably be a need to determine vocational skills, aptitude, and employability. A drug rehabilitation program would focus on the nature and seriousness of drug use. Correctional programs would be concerned about the criminal background of their clients.

It is often informative to simply know the characteristics of the population being served by the program. Such data provide the basis for· determining whether the program is reaching the relevant people. At the most basic level, is it involving the relevant age group, ethnicity, regions, and so on? A more complex question is whether the program is serving those who are most in need. In this regard, services are often provided to people who could manage without the program or to a clientele that the public is willing to support. For example, a major study of services to the blind showed that although blindness is scarce among children, services are mainly directed at them and young employable adults, rather than at the much larger population of elderly blind persons. In their campaigns for funds, these agencies convey the image of young employable adults who can be helped to become productive, and then search for the relatively few blind people who have these personal attributes.[7]

Another purpose for collecting data on the clients is to focus more specific attention on the causal assumptions made by the program. Several questions can be posed: Are program activities directed at the identified needs or problems? Does the program make realistic assumptions about the nature of these needs or problems? To what extent are the goals realistic for the program? The central question of this analysis is whether the program activities that are directed at the specified effects make plausible causal assumptions about the problems being addressed.

An Employability Assessment Scale developed by Estes and his colleagues illustrates the usefulness of data collection on clients to identify the nature and severity of problems which the program aims to address.[8] Twelve employability indicators are considered, including, among others, education, language difficulties, health barriers, legal barriers, work history, military status, age, motivation, transportation, child care needs, and job market. Each of these indicators is operationalized for a total of fifty characteristics. For example, language skills are assessed in terms of a client's ability to read, write, and speak English. Each of the fifty characteristics is rated as "low," "moderate," and "high." The claimed advantages are that this assessment can: (1) provide continuous data on individual and aggregate cases served by the agency; (2) contribute toward identifying the potential employability of individuals; (3) help isolate especially difficult employment barriers common to a large group of clients; and (4) identify major gaps in the social welfare service delivery system which, if permitted to continue, would frustrate both the client and agency occupational goals. In other words, the nature of the employability problem is assessed according to the relative potential of individual clients as well as the external barriers.

There are various means of obtaining data on the characteristics and problems of clients served by programs. Files can be used if available and considered adequate for this purpose. Record-keeping can often be modified to provide a better understanding of client needs and problems. Precoded reports in standard categories which staff can simply check to record information can be a substitute or supplement to narrative reports. The problem-oriented record, an instrument originally designed for general hospital use, is now being used extensively in the field of human services (a coding system is established for particular problems for each client in the program). These varied instruments can be administered to new clients or those already involved in the program to identify needs or document problems.

INCREASING THE EVALUABILITY OF PROGRAMS

Aside from determining whether a program meets the preconditions of evaluability, formative research can be used to increase the evaluability of programs. It does so by (1) identifying factors that appear to influence the program's operation and effects; and (2) allowing managers to try different methods of implementing a program and observing the effects of each alternative.

To contribute to a better understanding of a program, formative research collects data on program personnel, organizational structure and climate, policy, and the context within which the program operates. The level of detail which is given to any of these issues can vary widely, depending on such considerations as the presumed salience of the issue for a particular program, the availability of time and resources, and the degree of commitment to the developmental tasks of the program.

PROGRAM PERSONNEL

The potential benefits of a program can be facilitated or impeded by the people who carry it out. Depending on the particular program, some of the following factors may be considered relevant: demographic characteristics (age, sex, marital status, race, ethnicity, etc.), type of training, work experience, particular attitudes, and so on. Work by Truax and Carkhuff shows the importance of considering the characteristics of personnel in regard to the effectiveness of psychotherapy.[9] Their findings showed that patients whose therapists offered a high level of unconditional positive warmth, self-congruence or genuineness, and empathic understanding showed significant positive personality and behavioral changes on a wide variety of indicators.

ORGANIZATIONAL STRUCTURE AND CLIMATE

It is widely recognized that organizational factors have a major influence on the program's operation. Considerable research has been done on the influence of organizational structure on the accomplishment of goals.[10] Relevant questions pertaining to organizational structure include hierarchical levels, span of control, size, complexity, and centralization of authority. In addition, information can be collected on the organizational climate—i.e., the atmosphere which is the characteristic way of working within an organization. For example, Moos has used instruments to measure the social environment of wards in mental hospitals to identify the factors which facilitate or hinder the accomplishment of treatment goals.[11]

POLICY

There is usually some policy which serves as the mandate for a program (e.g., legislation, cabinet memorandum, decisions of a Board of

Directors). In these policies, there are often formal guidelines which determine the manner in which the program is conducted. The policy can provide rules of eligibility, length of time for a service, the level of provision, and so on.

Formative research can focus on the manner in which the policy is implemented by the program. Thus, it is possible to determine the extent to which the operation of the program is in accordance with the policy guidelines. This is a particularly important concern where there is a high degree of discretion in implementing the program, such as the approval of grants or the administration of public assistance.

CONTEXT

A better understanding of the program can be gained by determining the context within which it operates. An effort is made to identify the political, economic, and social factors relevant for the particular program. The concern here is with the environmental realities that may have an influence on the manner in which the program is implemented and may impact on the expected results. Since this is the broadest area of concern, it is the most difficult for providing specific direction. The evaluator must attempt to uncover pertinent variables by determining which factors impinge upon the program. For example, the context for manpower programs would probably include such considerations as characteristics of the employment market, socioeconomic factors (e.g., social class, racial and ethnic composition of a community), the presence of training programs and placement services, availability of day care, and so on.

Formative research can make a contribution to those programs which are still in the process of development and not ready for an effectiveness evaluation. The research on *Sesame Street,* the educational program for children, illustrates how formative research provides opportunities for trying different methods and then determining the effects of each alternative.[12] For example, before *Sesame Street* was evaluated for its effectiveness, some formative research was conducted to determine which methods of presenting content best held the attention of children. This was studied by having observers rate the degree to which different approaches of presenting the program held the attention of economically disadvantaged children.

In summary, to determine whether a program is evaluable there is attention paid to: (1) monitoring the program's activities; (2) identifying the program's effects; and (3) determining the needs or problems which the program aims to address. However, if the purpose of formative research is to increase program evaluability, then there are additional tasks. An effort is made to determine the influence of personnel, organizational structure and climate, policy, and context. Attempts should also be made to observe the effects of different ways of implementing the program.

METHODOLOGICAL CHARACTERISTICS OF FORMATIVE RESEARCH

Since the purpose of formative research, which is the development of an evaluable program, differs from that of evaluation research, which tests for program effectiveness and efficiency, there are also differences in their respective approaches to research.[13] Formative research is mainly aimed at discovery and relies largely on an inductive approach. The study of the program affords a learning opportunity with research used as a tool for collecting data to assist in the conceptualization and operationalization of a program, its goals and effects, and the assumed causal relationships. On the other hand, evaluation research as normally viewed attempts to verify through measurement the relationship between the experimental variable (i.e., the program) and the dependent variables (i.e., goals and outcomes). Whereas formative research searches for causal relationships, evaluation research attempts to test hypotheses.

Formative research is not a particular methodology of social research. Rather, it refers to the purpose of the research—namely, the development of the preconditions of an evaluable program. This purpose is pursued through the use of different types of commonly accepted research methods and data-gathering approaches which can be used creatively, including, among others, especially prepared administrative forms, audio visual aids, participant observation, program documents and records, questionnaires, unstructured interviews, and analysis of the literature and related research. These data can be collected from such sources as clients when they arrive at the program and at a follow-up period; interviews, records, and/or observations of program personnel; and monitoring the operation of the program.

In effectiveness evaluations, there is consideration of research designs which provide the greatest possible assurance that the program produced the measured results and that they are not due to other factors. To safeguard against alternative explanations of the outcomes (i.e., other than the program), attempts are made to approximate experimental designs, involving randomization to experimental and control groups with "before" and "after" measures. On the other hand, because formative research does not attempt to determine whether the program was successful, it is usually unnecessary to use experimental designs. The data are recognized as being equivocal and suggestive rather than definitive. Nevertheless, this is all that should be expected when an attempt is made to get a handle cn the program rather than to rigorously examine it.

Since evaluations of program effectiveness draw conclusions about programs and their effects, there is great concern about assuring the highest practical degree of reliability and validity of the measures. Formative research relaxes these demands to some extent and places heavier reliance on "soft" approaches for data collection (e.g., unstructured interviews and observation) and the measures used (e.g., attitudes, felt needs, subjective estimates, personal opinions, and recollections). During this period of formative research, it is appropriate to refine the measures through practice and lessons learned from experience.

In effectiveness evaluations, there is concern about having a controlled situation—i.e., holding the program constant and withholding data during the experimental period. Otherwise it is impossible to know what was evaluated since the program is continually changing. However, formative research provides information to the program on an ongoing basis so as to clarify, develop, and operationalize it and its goals.

The desirability of using "inside" rather than "outside" evaluators is an issue which has received widespread debate. The major argument in favor of outside evaluators is that this would result in less bias and a more penetrating analysis of the program. In effectiveness evaluations, this is obviously an important consideration because the credibility of the findings about the program's impact is at stake. However, since formative research does not attempt to draw conclusions about the worth of a program, there is not as much concern about the "objectivity" of the researchers. Moreover, formative research is an important part of program development. The use of internal researchers is not problematic, but quite desirable.

CONCLUSION

Formative research has been described as a procedure for determining program evaluability as well as increasing the evaluability of a program. Many programs use the notion of formative research as an excuse for avoiding an evaluation of effectiveness. In such instances, evaluation is considered as an ongoing process which guides decisions about program changes. At some point, however, it is necessary to put a program to the test. Formative research should therefore be viewed as an approach which prepares programs for subsequent effectiveness evaluations.

NOTES

1. Leonard Rutman and Dick de Jong. *Federal Level Evaluation.* Ottawa: Carleton University, 1976, Chapter 4.

2. James L. Wilkins. *Legal Aid in the Criminal Courts.* Toronto: University of Toronto Press, 1975.

3. Avedis Donabedean, "Evaluating the Quality of Medical Care," in (eds.) Herbert C. Schulberg, Alan Sheldon, and Frank Baker. *Program Evaluation in the Health Field.* New York: Behavioral Publications, 1969.

4. Robert F. Mager. *Goal Analysis.* Belmont: Fearon Publishers, 1972.

5. Daniel Glaser. *Routinizing Evaluation.* Rockville, Md.: National Institute of Mental Health, 1973, p. 5-6.

6. Michael Scriven. "Pros and Cons about Goal-Free Evaluation," *Evaluation Comment* 3, 4, 1972.

7. Robert A. Scott. "The Selection of Clients by Social Welfare Agencies: The Case of the Blind," *Social Problems* 14, November 3, 1967.

8. Richard Estes. "Welfare Client Employability: A Model Assessment System," *Public Welfare,* Fall, 1974.

9. C. B. Truax and R. R. Carkhuff. *Toward Effective Counseling and Psychotherapy.* Chicago: Aldine, 1967, pp. 12-14.

10. See, for example, Joseph A. Olmstead. *Organizational Structure and Climate.* Washington: Department of Health, Education and Welfare, 1973.

11. Rudolph H. Moos. *Evaluating Treatment Environments.* New York: John Wiley & Sons, 1974.

12. Thomas D. Cook et al. *Sesame Street Revisited.* New York: Russell Sage Foundation, 1975.

13. See Leonard Rutman. "Evaluating Explorations and Demonstrations for Planning in Criminal Justice," *Criminal Justice Research* (ed.) Emilio Viano. Lexington, Mass.: D. C. Heath, 1976, pp. 235-246.

The conduct of an evaluability assessment and/or formative research should uncover the variables for inclusion in the evaluation. If these pre-evaluation approaches have not been undertaken or if the evaluator wishes to check whether all relevant variables have been identified, the following categories can be used to identify what is to be measured in the evaluation: antecedent variables, the program process, intervening variables, goals, and effects.

Once variables are identified, it is necessary to select appropriate indicators. What are the indicators of such variables as lower recidivism, improved social functioning, reduced alienation, and so on? These indicators must be clearly specified and operationalized so that reliable and valid measures can be developed.

The technical considerations of reliability and validity are of central importance for the various sources and types of data (i.e., interviews, agency files, official government statistics, or observations). Caution must be exercised in developing the measures as well as in collecting and processing the data to ensure the greatest practical degree of reliability and validity. There are numerous standard texts on basic social research methods which provide excellent discussions of these issues. In this chapter, the focus is on the more practical problems facing evaluators who wish to measure and account for changes that the program is expected to produce. A case study of an evaluation of a Restitution Center, a novel community-based residential corrections program, is used to illustrate the identified practical measurement problems.

4

PROBLEMS OF MEASUREMENT IN CRIMINAL JUSTICE

Joe Hudson

Increased interest is being demonstrated in applying the principles and methods of research to social programs for the purpose of documenting the relative level of effort expended and outcomes achieved. Central to the main purpose of evaluation research is the assessment of the relative extent to which a social program achieves its goals and demonstrating that movement toward program goals actually resulted from the program or activity under study. Our major focus here will be on identifying some practical problems associated with attempting to measure change in criminal justice programs; a case study of a community-based corrections program, the Minnesota Restitution Center, will be used to illustrate the identified problems.

PURPOSES OF MEASURING CHANGE

A variety of both covert and overt purposes can be given for an evaluation research project. These purposes may have serious implications for the measures used, the results obtained, and the utility of the information for modifying the set of intervention activities. Scriven, for example, has distinguished between two largely incompatible overt purposes for conducting an evaluation research project—formative and summative.[1] Formative evaluations are designed to provide for the ongoing feedback of measurement results to the program so that appropriate program alterations can be made. In contrast, measurement results from a summative evaluation are fed back at a much later stage in the life of the project. In many cases, the results from a summative evaluation will not be provided to the ongoing program due to the possibility of contaminating the independent variable if consequent alterations were to be made in the set of intervention activities. The basic distinction, therefore, is primarily that of the stage of program implementation at which measures are applied and findings fed back to effect changes in the form or content of the intervention activities.

This distinction of Scriven's seems especially germane to evaluation research conducted on the relative efficacy of correctional treatments. By their very nature, evaluations of correctional treatments tend to rely primarily on outcome measures associated with repenetration of the criminal justice system—arrests, convictions, revocations, or reimprisonment. The use of such measures is usually predicated upon some period of post-program community exposure, the usually accepted follow up being set at three years. Clearly, this type of outcome measure and length of follow up are primarily appropriate for summative evaluations; there are few very valid or reliable indicators of the intermediate forms of outcome success which would be useful in a formative evaluation.

In this connection, Suchman[2] has suggested that the purpose of an evaluation project should, most appropriately, be closely related to the particular developmental stage of the program. Thus, he notes that in the early "pilot" stage of a program, a flexible, "quick-and-easy" evaluation should be conducted with the primary emphasis placed upon the feedback of results for program changes. In this stage of program development, relatively short-term indicators of success are required in order to provide approximations, as opposed to a high degree of precision. In turn, the "model" stage of program development calls for a carefully controlled experimental design. Finally, the "prototype" and "operating" stages of program development are seen as requiring a continuous feedback of information on a systematic basis rather than the simple application of a set of before-and-after measures. The politics of implementing social programs can often cloud these distinctions and, in later sections of this chapter, an example of such situations will be provided.

The purpose of an evaluation research project can also be regarded from the perspective of the form the evaluation is to take or the type of questions to be answered. While different writers use somewhat different categories, the assessment of program effort, program effect, and program efficiency are three major forms which an evaluation may take.

PROGRAM EFFORT

Measures of program effort or program input aim at providing information on the nature of the effort expended in the program which, presumably, is related to the achievement of desired program outcomes. While an evaluation aimed at assessing program effort will not empirically test out the presumed causal relationship between inputs and outcomes, it is a necessary prerequisite to such an assessment. Measures of program effort can usually be viewed as falling into two major categories: measures of program characteristics and measures of the conditions of the target group of clients prior to exposure to the set of intervention activities.

Measures of the specific content of the program may encompass such factors as the time, frequency, and duration of program involvement, number of staff, qualifications and experience of staff, and the level and allocation of material resources. Because of the expense and time involved, it is usually not practical to attempt collecting vast amounts of information on the wide number of program inputs. Therefore, a crucial consideration in the selection of measures designed to assess program content is the collection of basic information on those aspects of the program which one reasonably expects are causally related to the desired changes in the client group. In turn, this requires that careful attention be paid to assessing the nature of the program to be evaluated. Without careful program specification, it will be difficult to develop program-relevant measures, to know to what to attribute any program effects that may be obtained, or to identify the appropriate program variables for which measures will need to be developed. Clearly, the inadequate knowledge available specifying how change in client groups is to be brought about has direct implications for specifying what are the significant variables to be measured.

Uncritical assumptions that the set of intervention activities is being implemented within the daily operation of the program in a manner consistent with the original plan or program conception can lead to the development of measures which may be relatively foreign to the operational reality of the program. Transforming a set of program concepts and ideas into an operational entity providing some form of service to a client group can be an extremely complicated and difficult task; as a result, what may be forthcoming from the program on a daily basis may have little resemblance to the original program conception.

Related to the potential discrepancy between program concept and program reality is the possibility of the program undergoing major changes over time. Characteristics of the program at any particular time may bear only a slight resemblance to the program at subsequent times. This may be particularly the case in social programs for which there is little empirical evidence to support desired outcomes of particular types of interventions. Furthermore, social programs often are highly visible and generate strong and conflicting attitudes on the part of influential publics. Consequently, such programs are commonly forced to adapt to the changing demands placed on them by significant interest groups. It is this process of program adaptation and change over time that is likely to have negative effects upon the measures used. In other words, while the program undergoes significant change in form and content, the measures may not change and, as a consequence, will lose much of their original relevance.

A second major category of necessary measures in the assessment of program effort are those regarding the clients exposed to the program. Just as with staff and material resources, clients can be regarded as important program inputs. Within criminal justice evaluations, for example, important measures of client input characteristics would have to include variables significantly related to expected outcomes such as present age, age at first court appearance, age at first adjudication or conviction, race, sex, number of prior adjudications, convictions, or institutional commitments, and factors related to employment history, such as skill level and length and type of employment.

PROGRAM EFFECT

As compared to the assessment of program effort, measures of program effects or outcomes aim at providing information on the relative extent to which the effort expended impacted upon program goals. Within criminal justice programs, for example, the most common measures of effectiveness are those concerning the behavior of offenders following some type of program exposure. The program is then defined as "successful" or "unsuccessful" relative to client change on indicators of desired program outcomes. Crucial measurement problems, then, are those of defining appropriate criteria of program "success," developing valid and reliable measures, and determining appropriate follow-up periods.

PROGRAM EFFICIENCY

Given the assessment of program effect, a logical concern then becomes the relative extent to which the outcomes achieved could have been attained at lower cost and with greater efficiency. As greater demands are placed on limited financial resources, questions of program efficiency will demand and receive closer consideration. Evaluations of efficiency focus on the extent to which comparable levels and types of effort achieve relative outcome levels. In this sense, efficiency represents the ratio of effort to effect. The question to be answered by evaluations of efficiency is whether the same outcome could have been achieved at less cost.

Research aimed at the evaluation of the effort expended, effect achieved, or efficiency of a social program should also assess the process by which interventions are implemented. Emphasis placed upon developing and implementing measures of program process in evaluation research would aim at explaining how and why change does or does not occur. Sarason, for example,[3] has noted that how a human "setting" is created has been largely ignored. As a consequence, we lack basic understanding as to why the intent to create new human service programs and settings generally results in a confirmation of the notion that the more things change, the more they remain the same.

It is only on the basis of careful attention to measures of program process that an adequate understanding of program outcomes is likely to be achieved. A number of different approaches to measuring program process have been described in the literature. For example, Kiesler[4] divides programs into the stages of candidacy, selection, treatment, termination, and follow up, and then defines the major variables of interest as program, staff, clients, and time. Weiss and Rein[5] suggest that the evaluator's major question should be: "What happens once a program is introduced?" These authors then suggest that the general evaluation methodology would be inductive and concerned with assessing the unfolding form of the intervention activities, especially in relation to the reactions of those subjected to them. Weiss and Rein particularly emphasize measurements based upon participant observation and interviews. Other authors have suggested alternative types of measures. For example, Klein and Snyder[6] have demonstrated the utility of detached delinquency workers keeping a detailed log of their activities. Empey and Lubeck[7] have suggested that a useful technique might include the writing of personal diaries by individuals in a treatment program. Because of the possibility of overburdening subjects and staff members in social action programs, careful consideration is needed in the development of unobtrusive measurement techniques by which program process can be assessed without directly affecting the respondents. Thus, Empey and Lubeck have suggested that such techniques might include the use of concealed videotape cameras and sound systems in order to collect information on group development. An additional benefit of this approach is that the information collected could be used as information feedback to the respondents. Similarly, as demonstrated in the work of Polsky,[8] the use of unobtrusive ways of measuring power groupings within institutions might involve observations of seating patterns. Additionally, sociometric techniques could be used for developing measures of friendship patterns, while measures of the amount and nature of interaction between staff and clients can be achieved through participant-observation.

In short, there are a variety of ways to collect information that can be used as measures of how the program operates, as well as to help explain program outcomes. It would seem at least equally important to understand, for example, how a total institutional setting affects the inmate as it would be to understand the relative extent to which such an organization achieves formally specified goals.

COMMON PROBLEMS IN MEASURING CHANGE

PUNY INTERVENTIONS

As formally reflected in commonly articulated social program goals, optimism about man's propensity to change is exceeded only by the accumulation of negative evaluation findings. Man is a perverse creature and highly resistant to change; consequently, it is probably foolish to expect that massive change will occur in client groups on the basis of relatively weak and diluted intervention activities. For example, what reason is there to expect that twice-weekly group meetings within a prison setting will result in significant changes in inmate behavior upon release, or that a reduction in the size of parole or probation caseloads will massively impact upon parolee or probationer behavior? If one accepts the idea that a large proportion of the individuals caught up in human service systems are products of total environments of deprivation and lengthy periods of training and socialization, it appears

rather naive to expect that relatively anemic and time-limited intervention activities will result in major positive outcome effects. Such
expectations are as much a commentary upon the naivete of people
responsible for framing social program goals as on the evaluator who
uncritically accepts such goals and sets about the task of measuring
their relative accomplishment. A pre-evaluation assessment by the
investigator of program activities and goals conducted prior to mounting a full-blown evaluation research effort may prove extremely useful
and save considerable time and expense.[9]

MIXED PROGRAM INGREDIENTS

Not only are social programs often lacking in a reasonable potential
for significantly affecting client groups, but they also commonly constitute an extremely mixed and cluttered assortment of activities. For
example, corrections programs are usually quite varied in nature, and
within any operating program there can commonly be found a variety
of intervention activities—from group treatment of various sorts to
individual treatment approaches, to job counseling, to the use of
volunteers. The problem confronting the evaluator, then, is to take the
"program" as the independent variable and develop and implement an
appropriate research design so as to be able to test the relative effects of
the mixed collection of components on the limited number of individuals exposed to them. The problem is obvious and the solution is far
from simple. Because of the number and variety of intervention activities commonly found in social programs, a variety of measures is
usually called for, corresponding to the major program components.
What Suchman[10] refers to as "component" or "variable" testing as
opposed to program testing is the preferred measurement approach.
Unfortunately, however, the development and use of program component measures is commonly complicated by the problem of isolating
the varied component effects relative to overall program outcomes.

FLEXIBILITY DEMANDS

The problem of mixed and diluted independent variables is frequently compounded by the administrative requirement for flexibility
in modifying programs as required by changing circumstances. As a
consequence, the mixed collection of program components is often
differentially modified in both form and content. Thus, within any
program, staff members may come and go, different program components take precedence at different times, program components are
changed or dropped completely in response to the changing nature of

the clientele or different treatment preferences of staff. Such practices have serious implications for the evaluation research and are commonly associated with management needs for relatively quick answers to pressing and immediate problems. Quick answers are not likely to be forthcoming from rigorous evaluations that involve extensive follow-up periods. In addition, the unwillingness of administrators to radically alter managerial practices in order to comply with the formal research design requirements of the evaluator, are notorious and cause serious problems for the research.

MODELS OF CAUSATION

A related problem confronting the evaluator in transforming a practical problem of social action agencies into a problem amenable to measurement is the inadequacy of the model and methodology which underlie evaluation efforts. For the most part, evaluation research projects involve a simple model of causation assuming a linear relationship between exposure or involvement in a set of intervention activities and certain desired outcomes. Simple linear relationships, however, may be only one, relatively rare type of function that can be used to explain the relationships between program input, processing, and outcome. Other types of relationships need considerations: These include curvilinear relationships or nonlinear step functions in which a particular level of program effort may have no appreciable effect on the desired outcome until its value has reached a certain level. As a consequence, research may show no significant relationship between intervention activities and program outcomes, even though a large potential effect may, in fact, be generating.[11]

One example of current attempts to improve measurement efforts within evaluation research is that of matching particular types of clients with particular types of intervention activities. In more complicated form, such approaches may involve matching type of client with type of treatment person, type of treatment intervention, and context within which the treatment process is conducted. While the results that have been achieved thus far are not encouraging, the idea makes so much good sense that it continues to survive. For example, in the corrections field, the idea is that for any type of offender, there is a type of treatment or punishment that is most effective. Viewed from this perspective, the evaluation of correctional treatment outcomes has, for the most part, simply involved showing that different types of offenders respond differentially to the same form of treatment and, as a consequence, has only demonstrated that a particular form of treatment which is effective in reducing the recidivism of one type of offender may, in fact, increase the chances of recidivism of different types of offenders. In short, measurement results may tend to mask the differential program effects on clients served.

REACTIVITY OF MEASURES

Many of the measures suggested for the evaluation of process are nonreactive in nature as compared to the more commonly used reactive types of measurements designed to assess program outcomes. Webb and others[12] have noted, for example, that an awareness of being tested may result in reactive effects on the measures used so as to threaten the internal and external validity of the study. In an experiment involving pre- and post-measures in experimental and control groups, it is plausible to expect that reactivity is likely to be equally present in both measurement situations and therefore the primary threat to the research is to external validity. However, if there is in fact a variable reactive effect resulting from the application of measures, problems of internal validity are likely to arise. Thus, outcome differences may be a pseudo-difference resulting from differential reactivity of measures.

Evaluative research studies which rely upon interview or questionnaire methods are particularly open to reactive efforts, especially in those social programs in which power is exercised by staff over the lives of clients. In the correctional field, for example, much of the information utilized in evaluation studies have been collected by probation/ parole officers or caseworkers within correctional institutions. Such officials possess significant levels of authority and power over the life situation of offenders and, as a consequence, are likely to have significant reactive effects on the quality of the information obtained. Guarantees of anonymity as a safeguard against reactive bias are not likely to occur in the normal operation of correctional organizations because, most characteristically, the information collected by officials is related specifically to decisions to be made about a particular individual. Without the identification of the individual offender, the information loses most, if not all, of its utility for decision-making—whether to release on parole, provide alternative judicial dispositions, return to an institution, and so on. As a result, it is reasonable to expect that there is a relationship between the awareness of being tested and the tendency to bias answers by responding in a socially desirable form.

Another way in which an awareness of being measured can produce differential reactions among respondents is that of differential role selection by individuals being measured. In this type of situation, the fact of measurement may force the individual into taking on a different social role from that which would ordinarily be performed. Consequently, the validity of the measure decreases proportionate to the extent that the role being performed in the measurement situation varies from the usual role present in a comparable situation outside the measurement setting. The effect of using such measurements is to call into question the internal validity of the study. The relative lack of familiarity of clients in many types of social programs with formal testing situations may well result in highly unrepresentative responses. Sykes and Matza,[13] for example, have listed a number of stereotyped responses commonly forthcoming from delinquents questioned about the reasons for their delinquent acts. To some considerable extent, the youth take on social roles for the purpose of neutralizing societal disapproval. Similarly, the interview setting can have the effect of eliciting different roles on the part of the individual as compared to those which may be elicited in more natural situations.

A major implication of the potentially reactive effects of different measures is the importance of utilizing combined or triangulated measurement. Research instruments need to be constructed with consideration for their use in combination with other techniques. This could involve triangulation within classes of measurement in the form of using several different measures to assess the same phenomenon, or it may involve between-class triangulation, in which case several different methods and measures are combined to assess a particular phenomenon.[14]

PROBLEMS WITH STATED GOALS

Measures of program effects most commonly and directly relate to the relative achievement of program goals. In this sense, goals are the intended consequences of the program, and unless they have been articulated in clear, specific, meaningful, and measurable terms, the development of adequate measures can be difficult, if not impossible. Among the major problems associated with formally stating program goals and developing measures relevant to these goals are those of vagueness or imprecision, multiple and conflicting goals, and goals which are irrelevant to the program under study.

Vaguely stated program goals are more often the rule than the exception within social programs. While such ambiguous goal statements as "preventing delinquency," "reducing recidivism," and "enhancing pro-social behaviors" may serve useful purposes for programs in receiving support from different and potentially conflicting interest groups within the community, such statements are essentially useless for the evaluator confronted with the problem of developing appropriate measures.

For the evaluator confronted with fuzzy goals, Weiss[15] has listed four possible courses of action. As one alternative, she notes that the evaluator can raise the question as to what the goals mean in operational terms and simply wait for program staff to formulate agreed-upon goal statements in an appropriate manner. A long wait may then be forthcoming. A second alternative is for the evaluator to simply proceed in framing the program goals, develop relevant measures, and carry out the study. The obvious problem with this alternative is the likelihood of the research imputing inappropriate goals to the program, and as a consequence, developing irrelevant measures. A third alternative is for the researcher and program staff to jointly collaborate in the formulation of operational goals. In this joint venture, the program staff can provide their informed view of what the program is attempting to accomplish, while the researcher can relate to measurement problems posed by the evolving goal statements. A fourth course of action is to orient the evaluation toward discovering goals rather than verifying the relative achievement of goals. Given a lack of knowledge about the relationship between intervention activities and outcomes, as well as the ever-changing nature of social programs, an evaluation strategy focused on an inductive "discovery" stance may be more feasible than a strategy of verification. Clearly, however, the issue as to whether the evaluation will focus on verifying the relative achievement of formally stated program goals or concentrate on "discovering" program goals should be resolved on the basis of the formally agreed-upon purpose of the evaluation.

The multiple goals commonly held by social programs often cause major measurement problems for the evaluator. For example, police programs are often expected to achieve goals of preventing or reducing crime, providing social welfare services, protecting individual liberties, and so on. Similarly, the courts are expected to convict the guilty, protect the innocent and conduct proceedings with fairness and restraint. Finally, correctional organizations commonly hold such goals as containing dangerous offenders, reducing recidivism through rehabilitation, deterring crime incidence through general methods, maintaining order in institutions, and providing due process protections. Moreover, at an individual level, social programs are often concerned with many kinds of program outcomes—educational, vocational, familial, interpersonal. Consequently, it is important that the evaluation researcher within such agencies be sensitive to the variety of potential program effects and develop appropriate measures that can be used to separately assess the relative achievement of the various program goals.

Conflict between goals frequently compounds the problem of developing appropriate measures for the multiple goals of social programs. The relative achievement of one goal may have negative implications for the relative achievement of others. For example, the goal of reducing prison escapes may conflict with the goal of providing greater degrees of freedom to inmates. Similarly, the goal of providing high-intensity police patrols within high-crime neighborhoods may conflict with the goal of reducing crime as measured by police clearance rates. A partial solution to the problem of attempting to evaluate a plurality of conflicting goals within human service agencies is for the researcher to work closely with program personnel in establishing the logical relationship between multiple goals, as well as the priorities among goals. Most appropriately, this should occur at the pre-evaluation planning stage and take the form of a critical analysis of the set of intervention activities in relation to the stipulated goals. At this stage of the research, multiple goals can be identified, possible conflicts established, and decisions made concerning priorities among the goals, as well as the appropriate measures that will need to be developed and implemented.

It may be particularly important for evaluation researchers to keep in mind the multiple goals associated with human service agencies and the need to develop a variety of measures to assess their relative achievement in light of the problem of goal distortion which has been noted by Etzioni.

> Curiously, the very effort—the desire to establish how we are doing and to find ways of improving if we are not doing as well as we ought to do—often has quite undesired effects from the point of view of organizational goals. Frequent measuring can distort the organizational efforts because, as a rule, some aspects of its outputs are more measurable than the others. Frequent measuring tends to encourage over-production of highly measurable items and the neglect of less measurable ones. . . . The distortion consequences of over-measuring are larger when it is impossible or impractical to quantify the more central, substantive output of an organization, and when at the same time, some exterior aspects of the product, which are superficially related to its substance, are readily measurable.[16]

The need for developing and implementing diverse measures to assess the variety of organizational goals may be particularly relevant to criminal justice agencies. Within corrections organizations, for example, an exclusive reliance on measuring the goal of reducing recidivism, however this may be defined, may have the distorting effect upon the organization of placing relatively less emphasis upon such difficult to quantify goals as justice, fairness, decency, and civility. One could speculate that to some extent the contemporary disillusionment with the rehabilitation ideal has resulted from an overemphasis placed upon the negative evaluation research findings of easily quantified recidivism goals to the relative disregard of less-easily-quantified goals concerning humaneness and justice.

The distinction between officially held and unofficially practiced goals is a further issue holding implications for measuring the effects of social action programs. Like most organizations, human service agencies are highly complex and ever-changing. Consequently, organizational goals may best be viewed as evolving over time. As a result, officially prescribed goals may not be modified in relation to the changing practices of the organization. Thus, if the evaluator is not sensitive to the changing nature of the organization and measures are developed only in relation to the formal or official goals of the agency, such measures may have little relationship to actual or unofficial agency goals.

RELIABILITY AND VALIDITY OF MEASURES

The most commonly used outcome indicators of program success in criminal justice agencies are measures of "recidivism." A major problem associated with the concept of recidivism, however, is that it is extremely vague and ambiguous and commonly used to communicate different meanings. Recidivism can be used to refer to re-arrests, revocations, reconvictions, or re-imprisonment. Furthermore, each of these measures is often defined in several different ways.

Vasoli,[17] for example, has provided a striking illustration of the lack of common definitions and outcome measures of probation success. In his study of 814 federal offenders probationed between 1946 and 1960, Vasoli found that 155 or 622 probationers officially counted as "successes" had committed at least one felony during their probation term—including one homicide, two rapes, twelve robberies, thirty-one burglaries, and thirty-four auto thefts. To a considerable extent, this was found to be a function of the manner in which probation outcome was defined. Thus, when a federal probationer was convicted and imprisoned for an offense falling under state jurisdiction, the federal probation officer terminated probation and relinquished jurisdiction over the offender to the state authorities. Officially, therefore, the offender was classed as a "success" because he had not been found guilty of committing a federal offense while on probation, even though he had been convicted of criminal offenses falling under state jurisdiction. A further example of this situation is common within parole agencies dealing with juvenile offenders. In many of these jurisdictions, it is a common practice for the paroling or releasing authority to relinquish jurisdiction over juveniles when they reach the age of majority and are charged with new offenses. In such cases, the parolee is usually discharged from parole status and defined as a "success" for administrative purposes even though he may subsequently be convicted of an offense which, in fact, occurred while on parole. In both cases, the imprecise manner in which important outcomes are defined will seriously affect the success rate of a program.

Another major validity problem associated with the use of common measures of program outcomes in criminal justice programs is that they are based upon information collected and reported by the criminal justice agencies themselves, usually as a routine part of their everyday activities. This is not so commonly the case in evaluation research completed in other fields where researchers more frequently collect information and develop measures independent of information collected and provided by the agencies themselves. This feature of the measures used in criminal justice evaluation poses several problems. First, officially collected information used as measures of program outcomes are, by their very nature, indirect measures of behavior. For example, we have no practical or direct way of measuring the actual extent to which graduates of correctional programs commit new crimes. Second, the measurements provided are commonly open to serious problems. For example, the number of crimes known to authorities in most situations is only a fraction of the number of crimes committed, although that fraction varies from crime to crime. This problem is compounded by the fact that the relationship between reported and unreported crime is not constant but variable over time. Thus, changes in policy and public attitudes can result in changes in the proportion of reported crime between both different geographical jurisdictions, different times, and different types of reported crime. The growing willingness of victims of sexual assault to report their crimes to the police and actively cooperate in prosecution is an example of the manner in which public attitudes can affect officially recorded rates of crime.

Of the various criteria used to measure recidivism, that of arrest appears to be especially problematic. The use of arrest as a measure of recidivism seems to fly in the face of the principle that an individual is presumed innocent until proven guilty. Recidivism rates based on arrest do not tell us whether those arrested have, in fact, returned to criminal behavior but only that they are presumed to have done so. At the same time, however, one might suggest that arrests may be the most accurate measure of return to criminal behavior on the grounds that it is the institutional response closest to the individual's behavior. In other words, it is argued that the further one is processed through the criminal justice system, the more likely it is that the institutional response will not be descriptive of the individual's behavior. For example, an individual convicted of trespassing may have been arrested in the act of committing a burglary and plea bargained the offense down.

The widespread discretion exercised by the police to arrest is a further source of invalidity. For example, it is probably reasonable to expect that the number of individuals arrested for a particular type of crime within a jurisdiction is to some extent a direct reflection of changing police policies and not totally the function of changing patterns of law-violating behavior. In addition to the power of deciding when to arrest, police also have discretionary authority to determine which of a number of crimes an individual will be arrested for in a particular situation. Thus, if policy emphasis is placed upon combating burglary, this may affect the decisions as to whether an arrestee is to be arrested for burglary, simple larceny, or criminal damage to property. In short, the discretion of the police to control both the number and type of arrests raises serious validity problems in evaluations which attempt to use this measure of program outcome.

In most jurisdictions, the probation or parole status of an offender can be revoked for a number of reasons, including conviction of a misdemeanor or felony, the admission of such an offense, the parole or probation officer's allegation that a criminal offense was committed or the offender's violation of technical rules of probation or parole. A major problem with the use of revocation rates as a measure of recidivism is the extent to which such rates are open to manipulation through agency policy. An example of such manipulation has been provided in reassessments of the measures obtained in the evaluation research conducted on the California Community Treatment Project. The research conducted on this project included randomly selected experimental and control groups, with the experimental group released to the community where each offender was diagnosed according to his maturity level and, on the basis of this diagnosis, assigned to a parole officer who was defined as particularly skilled in working with that type of delinquent. The control group was assigned to one of the state correctional institutions where, after the normal length of confinement, the members were released on regular parole. Experimental caseloads in the community were small, from nine to ten offenders per officer, as compared to regular parole caseloads of approximately fifty-five offenders per parole officer. Robison and Smith have noted that a follow up of the two groups strongly favored the experimental community program:

> At the 15-month period, 30% of male experimentals had "violated parole or had been unfavorably discharged," compared with 51% of male control . . . at the 24-month period, these outcomes were 43% and 63%, respectively, again favoring the experimental group. If we take these findings at face value, we are forced to conclude that probation has been proven to be a more effective correctional program than imprisonment for reducing recidivism. But has it?[18]

In fact, as these authors go on to indicate, considerable evidence has been established to indicate that the reported figures were a function of the discretionary authority exercised by parole officers. Clearly, since the primary dependent measure was revocation of parole, the findings are to some undetermined extent a function of parole officer discretion. Thus, Lerman[19] has shown that parole officers responsible for dealing with control group members were much more inclined than parole officers dealing with experimental cases to revoke parole for low or moderately serious offenses. Furthermore, Lerman has demonstrated that parole officers working with experimental group members were far more inclined to use temporary detention and retain the offender on parole than was the case with parole officers dealing with control group members.

Consequently, in order for revocation rates to have much use as measures of recidivism, it is important to note the reason for the revocation. It is also important to distinguish between revocations for new offenses and revocations for technical violations of parole or probation. Without such distinctions, there are serious problems involved in using revocation rates as a measure of return to criminal behavior. Furthermore, in using such rates, it is necessary to keep in mind that parolees and probationers may in fact commit new offenses without being revoked. Finally, it is important to note that this measure cannot be applied to those receiving flat discharges from institutions. In this respect, one common fallacy is to compare revocation rates with the return to prison rates of inmates released on flat discharges from institutions. Thus, the return to prison rate for a group of men released on parole is compared to the return rate for a group of men released on mandatory discharge, and the positive findings are used to support the claimed superior effects of parole. The biased nature of the sample is lost sight of in such conclusions.

The conviction rate for new offenses is commonly used as a measure of the frequency of return to proven criminal behavior. When this measure is used, distinctions are commonly made between types of offenses and types of dispositions resulting from the offenses. For example, a variety of offense seriousness scales have been developed to refine measures of recidivism based upon conviction. Similarly, levels of severity of disposition have been used in a number of outcome studies. For example, the distinction would be made between convictions resulting in a disposition to a state prison as compared to probation. Conviction rates do offer an advantage over the use of revocation rates as a measure of recidivism because they include convictions for all ex-offenders and not just those placed on probation and parole. Furthermore, such rates do not include the often arbitrary category of technical parole or parole violations. Clearly, however, this measure is open to the confounding effect of plea bargaining which may result in the conviction offense having little relationship to the offense actually committed.

Incarceration rates provide a measure of the frequency with which a population of offenders is placed in correctional institutions. Such rates usually include those offenders returned to institutions as a result of parole revocations as well as those who are sent to an institution partly because of probation revocations and partly for commitments arising out of convictions for new offenses. Because not all offenders who are convicted of new offenses are sentenced to correctional institutions, incarceration rates will be lower than conviction rates.

Correctional administrators are particularly interested in incarceration rates being divided into the categories of "return" rates for those who have previously been housed in a correctional institution and a "new admission" rate for those entering such institutions for the first time. The return rate will be of particular interest to the correctional agency because it is this group of offenders who have been previously exposed to the institutional program but who failed in adjusting to the larger community upon release.

In summary, a number of different measures can be used to determine the recidivism rate of categories of offenders. While each

measure may have some degree of utility for different agencies within
the criminal justice system, each of the measures also has drawbacks to
accurately determining the rate of return to criminal behavior by
products of the system. Consequently, different measures will no doubt
continue to be utilized and emphasized by different officials within the
criminal justice system.

CASE EXAMPLE: THE MINNESOTA
RESTITUTION CENTER

Beginning in September 1971, the Minnesota Restitution Center was
developed as a community-based residential corrections program for
adult males committed to the Minnesota State Prison. The program
aims at diverting selected property offenders from the state prison and
into the Center four months after admission to the prison. A central
focus of the program is on the active collaboration of the offender and
his victims in the development of a restitution agreement specifying the
amount of damages sustained as a result of the victimization and the
amount, form, and schedule of restitution to be made. Staff at the
Center are responsible for helping mediate the restitution negotiations
and, following the parole of the offender to the Center, helping facilitate the offender's completion of the agreement. In this respect, staff
members are responsible for monitoring the restitution schedule, helping residents obtain and maintain work, and providing necessary assistance required by residents in utilizing community resources.

The evaluation research design for the program during the first
twenty-four months of program operation took the form of a before-
after experiment with the random assignment of men from within a
specified population of recent prison admissions. The randomly selected experimental and control group members were, respectively,
designated to enter the Restitution Center after four months in prison
or remain in the conventional prison program until normal release date.
The difference between the two groups on outcome measures would
then be used to assess the effects of the experimental program relative
to the alternative prison program. While the logic of the design was
sound, the task of integrating the research design with the operational
program raised a variety of measurement problems each having major
implications for the assessment of change.

As initially conceptualized, the major intervention activity within
the Restitution Center program was to be offender restitution to crime

victims. More specifically, the process of offender restitution as operationalized in the program involved three major phases: direct victim/
offender meetings for the purpose of negotiating restitution agreements
involving the amount and form of restitution to be made; the ongoing
repayment process involving person-to-person offender/victim contacts;
the completion of restitution in accordance with the written restitution
agreement. Clearly, restitution was designed to be the sole sanction, and
upon the offender's successful completion of the agreement, it was
anticipated by the program designers that the offender would be
released from supervision.

As previously noted, the eligible population for the program were
property offenders who had been recently admitted to the prison. Both
the nature of this population and the perception held toward the
restitution sanction by members of the parole board has confounding
implications for the research design.

Almost totally, the men meeting the eligible criteria, randomly
selected and admitted to the Center, had criminal records involving a
long list of convictions and multiple incarcerations. None of these men
had a record of violent crimes against persons but, in common with
most property offenders who have high return to prison rates, they
were extremely poor risks for remaining out of future difficulties with
the law. At least as a partial result of their prior criminal records, the
Restitution Center residents had received fairly lengthy prison sentences. Thus, the men admitted to the Center during the first year of
program operation had prison sentences averaging four years. The
Restitution Center obtained these offenders four months following
prison admission.

PUNY INTERVENTION

In common with information available on the general amount of
damages usually incurred in property crimes, the group of men admitted to the program had been convicted of crimes involving only
limited amounts of damages. Undoubtedly, the inefficiency of law
enforcement in apprehending the offenders, coupled with the process
of plea bargaining, had reduced the actual true amount of criminal
damages done. In any case, the mean average amount of restitution to
be made by program participants only approximated a few hundred
dollars. Thus, a situation existed in which a group of offenders having
long criminal histories and with long prison sentences were obligated to
complete only relatively small amounts of restitution.

MIXED PROGRAM INGREDIENTS

Relative to both the offender's prior record and the length of the prison sentences received, the restitution sanction appeared inconsequential to the members of the parole board. As a result, the politically sensitive members of the parole board refused to discharge program residents from parole status upon completing the agreed-upon amount of restitution. In order to deal with residents who had completed restitution obligations and at the same time comply with Parole Board policies concerning parole supervision, these offenders were provided with conventional parole supervision in the community by Restitution Center staff. Requiring Center residents to remain under the parole supervision of the program helped extend the span of control exercised by the program over residents. Furthermore, restitution was no longer the sole or even primary sanction (intervention activity—independent variable) in the program. The more ambiguous and diffuse set of activities commonly contained in the process of conventional parole supervision became a more integral part of the program. Not only are these activities difficult to operationalize, but they raise serious problems for measurement. To carefully assess the variety of activities commonly engaged in by parole officers would have taken more research staff than the program could afford.

The problem then became one of how to isolate the differential impact of various types of program interventions relative to the overall aggregate impact of these activities in the form of the "program." An equally and perhaps more vexing problem was that of generalizing the research results obtained to other settings or populations. Two major problems are involved here: First, the fact that the different intervention activities were introduced serially over time and, upon being introduced, were then modified and refined as staff became more familiar and skilled in their use. A complicating problem was that different intervention emphases were used by staff with different residents, and this frequently appeared to change over time according to staff perceptions of offender needs.

In short, the Restitution Center program at the end of the first year of operation consisted of a variety of different intervention activities implemented at different times by different staff with different emphases and skills over time to a group of men randomly selected from a newly admitted population of prison admissions during a twelve-month period. One would be hard put to find a larger universe to which any measurement results obtained from this evaluation could be generalized, and the probability of replicating the project in other settings with

any degree of similarity is highly doubtful. Even given these qualifications, it is probably safe to assume that the evaluation results from this
project will be construed and used by significant audiences to "prove"
that restitution is or is not an effective correctional sanction.

Not only were the changing perceptions of the parole board important in transforming the character of the program, the perceptions of
Center staff concerning resident needs relative to the restitution sanction also tended to lead into a further dilution of the role of restitution
in the program as compared to the increasingly more central place of
more conventional types of intervention activities.

In common with a great proportion of men convicted and incarcer-
ated for offenses against the property of others, many Center residents
had long histories of chemical dependency problems. Coupled with the
tendency of program staff to perceive such problems as symptomatic of
intrapsychic needs, pressures were generated to include a structured
form of group counseling in the program of the Restitution Center.
Twice weekly two-hour group therapy or counseling sessions were
initiated. The effect on the evaluation research was one of further
complicating the independent variables. The problems caused for the
research of mixed program interventions were complicated by the serial
introduction of these different interventions into the program. The
different interventions were not introduced as a program package with
the inception of the Center; residents admitted to the program experienced different "pieces" of the program according to their time of
admission.

With respect to the mixed nature of the different set of interventions
introduced in the form of the Restitution Center program, Suchman's
previously noted point about the importance of relating the purpose of
an evaluation to the developmental stage of a program appears germane.
While technically correct, however, it does fail to consider the practical
realities of developing and operating social programs. For example,
program stability can work against the use of rigorous evaluation
research. A newly implemented social program at the pilot stage of
development and utilizing a nonrigorous evaluation research design
may, upon achieving program stability at the model stage of program
development, find it virtually impossible to radically alter accepted
practices. Once continuity and relative stability of program inputs have
been attained, significant publics, client groups, and staff members have
all become accustomed to evaluation research procedures as they have
been customarily articulated with program practices. Likely to be
discouraged, for example, is any attempt to shift the accepted practice

of purposively selecting clients to a practice of randomly selecting clients for the program.

FLEXIBILITY DEMANDS

The evaluation research conducted on the Restitution Center program is an example of this point. An experimental design was used and implemented concurrent with the program. In short, an evaluation design suggested as being compatible with the model stage of program development was, in fact, utilized during the initial pilot stage of development. Following Suchman's logic, one might argue against such a practice on the grounds that the new and unstable Restitution Center program should have set as an initial goal the development of program stability along with general community acceptance before attempting to implement a rigorous evaluation design involving random selection procedures. Quite clearly, however, any attempt to change radically the accepted research and operational procedures once the Restitution Center program achieved a level of relative stability and acceptance would be likely to be strongly resisted by significant publics, not least of whom would have been the parolling authority. Consequently, the alternative of organizing and implementing rigorous research procedures concurrent with the program was pursued in this project. The problems caused for the research by the lack of program stability have been previously noted.

MODEL OF CAUSATION

The primary causal relationship originally designed to be measured in the evaluation of the Restitution Program was (1) whether a specified sample of prison inmates released to the Restitution Center after four months in prison and after having developed a formal restitution agreement with their crime victims would pay back damages, and (2) whether this action would be significantly and positively reflected in outcome measures for this group as compared to another sample of men who completed full sentences in prison followed by supervision within the community on conventional parole. There are a number of problems with this type of causal relationship, most notably the likelihood that any measurement results obtained might mask differential program effects. For example, the longer prison sentences received by some members of the control group might reduce or eliminate contacts with the criminal subculture and consequently reduce the rate of return to crime when the inmate leaves prison. For others, however, long prison sentences might isolate them from family, job opportunities, and so on, and therefore make them more likely to commit further offenses after being released from prison.

Once the likelihood of differential effects is accepted, several major implications for measurement results need to be considered. First, interaction effects of treatment may offset one another and as a result, mask similar overall outcomes for two or more types of treatment. For example, the overall success rates for the two different sets of intervention activities to be found in the Restitution Center/Prison experiment might be shown to be the same. It could then be concluded that there was no difference in effectiveness between the two. However, classifying the two groups of offenders into different types might bring out differentials in program outcomes. Clearly, then, the number of offenders of each type that a program deals with is likely to directly affect differences in program outcomes. Quite obviously, the measurement problems caused for an evaluation by the possibility of interaction effects between type of treatment and type of client can be further compounded by the need to also consider the possibility of matching the type of treatment person dispensing the intervention activity as well as the context within which the treatment or intervention is being provided. Just as all plumbers, electricians, and auto mechanics are not equally skilled in dealing with all types of problems common to their fields, so it may not be wise to assume that all human service workers are equally skilled and competent to deal with all types of clients or client problems. Similarily, the context within which the intervention activity is being provided is likely to directly impinge upon the treatment service itself. For example, a specific type of psychotherapy provided within a penal setting may have strikingly different effects as compared to the same intervention provided within a mental health center in the community.

In summary, when we begin to fully consider the present state of our intervention activities in relation to questions about who gets what from whom and in what context, we can begin to grasp the complexities involved in measuring change through the conduct of evaluation research.

GOALS—MEASURES OF RECIDIVISM

In common with most evaluations of criminal justice programs, the research conducted on the Restitution Center made use of indices of recidivism. A major confounding problem for such measures concerned the residential nature of this program and the close supervision provided to the residents. The highly intrusive character of residential corrections programs coupled with the fact that program clients were released from prison on parole to the Center four months following admission to the prison, helped to ensure that considerable staff attention was given to actively supervising program residents—(i.e., direct and indirect talking with or about the client concerning varied aspects of his contemporary or historical life situation with particular attention to program rule violations, inclusive of the larger societal sanctions against criminal behavior).

On the one hand, relatively intensive parole supervision could have potentially negative effects on the measures used to assess program impact. For example, from relatively more intensive degrees of parole supervision, one might expect some corresponding changes in parole revocation rates. The logic is that relatively close supervision affords the parole officer greater amounts of time and energy to give to learning about the activities of the offender. In addition, there may be a tendency on the part of staff within a recently opened community corrections center to be particularly vigilant about the specific mental and physical location of each resident. Furthermore, such a program may be particularly concerned with demonstrating credibility to the referral source (parole board) as well as to present and future clientele by recommending that parole be revoked for certain nonconforming clients.

An alternative and quite different view of the likely effects of close parole supervision within the context of a residential community corrections center follows from the logic inherent in the crime control through deterrence argument. Thus, the close supervision afforded Restitution Center residents could have had a potential deterrent effect upon their individual susceptibilities to commit crimes. Putting this in treatment terms, the close supervision provided in the combined form of counseling or treatment techniques and surveillance activities acts as a specific form of deterrence on the offender's tendency toward committing criminal acts.

Regardless of whether the offender is to be regarded as "cured" of the purportedly irrational motives lying behind manifestations of criminal behavior or whether he has been deterred through fear of criminal sanctions, a deflationary effect on official indices of criminal behavior for the recipient of intensive parole supervision is likely to result. Given the relative lack of documented outcome effects of corrections programs, perhaps the most significant point in support of the notion that intensive parole supervision leads to relatively deflated indices of parole failure is the evidence presented by Lerman which indicates that both parole officers and parole boards exercise their discretionary authority to recommend parole violations in a variable manner relative to a host of criteria. Predominant among these may be the nature of the program context within which parole supervision is being dispensed. Operating within the context of an "experimental" program, parole officers are less likely to recommend parole revocation for particular forms of misbehavior than are their counterparts assigned parolees designed to receive the conventional form and amount of parole supervision. In short, a Hawthorne effect can be attributed to the experimental program. The result for the research conducted on the Restitution Center is that the parole outcome measures of the experimental group as compared to the controls is to some undetermined extent a function of the interaction of parole officer behavior and parolee behavior and not solely one of a neutral parole officer objectively and consistently responding to actual parolee behavior.

In summary, logical argument and empirical documentation can be used to support notions about the relative measured effects of providing intensive parole supervision. As a result, the question as to whether the measures of parole outcome performance used in the evaluation of the Restitution Center are inflated or deflated can only be indirectly answered. The discretion of the police officer to arrest or not and instead take the presumably offending program resident back to the Center; the discretion of the prosecutor to prosecute or to plea bargain in a differential way according to whether or not the accused is a resident of the Center; the discretion inherent in judicial dispositions all tend to affect problems of the validity and reliability of official statistics when used as proxy outcome measures of program success.

CONCLUSION

Some practical problems associated with measuring and attributing change to social program interventions have been identified in this chapter. As an illustration of these problems, the evaluation conducted on a community residential corrections program has been used. Most generally, measurement problems appear to follow from a lack of congruence between the purpose of the evaluation and the developmental life of the program, especially in relation to the nature of the program interventions, the articulated goal statements, and the validity and reliability of measures.

NOTES

1. Michael Scriven. "The Methodology of Evaluation," in Carol H. Weiss (ed.) *Evaluating Action Programs.* Boston: Allyn & Bacon, 1973, pp. 123-126.

2. Edward A. Suchman. "Action for What? A Critique of Evaluative Research," in Carol H. Weiss (ed.) *Evaluating Action Programs.* Boston: Allyn & Bacon, 1973, pp. 52-84.

3. Seymour B. Sarason. *The Creation of Settings and The Future Societies.* San Francisco: Jossey-Bass, 1972.

4. Donald J. Kiesler. "Experimental Designs in Psychotherapy Research," in Allen E. Bergin and Sol L. Garfield (eds.) *Handbook of Psychotherapy and Behavior Change: An Empirical Analysis.* New York: John Wiley, 1971, pp. 36-74.

5. Robert S. Weiss and Martin Rein. "The Evaluation of Broad Aim Programs: A Cautionary Case and a Moral," in Francis G. Caro (ed.) *Readings in Evaluation Research.* New York: Russell Sage Foundation, 1971, pp. 175-184.

6. Malcolm W. Klein and Neal Snyder. "The Detached Worker: Uniformities and Variances in Work Style," *Social Work* 10, October 1965, pp. 60-68.

7. LaMar T. Empey and Steven G. Lubeck. *The Silverlake Experiment.* Chicago: Aldine, 1971, pp. 312-319.

8. Howard W. Polsky. *Cottage Six.* New York: Russell Sage Foundation, 1962; Howard W. Polsky and Daniel S. Claster. *The Dynamics of Residential Treatment.* Chapel Hill: University of North Carolina Press, 1968.

9. See, for a similar point on the need for "informed rational analysis" in evaluation research, Ronald L. Warren. "The Social Context of Program Evaluation Research," in William C. Sze and June G. Hopp (eds.) *Evaluation and Accountability in Human Service Programs.* Cambridge, Mass.: Schenkman, 1974, pp. 13-35.

10. Edward A. Suchman. *Evaluative Research.* New York: Russell Sage Foundation, 1967, pp. 77-79.

11. See, for example, Walter Buckley. *Sociology and Modern Systems Theory.* Englewood Cliffs, N.J.: Prentice-Hall, 1967.

12. Eugene J. Webb, Donald T. Campbell, Richard D. Schwartz, and Lee Sechrest. *Unobtrusive Measures: Nonreactive Research in the Social Sciences.* Chicago: Rand-McNally, 1972.

13. Gresham M. Sykes and David Matza. "Techniques of Neutralization: A Theory of Delinquency," *American Sociological Review* 22, December 1957, pp. 664-670.

14. Donald T. Campbell and Donald W. Fiske. "Convergent and Discriminant Validation by the Multitrait-Multimethod Matrix," in William A. Mehrens and Robert L. Ebel (eds.) *Principles of Educational and Psychological Measurement.* Chicago: Rand-McNally, 1967, pp. 273-302.

15. Carol Weiss. *Evaluation Research: Methods of Assessing Program Effectiveness.* Englewood Cliffs, N.J.: Prentice-Hall, 1972.

16. A. Etzioni. *Modern Organizations.* Englewood Cliffs, N.J.: Prentice-Hall, 1964, pp. 9-10.

17. Robert H. Vasoli. "Some Reflections on Measuring Probation Outcome," in Robert M. Carter and Leslie Wilkins, *Probation and Parole.* New York: John Wiley, 1970, pp. 327-341.

18. James Robison and Gerald Smith. "The Effectiveness of Correctional Programs," *Crime and Delinquency* 17, January 1971, p. 73.

19. Paul Lerman. *Community Treatment and Social Control.* Chicago: University of Chicago Press, 1975.

Having identified and developed measures for the variables which will be included in the evaluation, attention can now be paid to the concern of research design. The major focus of this chapter is on internal validity—i.e., concerns about causal relationships. To ensure internal validity, attempts are made to rule out alternative explanations of the measured effects, leaving the program as the plausible cause. The authors show how an experimental design, involving random assignment to an experimental and control group, safeguard threats to internal validity.

In the "real world," there are numerous obstacles and sources of resistance to randomization. These are identified and some solutions are provided. The authors then describe quasi-experimental designs which can be implemented when resistance to randomization is too strong, if a program has to be implemented universally, or if one wishes to investigate the impact of a change after an intervention has already taken place.

The focus of Chapter 5 is on research designs aimed at providing relatively unequivocal causal inferences. Less attention is paid to external validity which is concerned with the design features which permit generalizations across different people, times, and settings. There is a dilemma in that the controls necessary to ensure internal validity often limit the generalizability of the findings (i.e., threats to external validity). Since this chapter is primarily concerned with design issues relevant for making causal inferences about the program's effects, attention is focused on internal validity.

5

RANDOMIZED AND QUASI-EXPERIMENTAL DESIGNS IN EVALUATION RESEARCH: AN INTRODUCTION

Thomas D. Cook, Fay Lomax Cook, and Melvin M. Mark

INTRODUCTION

Demands to assess the impact of new and existing social programs continue to grow. The field of evaluation research has attempted to meet these demands, but many programs, including pilot ones, are still not empirically evaluated (Rutman and deJong, 1976). In addition, some evaluations are so methodologically flawed that it is difficult to draw inferences about whether the program *has caused* the impacts claimed for it (Bernstein and Freeman, 1975; McTavish et al., 1975; Rutman and deJong, 1976). The primary purpose of this chapter is to suggest methods for decreasing the ambiguity of causal inferences in evaluation research.

Our focus is on the design of *summative evaluations* rather than formative evaluations. Formative evaluations are conducted to provide

AUTHORS' NOTE: The authors are grateful to Deborah Potts, Vita Carulli Rabinowitz, and Myra Roche for their comments on an earlier version of this chapter.

a program director or manager with ways to improve the program or its management. Such research is usually undertaken by in-house staff members who place less emphasis on scientific propriety than on the immediacy of feedback. Summative evaluations, on the other hand, are conducted to assess the impact of a program and are usually designed and carried out by researchers who do not belong to the organization being evaluated. The concern for scientific validity is usually greater in summative evaluations than in formative evaluations.

Most summative evaluations require collecting data within a planned experimental framework. We define an experimental framework as one involving (1) the intervention of some event which can be called a "treatment"; and (2) an assessment of the effects of that treatment by means of (a) the systematic scheduling of control groups and/or (b) the systematic scheduling of the measurement of the units in the study. (These units are usually persons, but need not be so. Treatments can also be assigned to neighborhoods, work groups, schools, or other intact units).

Experiments can be broken into two major classes. In *true experiments,* the experimental units are randomly assigned to treatments. In *quasi-experiments,* assignment to treatments occurs in some nonrandom fashion, usually because individuals choose the treatment they receive or are assigned to a treatment by officials or professionals who believe that certain kinds of individuals should receive particular treatments. Randomized experiments nearly always permit more confident causal inference than quasi-experiments (Campbell, 1969; Rivlin, 1971), but there are numerous factors that make random assignment difficult to implement initially or to maintain over time. This chapter will deal with how to anticipate and deal with these obstacles. However, in some situations true experiments are simply not possible, or they break down after they have been implemented. Therefore, the second major focus in this chapter will be on the design and interpretation of quasi-experiments. First, though, we will introduce four kinds of validity.

FOUR KINDS OF VALIDITY

The ability to make causal inferences is crucial in summative evaluations because the research goal is to learn what effects a program is causing. We do not want to go into a long philosophical discussion of the nature of cause here. Let it suffice to say that causal inference depends on showing that (a) a cause is related to a presumed effect; (b) variation in the cause precedes variation in the effect; and (c) no alternative interpretations of the relationship are possible other than that the cause-as-manipulated influenced the effect-as-measured.

Given these three requirements, it is important to make valid inferences about whether a treatment and possible effect are *related* at all, irrespective of whether the relationship may be causal. Inferential statistics are used for drawing conclusions about simple association. Unfortunately, though, they can be used incorrectly; even when they are correctly used, their probabilistic basis means that false positive and false negative conclusions will sometimes be made (i.e., Type I and Type II errors will occur). We shall use the term *statistical conclusion validity* to refer to the validity of conclusions about the statistical association of a presumed cause and a presumed effect.

To infer statistical association with a high degree of confidence does not logically permit inferring that the association is causal. Causal inference follows only after all competing explanations of why the treatment-as-implemented and the effect-as-measured are associated have been ruled out. They might, for instance, be associated because something that occurred at the same time as the treatment affected the outcome measure, or because taking a pretest increased performance on a posttest measure. We shall use the term *internal validity* to refer to the validity of conclusions about whether the statistical association of a treatment-as-implemented and an effect-as-measured can reasonably be considered as a causal association.

Rarely are we interested in drawing conclusions about a treatment-as-implemented or an effect-as-measured. Instead, we want to refer to a general construct rather than to a particular single way a treatment is implemented or a particular single way an outcome is measured. For example, we want to draw conclusions about "brief casework," as opposed to "John and Jane Doe delivering casework in a supportive atmosphere where they help the client learn to cope with concrete issues such as money management, the handling of landlords, etc." The problem concerns how to use particular manipulations and measures for making inferences about more generalized, hypothetical, and theory-relevant constructs. We shall refer to *construct validity* as the validity with which inferences are made about constructs on the basis of particular manipulations and measures of particular sets of manipulations and measures. For simplicity's sake, we shall restrict ourselves to the construct validity of causes and effects, though it must be acknowledged that the problem of labelling is more general than this.

External validity also deals with the question of generalizability. Here, though, the question is not one of generalizing from specific treatments and measures to more general constructs. Rather, the targets of our attempts to generalize are persons, settings, and historical times, and the validity issue is: To what extent can a causal relationship be generalized to, or across, persons, settings, or times? We mention generalizing both *to* and *across,* since some research questions demand generalizing to specified populations of persons and times (e.g., Is brief casework effective with adolescents in a high school setting?), while others are less specific and require generalizing across a variety of populations (e.g., with which groups is brief casework effective?). Further, even though a researcher may tailor the design so as to facilitate generalizing to a specific population, other researchers or sponsors of research may be more interested in other populations, and they may say: Granted that brief casework is effective with adolescents in a high school setting, and granted that that was the original researcher's main research question; nonetheless, I would like to know whether it will be effective with the working poor, middle-class neurotics, etc.

Programs are evaluated to see if they are *causing* certain effects. Accordingly, internal validity plays a special role in summative evaluations because it is addressed to determining whether relationships are causal. In line with this, most of the discussion that follows will deal with internal validity. However, it is important not to confuse the primacy of internal validity with the unacceptable costs that can accrue if other kinds of validity are sacrificed in the service of increasing internal validity. To take an extreme instance, an uncritical preference for internal validity would lead one to conduct only randomized experiments, and then with short-lasting treatments in settings that maximize the experimenter's control. The ultimate in this is the fifty-minute laboratory experiment with college sophomores—an experimental situation that is clearly less than optimal for drawing inferences about social welfare policy. Research objectives, common sense, and checks with colleagues dictate how far the primacy of internal validity should be compromised in the service of increasing other kinds of validity, when and if any compromise is necessary at all.

INCREASING VALIDITY

In this setting, we shall briefly present suggestions as to how each of the four kinds of validity can be maximized. The reader should notice the extent to which research design is a question of tradeoffs—actions taken to increase one kind of validity may often decrease another.

Because the rest of our presentation deals with methods for increasing internal validity, a list of common threats to internal validity will be introduced.

INCREASING STATISTICAL CONCLUSION VALIDITY

Increasing statistical conclusion validity is accomplished by increasing the statistical power of analyses and by using inferential statistics in ways that do not violate important assumptions or capitalize upon chance. Problems associated with statistical power are minimized by

(1) having "large" sample sizes (the desired size depends, of course, on the expected size of the effect relative to the expected variance);

(2) decreasing extraneous sources of error (e.g., using homogeneous populations of respondents, and standardizing the measurement setting);

(3) accounting for extraneous sources of variance in the statistical analyses (e.g., by blocking or covariance analysis);

(4) increasing the reliability of outcome measures; and

(5) standardizing implementation of the treatment, preferably with a high level of exposure to the treatment.

Statistics are validly used (1) when the important assumptions underlying their use are demonstrably met (e.g., the assumption of homogeneous variances in analysis of variance or the assumption of uncorrelated errors in time-series analysis), and (2) when we adjust for the number of statistical comparisons that are made, since unless corrective steps are taken more than the expected percentage of comparisons will be statistically significant by chance at the chosen α level. Such corrective steps include adjusting α for the number of comparisons made; using Newman-Keuls' tests or some other multiple comparison technique; or basing inferences on multiple attempted replications of the same relationship across studies or across, say, separate sites within a single study.[1]

Though all these precautions may be taken, it is still possible to conclude that a treatment is related to a presumed effect when it is in fact not so related (Type I error), or that a treatment and effect are not related when in fact they are (Type II error). These last two threats are never ruled out, which is why inferences about covariation are ultimately probabilistic and not deterministic. Nonetheless, to ignore the methods of increasing statistical conclusion validity which we have so briefly outlined is to increase the likelihood of drawing an incorrect inference about covariation.

INCREASING EXTERNAL VALIDITY

External validity deals with the generalizability of a causal relationship to, and across, populations of persons, settings, or times. Generalizability is limited to the classes of persons, settings, or times represented in an evaluation *when it ends*. These may or may not be reasonable representations of the populations of *initial* interest.

Three major models can be followed to increase external validity. *Random sampling* from a designated universe allows us to generalize results to that universe (i.e., a randomly chosen national sample permits generalizing *to* Americans in general). Though random selection is desirable, its value for increasing external validity is limited, because random selection for representativeness is rarely possible. For instance, one is usually lucky to find any social work agency that is willing to cooperate with an experiment, let alone being able to select agencies at random from a known population (e.g., a whole state), or even being able to sample randomly from the clients at a particular agency. (Note that we are speaking here of random sampling from a population to determine who will be in the experiment—an external validity concern— and not of randomly assigning units to treatment conditions—an internal validity concern. This distinction will be discussed in greater detail later.)

A more practical model for extending external validity involves choosing *heterogeneous groups* of persons, settings, or times. For example, if we wished to study whether the provision of housing vouchers leads to renting better-quality houses that are better maintained, we might wish to include samples of female-headed households, elderly headed households, families with an underemployed head of household, and so on. We would then try to determine across which groups the treatment was effective, irrespective of whether the families were randomly chosen to be in the experiment and therefore irrespective of whether there is a *formal* correspondence between the sample and its referent population. (Of course, random sampling also allows us to generalize across those groups which are included in the sample).

Generalization to modal instances is another practical way of increasing external validity. It requires explicating how a treatment would most likely be implemented if it lost its "experimental" status and became formal policy, and then finding or creating at least one research setting where the treatment is implemented in a way that closely corresponds to the explication of the modal setting. For instance, if a widespread program of group counseling sessions for poor students with bad academic records in inner-city schools was under consideration, we would want to know about the effectiveness of group counseling for such students, and not for middle-class suburban children. Thus, this model requires one to specify targets of generalizability in advance, and then to plan the selection of persons, settings, and times so that there is a commonsense correspondence between the planned targets and the achieved sample.

INCREASING CONSTRUCT VALIDITY

Increasing construct validity is a matter of tailoring manipulations and measures to the rigorously defined construct they are meant to represent. Since any one operationalization of a construct is imperfect, it is extremely useful to measure or manipulate a construct in several different ways if possible. For obvious reasons, it is usually easier to measure several versions of the same dependent variable construct than it is to manipulate several versions of the same presumed causal construct. Accordingly, we will consider construct validity of the cause and construct validity of the effect separately, even though the same logic applies to both.

Increasing the construct validity of the effect is usually accomplished by demonstrating, first, that different measures of the same presumed construct covary and, second, that measures of the construct do not covary with measures of related, but different, constructs. Thus, the *logic* of factor analysis probably provides the best model of construct validity (because factor analysis is concerned with the degree to which several variables fit together as parts of common underlying phenomena, or factors). Two evaluations of the children's show "Sesame Street" provide an example of construct validity issues arising in an applied context. The original evaluations claimed that viewing "Sesame Street" taught children how to read (Ball and Bogatz, 1970; Bogatz and Ball, 1971). A secondary analysis (Cook et al., 1975) points out, however, that this claim is based on tests of letter recognition, and that *actual* tests of reading ability do not support this contention.

To increase the construct validity of an effect, we examine the relationship of different measures of the presumed effect construct with each other and with measures of similar but related constructs. For obvious practical limitations, we usually do not look at multiple manipulations of a causal construct and at manipulations of similar but related constructs. Thus, construct validity of the cause is most often increased by showing that a treatment varied what it is was supposed to vary, and only that. This is often called measuring the "take" of the independent variable. In the experimental evaluation of "Sesame Street," the construct validity of the cause can be called into question because some children were visited weekly or monthly in their homes by researchers who encouraged them to watch the show and who gave them series-related books, toys, and balloons (Ball and Bogatz, 1970; Bogatz and Ball, 1971). Obviously, this treatment varied more than the policy-relevant construct of interest—*viewing "Sesame Street."*

It should be pointed out that the methods available for increasing construct validity are not limited to the actual time an evaluation is under way. Rather, the best chance of increasing the fit between a construct and its operationalization comes if one pilot-tests before the evaluation begins.

INCREASING INTERNAL VALIDITY

Internal validity is concerned with the question of whether the treatment-as-manipulated caused any change in the effect-as-measured. Because most of this chapter deals with internal validity issues, we shall now briefly introduce some common threats to internal validity using the notation of Campbell and Stanley (1963). The list is not exhaustive, a larger list being in Cook and Campbell (1976).

History. History is a threat when observed effect might be due to some event, other than the treatment, which occurred between the pretest and the posttest.

Maturation. Maturation is a threat when an observed effect might be due, not to the treatment, but to participants growing older, wiser, more tired, etc., between the pretest and the posttest.

Statistical Regression. This is a threat when an observed effect might be due to participants being assigned to treatments on the basis of a fallible pretest measure (or any other fallible measure, for that matter). Because the measures are unreliable, high pretest scorers will tend to score lower at the posttest and low pretest scorers will tend to score higher. Such statistical regression often masquerades as a treatment effect.

Selection. Selection is a threat when an observed effect may be due to differences in the kinds of people in the different treatment groups rather than to the treatment.

Interactions with Selection. Many internal validity threats can interact with selection to create spurious effects. Probably the most common is a "selection-maturation" interaction, in which experimental groups are composed of different kinds of persons who are maturing at different rates. Another might be called "selection-history" and is involved when the different experimental groups experience different events between the pretest and the posttest, and this dissimilarity in historical events might differentially affect posttest scores.

Each of these particular internal validity threats is rendered implausible by randomly assigning experimental units to treatments. In quasi-experiments, however, since there is no random assignment, they must be ruled out individually. This is usually accomplished (a) by the wise inclusion of design features that we shall later list, and (b) by examining additional data which might bear on the plausibility of each threat; or (c) by assuming, because of theory or common sense, that a particular threat—while possible—is not plausible as an alternative interpretation in the particular evaluation under discussion.

RANDOMIZED EXPERIMENTS

Randomization serves two purposes in research. The first, *representativeness*, was mentioned as a method of increasing external validity. By drawing a random sample from a well-designated universe, we can generalize our results (within known limits of sampling error) from the sample to the universe. Although the universe usually consists of individuals, it could also be composed of settings (e.g., public social agencies, schools, or hospitals). But while random sampling for representativeness is a good method of increasing external validity, it is often impractical.

The second purpose of randomization, *comparability*, is achieved by randomly assigning experimental units to treatments. Random assignment for comparability is the defining characteristic of a true experiment. It is important because it assures that the various treatment groups do not differ from each other, *on the average*, at the start of an experiment. Such comparability rules out most of the internal validity threats which we mentioned above because they were based on treatments being assigned to noncomparable groups (e.g., selection, selection-maturation, selection-history, and statistical regression). Given random assignment to treatment groups and the pretest comparability that follows from this, we know that any observed posttreatment differences between different treatment groups are not attributable to differences in the composition of groups. Therefore, few alternative interpretations of the posttest difference are viable—certainly fewer than with quasi-experiments, where the researcher has to list all the relevant internal validity threats and then rule them out one by one.

The preceding discussion does not imply that planning a true experiment will necessarily lead to a successful summative evaluation. Several problems beset random assignment. In particular: (1) The program planners and staff may resist randomization as a means of allocating treatments, arguing for some other allocative criterion—e.g., need or merit. (2) The randomization process may not be correctly carried out, resulting in nonequivalent experimental groups. (3) The randomization may break down because different kinds of persons may refuse to participate in or may drop out of the different treatment groups. (4) Randomization creates a focused inequity because some persons receive treatments that are more desirable than others, and this inequity can cause reactions that may be falsely interpreted as treatment effects. We shall now consider each of these four difficulties in turn, detailing ways in which they can sometimes be overcome.

SOURCES OF RESISTANCE TO RANDOMIZATION

There are two common reasons why program sponsors and personnel may object to the use of randomization for treatment assignment. One is the belief that more appropriate criteria for allocation (e.g., need or ability) are available and should be used. The other is the related belief that the treatment should not be withheld from any potential recipient, particularly if the treatment promises to be ameliorative in some way.

Resistance based on the belief that the treatment should not be withheld from the controls is fairly common. Indeed, when he evaluated a clinical counseling program for criminal offenders, Ward (1973) found such resistance even though his work had initially been solicited by the same project personnel! In some cases, the problem can be solved by comparing one type of treatment, such as individual counseling, with another, such as group counseling. This obviously does away with the need for a no-treatment group and is useful when an evaluation of the relative merits of alternatives is called for or is at least acceptable. At other times, resources are not available in sufficient numbers so that all who want or need the resource (or treatment) can obtain it. When this happens, a good case can be made that the lottery (i.e., randomization) is the most ethical principle of distribution, especially when the positive impact of the resource is not definitely known and the possibility of negative side effects cannot be ruled out. *Moreover,* a case can often also be made that resources over and above the experimental ones are more likely to be made available in the future if valid unambiguous evidence regarding the effectiveness of the treatment is available. Such unambiguous evidence, we firmly hold, is more likely to be obtained when units have been randomly assigned to treatments than when they have been assigned by some other distributional criterion.

The most common argument against random assignment is that a scarce resource should be distributed to those who need or merit it most. This point of view assumes that merit and need are validly measured. To the extent that they are, randomization may not be appropriate. But to the extent they are not, randomization may be a fairer rule of distribution than the alternatives, which give only a spurious appearance of rational distribution. Even if considerable confidence is placed in the accuracy of a merit or need measure, recognition of its imperfection may allow us to institute a randomized experiment *over that part of the range of eligibility where uncertainty is greatest.* For example, a school district may wish to institute and evaluate a program designed to improve poor reading skills. A randomized experiment is likely to be opposed on the grounds that admission to the program should be based on need as indexed by low scores on reading tests. We might easily acknowledge that the very lowest scorers deserve to enter the treatment group. But if, say, only 100 children can get the new program, who is to say whether the children who rank 101st, 100th, and 99th are really different from each other in ability, or whether the 102nd and 98th differ, or the 110th and 90th, or even the 125th and 75th? In other words, a region of uncertainty can often be defined that allows the extreme scorers to get the treatment but also allows those scoring around the cutting point to be assigned at random to a new program.

Buttressing many of the sources of resistance to randomization is the implicit assumption that a new treatment will be beneficial. But this is merely an assumption, and pointing out the lack of a data base for such beliefs may help reduce some resistance. Additionally, it may help to illustrate that stringent evaluations of many programs in the past have proven them to be less successful than was initially believed by both the public in general and program advocates in particular. Most evaluations of the effectiveness of therapies or prison rehabilitation attempts would serve as examples. A cursory example of these literatures might reduce the naive confidence of some persons that a program will be beneficial, and may help convince them that rigorous evaluation of the program's value is worthwhile.

When initial resistance to randomization is expected, the acceptance of true experiments depends on convincing program personnel and sponsors that reality-testing evaluation is most validly achieved with random assignment, and that random assignment can be carried out in practice without too much inconvenience to the parties involved. It is to the researcher's advantage, therefore, to have prepared in advance: (1) simple explanations of the workings of randomization; (2) a list of evaluations in the particular substantive area in which a randomized experiment was successfully completed (see Boruch, 1974); and (3) statements in which randomization has been endorsed by respected figures (e.g., Campbell, 1969; Rivlin, 1971) who have pointed out the biases that usually operate in the quasi-experimental designs that would probably be used if randomization were not carried out.

Finally, resistance to randomization may be a symptom of a general resistance to evaluation. Developing good relations with the evaluated, appealing to their desire to improve their program if it demonstrates inadequacies, and showing that the evaluation outcome does not threaten anyone's job security may reduce this resistance.

FAULTY RANDOM ASSIGNMENT

Procedural difficulties in randomizing. Randomization is a procedure which ensures that each experimental unit has an equal chance of being selected for each treatment. In some cases randomization fails because of correctable flaws in the method of assignment. For example, in the 1969 military draft lottery, men with birth dates late in the year stood a higher chance of being assigned low draft numbers making them eligible for military service. The bias occurred because the dates of the year were placed, in order from January to December, into an urn from which they were then drawn. The urn was not adequately shaken, and the dates put in last tended to be drawn out first, thereby giving later-born persons a higher chance of being drafted (Feinberg, 1971; Notz et al., 1971). This problem is easily solved by consulting references about how to randomize correctly. For instance, a discussion of the mechanics of randomization is in Riecken and Boruch (1974).

Randomization sometimes breaks down because the personnel responsible for implementing the procedure do not fully complete their task. Often the job of processing applicants to a program falls to permanent organizational staff or to temporary help, and these individuals may either believe that some criterion other than chance should be used for deciding who enters the program (e.g., need or merit), or they may not be adequately committed to systematic assignment of any form. Random assignment may therefore be completely or partially "fudged" to accord with the processor's personal conception of how selection should take place or merely to satisfy "difficult" applicants who are particularly vocal in their desire to receive a certain treatment. Where possible, such well-meaning sabotage should be prevented by instituting randomization systems which are difficult to circumvent. A simple two-step randomization procedure frequently helps achieve this. The first step calls for the individual who processes applicants to take all of the needed information, and the second for subsequent assignment to conditions by someone who is unaware of the identity and characteristics of the applicant. Regardless of whether this, or some other system is used to reduce deviations from random assignment, careful supervision should be given to the randomization process. It should not be taken for granted that a planned process will be implemented in the form that was initially devised.

Sample size and sampling variability. Sometimes a decision will be made to deliver a treatment to units much larger than an individual. For example, all the welfare recipients in some cities might be assigned to a treatment condition dealing with the method of dispensing financial aid, while all the recipients in other cities would be selected to serve as a no-treatment control group. Such decisions are often made to reduce respondents' awareness of other experimental conditions, for such an awareness can lead to serious difficulties which we shall discuss below. Since the selection of larger units typically results in fewer units for assignment to each treatment, the random assignment of fewer but larger units is less likely to result in comparable groups.

One solution to this problem is to match units on variables that we strongly believe, on the basis of theory or common sense, are correlated with the major dependent variable. We then randomly assign to conditions from these matched sets. An alternative, albeit rather mundane-sounding approach, is to use a larger number of smaller experimental units. That is, rather than assigning *cities* to a particular method of dispensing aid, we might assign at the level of local welfare offices, having several within each city receiving different treatments. A third approach would be to use some form of a "switching replication" design. This entails that one delivery system would initially be used in one set of cities, and the other in different cities, after which the cities would switch from the system it had to the system the other had.

Alternatively, one might strive to implement a time series design, using archives either to collect repeated pretreatment measures of the dependent variable or else to collect repeated measures during the period of exposure to the treatment. The latter part of the series would be particularly useful if we expect a treatment effect to build up over time. Such a build-up would be tested by the statistical interaction of the treatment and the time of testing. That is, we would expect the difference between groups to increase steadily over time after the treatment by more than it may have done before the treatment.

TREATMENT-CORRELATED LOSS OF PARTICIPANTS

Treatment-correlated refusals. In some cases, experimental units will be randomly assigned to conditions and some individuals will choose not to receive the treatment selected for them. For example, Meyer and Borgatta (1959) report a study to determine the effectiveness of a particular method of rehabilitating individuals hospitalized with psychiatric disorders. The treatment was conducted at a live-in workshop at which the patients were expected to live for a year. Understandably, many people chose not to receive this assigned treatment, and only about a third of the assigned experimental subjects actually entered the program. Such self-selection is most likely in two circumstances: If prospective program participants perceive some sort of cost involved in receiving their assigned treatment or if the treatments differ intrinsically in attractiveness, as in the case with guaranteed income experiments that offer guarantees of, say $12,000 versus $3,600. Treatment-related refusals to receive the assigned treatment creates groups which, on the average, are composed of different kinds of individuals, thereby causing selection problems and making it difficult to interpret relationships between the treatment and any of the dependent variables.

Treatment-related bias in who enters treatment groups can arise from processes other than self-selection. It can, for instance, also result from pressures to ensure that certain groups or individuals (e.g., cronies of the project director) are overrepresented in a particular treatment condition.

Treatment-correlated attrition. Even though random assignment to treatments may be successfully implemented, program participants can still differentially drop out of a program before an evaluation is completed. This is primarily a problem in longitudinal research where participants perceive that differences in costs or gains are associated with different treatments. For instance, in the New Jersey Negative Income Tax Experiment, attrition from the experiment, after a three-year period, ranged from 25.3 percent in the control condition to 6.5 percent in the highest payment condition. Differential attrition of this sort leaves us with groups that differ in many important ways, and is a major threat to internal validity.

There are three primary methods of inspecting for differential attrition. The first, and simplest, is to test whether the percentage of lost units differs across treatment groups. The second is to elucidate the reasons for attrition in different groups. This is useful because it is possible to have equal rates of attrition even though different *kinds* of people may have dropped out of each treatment group. To illustrate this, imagine an effective ameliorative program for poor people. Members of a no-treatment control group might drop out because they could not afford to pay their rent and had moved, whereas the experimentals might drop out because they benefitted from the treatment and moved on to better jobs or better apartments. Unfortunately, this second method of inspecting for differential attrition requires direct measures of the reason for attrition or, when these are not available, informed speculation.

The third method of analyzing for differential attrition requires data collected prior to treatment. Usually these will be pretest data, but sometimes covariates or blocking variables are also available. These are then examined to test whether the pretreatment means are different across the treatment groups *after the individuals who did not provide posttest data have been deleted.* Such differences suggest that differential attrition has taken place and provide a first, though imperfect, estimate of the magnitude of any bias.

It should not be forgotten that, when random assignment has occurred initially, treatment-correlated attrition from an experiment implies that the treatment has *caused* differences in the willingness to stay in the experiment. This is often an interpretable and important effect. For example, if a program is instituted to encourage job stability, attrition from the experiment is the ultimate dependent variable of interest. In other studies, however, attrition is not a particularly interesting outcome and is usually a problem because it makes the treatment groups noncomparable, thereby making it difficult to draw unambiguous causal inferences about any outcomes other than attrition itself.

Possible solutions. Several methods exist for dealing with the problem of treatment-correlated refusals and attrition. Many sources of treatment-related loss can be identified prior to the evaluation, and corrective steps can be taken at this stage to overcome the anticipated difficulty. Thus, pressures to provide some individuals with a certain treatment might be foreseen. If so, then the selective assignment should be monitored and the persons who benefit from it should be dropped from the study, though not from getting the treatment. This effectively redefines the experimental population, and random assignment is restricted to persons in the refined population.

Alternatively, we could redefine the population even further by randomly assigning to treatments only those persons who agree to stay in the experiment, *regardless of the treatment to which they might be assigned by chance.* The question of when to randomly assign is a difficult one, and issues of internal validity, external validity, and ethics are involved. Logically, we can randomly assign to treatments at three alternative time points: (1) as soon as the pool of available and eligible units has been identified, irrespective of whether participants agree to being measured or "treated"; (2) when units have agreed to participate with all the measurement demands of the study even though they may discontinue receiving their treatment; and (3) when the units have agreed beforehand to participate in the evaluation and to be in any treatment condition to which they might be assigned. Randomization at the first time point presents the greatest threat to internal validity. This is because the participants have made no commitments and so the potential treatment-correlated dropouts have not been identified. However, assignment at this time point may present the smallest limit to external validity, since all of the available units are included in the study and the population is not redefined away from the population of initial research interest. However, we must remember that generalizability is limited to the range of persons represented in the evaluation when it ends, so external validity may be limited by the loss of participants in studies which randomize at this time point.

Random assignment at the third time point given above should reduce the treatment-related loss of participants more than the two others, and is ethically satisfying in that participants are fully informed about the evaluation, both about the treatments and about measurement demands. However, having fully informed participants may lead to other problems. For example, the controls may react to any inequities caused by the fact that they receive less than others, and these reactions could lead the researcher to make false interpretations of treatment effects. (Reactions to such focused inequities will be discussed later.) The second alternative strikes a middle ground between the more extreme positions and is often preferable. In many instances, individuals will be continuing in the measurement framework naturally, as in the case in educational settings, or will agree to meet the measurement demands of the evaluator for small financial inducements. However, concerns specific to a particular evaluation often suggest the use of one of the other alternatives, and each evaluator has to be sensitive to the tradeoffs implied by his/her choice of when to randomly assign.

Pre-experimental discussion can also help identify some sources of differential cost to participants which can be dealt with quite simply. For instance, Hudson (1969) wanted to evaluate the effects of an autotelic teaching device that was located miles from where his respondents lived. To alleviate the potential attrition of the treatment group members, who had to travel to the machine (control group members did not), he simply provided them with transportation to the device. Another related way in which the problem of treatment-related loss of participants can be minimized is by adding inducements to participate in the less-desirable treatment groups. In some cases, we may simply offer to pay those who are in less desirable groups for their cooperation. This seems to have reduced the rate of attrition from the control group in the New Jersey Negative Income Tax Experiment, which was initially much higher than from the experimental groups. At other times, we may be able to offer alternative treatments to participants, rather than having some people in a no-treatment control. To the extent that participants in the different treatments perceive the treatments as equally attractive, differential refusal and attrition should be reduced. Designs employing alternative treatments are often feasible. For instance, Atkinson (1968) studied the effects of computer-assisted instruction (CAI) by having children randomly assigned to CAI either in math or in English. Each group was tested on both math and English, so that the English scores of children receiving math instruction provided a no-treatment baseline for English instruction, and the math scores of children receiving English instruction served as a control for the math course. Alternatively, one can imagine situations where persons are assigned to one form of psychotherapy versus another, with everyone receiving some sort of treatment.

There is a problem with designs offering alternative treatments to all participants. It is that, while we can assess the effectiveness of the treatments relative to one another, we cannot readily assess their absolute effectiveness. This is particularly problematic if the treatments are in fact equally effective (or equally harmful), for without a no-treatment control group the effect of each treatment would go undetected. This is why it is particularly important to try to establish what a no-treatment baseline would be when using a design in which all units are to receive a treatment. Methods other than a no-treatment control group are available for achieving this. The most reasonable, but not necessarily the most available, is the use of a long pretreatment time-series as opposed to a single pretreatment measure. But one can also resort to one of the cohort strategies that we shall outline later when discussing quasi-experimental designs.

The treatment-correlated loss of participants can sometimes be reduced by the sensitive use of the power that most organizations have over the persons in them. For instance, schools can ensure that their students attend certain activities, within the limits of absenteeism, dropping out, and moving; the armed services can ensure that their members receive certain treatments, within the limits of differential desertion and discharge. But though the use of organizational *support* can be invaluable in eliciting cooperation and minimizing refusals, its *coercive* nature is sometimes problematic. First of all, construct validity is decreased because coercion is confounded with the treatment. Next, there are obvious ethical issues that often cannot be easily resolved, the major one being: Though power over individuals is the essence of such organizations, when—if ever—is it desirable to use such power for experimental purposes, particularly if the use of power increases resentment or passivity.

Despite the researcher's best efforts, participants may be lost for different reasons in different experimental conditions. When this happens, we must rely on post hoc data analysis strategies. One approach is to conduct the statistical analysis using all of the individuals who were assigned to a particular treatment group, even if some of them did not in fact receive the treatment. Thus, to go back to the earlier example of the live-in workshop rehabilitation treatment, the strategy would involve grouping together all those who were assigned to the treatment group, whether they attended the live-in workshop or had refused to, and then analyzing the pretest and posttest data they provided as the complete data from this group. Analyzing the data in this way is possible only when people self-select themselves out of the treatment *but do not leave the measurement framework,* and so provide posttest information. This situation occurs, for instance, in evaluations of educational innovations at the college level. Students might refuse to be in an experimental version of, say, accounting, but still take the same-titled course in a regular class from which they receive a final grade.

Including in the analysis all the persons who dropped out may seem like a bad idea because it introduces a conservative bias that will tend to make programs look less effective than they would otherwise appear. How, it will be argued, can a program be sensitively evaluated if the analysis includes persons in the treatment group who received little or none of the treatment? Against this it has to be argued that omitting persons who did not get the treatment from the analysis will introduce a selection bias that might result in spurious differences. The issue is: Which is preferable, a statistically conservative test with no bias or a statistically more powerful test with bias? One can, of course, do both analyses, one time including the persons who did not actually receive their assigned treatment and another time omitting them. If the analyses produce comparable results, causal inference is easy. If they do not, great caution is called for in drawing conclusions, particularly from the analysis where individuals have been omitted since selection biases have probably been introduced.

Another post hoc approach is to inspect the data to see if randomization has remained intact in some subgroups, while not in others. For example, in evaluations that are conducted at several sites, the randomization may have broken down in some places but not others, or it may have broken down with some age, sex, or race groups but not others. Once randomly intact subgroups are found, the data from them may be analyzed as coming from a randomized experiment, with all the advantages for internal validity that this confers. A post-hoc examination of the data was conducted for this purpose by Cook et al. (1975) in their reanalysis of the evaluations of "Sesame Street" by Ball and Bogatz (1970) and Bogatz and Ball (1971). Cook et al. discovered that randomization had remained intact at some of the experimental sites but not others, and the data analysis was made to center on the true experiment that was completed at some sites.

This subgroup method requires focusing on a subset of the total data, and thus can reduce statistical power. It should sometimes be used, therefore, together with quasi-experimental analyses that use all of the data but are not so powerful as randomized approaches for inferring cause. Using both a randomized approach on a subset of respondents and a quasi-experimental approach on all of the data gives clearer information about cause when the two analyses suggest a similar conclusion.

VARIATION IN TREATMENT IMPLEMENTATION

We have already discussed the problem of some participants not receiving the planned treatment to which they were assigned. A related problem occurs when program participants have the ability to determine how much of a treatment they wish to receive. For instance, in a test of an individualized counseling program for individuals newly on welfare, the number of face-to-face therapy contacts ranged from 1 to 129, with a median of 15; the number of telephone and mail contact ranged from none to 81, with a median of 9.5 (Mullen et al., 1972). Thus, exposure to the treatment ranged from no more than one initial face-to-face contact that was required of everyone to a rather high level of contact. Variability in exposure to the treatment is not necessarily due to self-selection by respondents. It can also occur because the people responsible for implementing the treatment—i.e., caseworkers, teachers, counselors, or whoever—differ in the degree to which they are available to individual respondents or to their caseload in general. Further, the persons implementing a treatment—e.g., some casework method—may differ in how well they conduct that treatment when contact occurs.

Standardization of the treatment delivery, extensive training of those responsible for delivering the treatment, encouraging participants to have high levels of treatment exposure, and continued monitoring of all of these, can greatly reduce the problem of heterogeneity in treatment implementation. Nonetheless, if such heterogeneity occurs despite these precautions, the best strategy is to perform an analysis analogous to the conservative analysis just discussed. That is, one should simply treat all those assigned to the treatment group as though they had received the (fixed) level of the treatment to which they were originally assigned. But to complement this analysis, a quasi-experimental analysis should also be conducted that relies on stratifying individuals according to the length or intensity of their exposure to the treatment. Many such quasi-experimental analyses would not be easy to interpret, but they will usually be more interpretable if the pattern of results is similar to that from the conservative analysis which preserved the planned random assignment. Similar, of course, does not mean identical, and common sense must be used for ascertaining how much similarity warrants concluding that the implications of one analysis correspond with those of another.

REACTIONS TO THE FOCUSED INEQUITY CAUSED BY RANDOMIZATION

The implementation of a randomized experiment creates inequities between groups, particularly when a no-treatment control is compared with a treatment group. Awareness of these inequities may cause reactions which can be mistakenly interpreted as treatment effects. Four such classes of reactions are discussed in the section below and, since they share a common set of solutions, the solutions will not be discussed until the end of this section. The four reactions can be classified as threats to internal rather than construct validity because their effects are not caused by the treatment. Rather, they are caused by some atypical reaction on the part of the members of control groups.

Diffusion or imitation of the treatment. Diffusion or imitation of the treatment occurs when units in the no-treatment control group learn of the other treatment (or treatments), and gain exposure to the events that were planned only for experimentals. Such exposure reduces the planned contrast between experiments and controls and hence tends to obscure true treatment effects. For example, a caseworker whose colleague is administering some experimental counseling technique may learn of the technique and employ it with his/her control group clients. Or the intended no-"Sesame Street" controls might spontaneously tune in the show given its popularity (Ball and Bogatz, 1970). In addition, legal, ethical, and public relations considerations can lead to some of the controls receiving treatment. For instance, in an investigation of the effectiveness of pretrial conferences between clients and their lawyers (Rosenberg, 1964), one randomly selected group had mandatory pretrial conferences, while the controls were only asked to forego the conference. For ethical and legal reasons they could not be denied the right to the treatment and over half of those assigned to the control group elected to have the experimental conference.

Compensatory rivalry. Members of a no-treatment control group sometimes learn that they are not receiving a treatment, but others are. This can sometimes motivate people to alter their behavior so that their group is not out-performed. This can happen if existing groups, such as work departments, are assigned to control conditions while nearby departments receive the treatments. It is also likely if members of the control group stand to lose something if the treatment proves effective. Saretsky (1972) cites the OEO Performance Contracting Experiment as a case to illustrate this last point. He reasoned that the teachers' job security would have been threatened if the results of the experiment had shown that outside contractors were more effective in teaching than regular teachers. The best way for teachers to deal with this threat was to do an atypically good job of teaching in the year of the experiment so as to decrease the possibility of the experimentals outperforming the controls at the posttest.

Resentful demoralization of participants receiving less desirable treatments. The knowledge that others are in a more favorable treatment group will sometimes lead to resentment and demoralization, rather than to compensatory rivalry. Imagine an attempt to assess the effect of physical recreation on the coping of depressed adolescents. Youths in the control group might observe the treatment the others receive, feel relatively deprived, and become even more depressed. If so, any posttest differences between groups would not really be due to the treatment but to the resentment or demoralization of the controls. Resentful demoralization, then, is likely to lead to pseudo-effects.

Compensatory equalization of treatments. The perception of un-
equal treatment of experimental units may cause an administrator,
perhaps under pressure from members of the group less favored by the
allocation of treatments, to distribute other similar goods at his/her
disposal in such a way as to equalize treatment groups. For instance, if
an experiment were conducted in a social work agency to evaluate the
effects of a reduced caseload, an administrator might take it upon
himself to reduce the workload of members of the control group so as
to avoid a focused inequity between people with different caseloads.
This type of administrative response is most likely when the administrator is not deeply committed to the evaluation and when it is
anticipated that members of the control group will be vocal about the
inequality. Compensatory equalization, like compensatory rivalry and
diffusion or imitation of the treatment, tends to equalize the experimental and the control groups.

Solutions. The four threats to internal validity that we are now
discussing are unlike the ones previously discussed because they are not
ruled out by random assignment. Instead they may be ruled out
individually, on the basis of background information that is available to
the researcher. The strongest such information is the awareness that the
experimental units were successfully isolated or did not communicate
with each other about the experiment. This is done by minimizing the
obtrusiveness of the experiment. When we isolate experimental units
from each other, individuals cannot react to inequities because they will
not be aware of them. Usually, separating the experimental units
involves using fewer, larger units (e.g., schools rather than individual
people) which do not communicate regularly with each other.

Pretest data, particularly time series data on the controls, is an
additional aid in determining whether one of these four problems
occurred. If imitation of the treatment, compensatory rivalry, or compensatory equalization occurred, then the control group should sharply
deviate from its pretreatment no-cause baseline. If it does, then these
threats are rendered all the more plausible. If it does not deviate, then it
is not likely that something atypical happened in the control group. It
is worth remembering that time-series data are valuable even if the
series is of abbreviated length, for even then they provide a reasonable
estimate of what a no-cause baseline would be. Thus, in the performance-contracting experiment, we find that control students improved
by more points on standardized tests of achievement during the experimental year than their cohorts had gained annually in two earlier years.
Such evidence strengthens the contention that compensatory rivalry
may have occurred in this evaluation.

The researcher can also search for additional data (again preferably time-series data) from units similar to the control units which were not in the experiment. For instance, if in the performance-contracting experiment we were to retrieve data from teachers' classes that were similar to the control classes, and if we were to find that these classes registered the same achievement gain in the year of the experiment as in previous years, this would be quite consistent with the interpretation that compensatory rivalry arose among the control teachers and classes.

Finally, a post-treatment series can also be useful in determining the plausibility of these threats, especially if the treatment is removed from some of the respondents. This presumably—but not invariably—ends the focused inequity between groups, and any forces operating to change performance in the control group should end. This being so, the control group performance should revert to the no-cause baseline level, and one can see whether performance does or does not stabilize at the level found during the time that the treatment was implemented.

PUTTING THE DIFFICULTIES OF ACHIEVING RANDOM ASSIGNMENT INTO PERSPECTIVE

The preceding discussion might make the reader wonder, if there are so many problems with implementing random assignment in evaluations, why not aim for a quasi-experimental design in the first place? One might reply to this: First, the problems that occur with random assignment are often manageable, provided they have been identified in advance and ways of overcoming them have been considered. Second, most of the problems that occur with randomized experiments can also occur with quasi-experiments. For example, members of control groups in quasi-experiments can also become aware of more desirable treatments, thereby experiencing resentment or demoralization; attrition can occur in quasi-experiments as well as in true experiments. Third, our previous discussion has highlighted threats to validity in a self-conscious way that may inadvertently give the impression that the bias which arises when a randomized experiment breaks down is of a greater magnitude than the bias which arises with feasible, alternative quasi-experiments. Our firmly held opinion is quite the opposite. The bias arising from an implemented true experiment which broke down will nearly always be less than the bias arising from the systematic self-selection and recruitment biases that characterize the treatment assignment processes in most planned or ex post facto quasi-experiments.

QUASI-EXPERIMENTS

Randomized experiments are not possible if resistance to randomization is too strong, if an innovation has to be implemented universally, or if one wishes to investigate the impact of a change after it has already taken place. Under such circumstances, a quasi-experiment has to be used. In a quasi-experiment, assignment to treatment occurs in some nonrandom fashion, usually because individuals choose the treatment they receive or are assigned to a treatment by officials or professionals who believe that certain kinds of individuals should receive particular treatments. The main problem with quasi-experiments is that this nonrandom assignment makes it difficult to draw causal inferences. However, there are design features which can help researchers rule out certain alternative interpretations of any obtained relations between the independent and dependent variables. They therefore enhance our capability to draw a less ambiguous causal inference.

Our attention here will not be on specific quasi-experimental designs themselves, as has been the case in earlier expositions (Campbell and Stanley, 1963, 1966; Cook and Campbell, 1976). Instead, we shall focus on particular design features which can strengthen causal inference in a quasi-experiment. This is consistent with the aforementioned authors' position that the designs they listed were not immutable, and that features from some of their designs could be profitably combined with others to meet the special needs of a particular investigation. In fact, the features discussed below should not be thought of as design features solely for quasi-experiments, for they can and should also be used to increase clarity of inference in true experiments.

Our focus, then, is on design features which can strengthen causal inferences in an evaluation. Despite this, certain frequently used quasi-experimental designs will be commented on to illustrate how the utility of a particular design feature depends on other features of the design.

THE PRETEST

A pretest is a pretreatment measure that is taken from respondents on the same, or an equivalent, scale to the one which is used at the posttest. A pretest is vital for most quasi-experiments, and its utility derives from it being an assessment of the initial difference between nonequivalent groups.

THE NO-TREATMENT CONTROL GROUP

A no-treatment control group is a collection of experimental units, usually individuals, who do not receive the treatment. Their posttest is compared with that of the experimental group in order to assess whether the treatment has had an impact. In a sense, therefore, the no-treatment controls function as a no-cause baseline. But since nonequivalent groups are used in quasi-experiments, measures of posttest performance only are particularly inappropriate as no-cause baselines. This is because, if posttest performance differed between the experimental and control groups, it would not be clear whether this was because of a treatment effect or because the composition of the groups differed from each other in ways that would lead to the obtained posttest difference.

Let us consider an example in order to demonstrate the usefulness of the pretest and of the control group, especially when they are combined. Consider a new recreational program to decrease the number of fights in a home for delinquent youths. If the program were implemented and the only measure was a posttest assessment of fighting, then one would have no real notion of the program's effect. The best one could do would be for the researcher to make subjective estimates of the level of pretreatment fighting, which might or might not correlate highly with actual fighting.

Adding a pretest allows one data-bound estimate of the program effect (i.e., the difference between pretest and posttest performance). But several serious internal validity threats plague the single-group design with pretest and posttest. Suppose, for example, that we find a statistically reliable decrease in the number of fights between the pretest and the posttest. Inferring that the program caused the decreased fighting may well be inappropriate, for the decrease may be due to some event other than the treatment which occurred between the pretest and posttest. Such alternative interpretations of "history" might include: surveillance of the youngsters increased between the pretest and posttest; rival gangs in the institution called a truce; living conditions in the home improved for reasons irrelevant to the treatment. Before researchers can reasonably claim that the recreational program decreased the amount of fighting, these and any other plausible alternative explanations must be ruled out.

History is not the only threat to internal validity when a single group is measured at the pretest and posttest. Statistical regression would be a plausible threat if the recreation program were started in response to an unusually high level of fighting. This high level could be due, at least in part, to random factors, including measurement error. To the extent that this is true, the level of fighting would be expected to decrease from its abnormally high level with or without a treatment.

The plausibility of history and statistical regression, as well as the possible operation of other internal validity threats (such as instrumentation, or the effects being due not to the treatment but to a change in the measurement instrument between pretest and posttest), render generally uninterpretable the design using only a pretest and posttest measure of one group.

Let us now consider an evaluation in which posttest values are measured for both the experimental and control groups, but in which there are no pretests. In our example, the level of fighting is measured after the treatment has begun in the experimental youth home and at the same time in a similar institution which had no such treatment. The threat of selection biases looms so large in this design that it is not possible to attribute to the treatment any observed differences between the number of fights in the two institutions. The differences may instead be due to differences in the composition of the two groups. In our example, more aggressive offenders might be sent to one institution than to the other, or there may be more youth gangs in one than in the other.

Combining the two designs just discussed—taking both pretest and posttest measures of a treatment and a control group—reduces the selection threat. Further, in this design, which we shall call the pretest-posttest control group design,[2] history, testing, and some other internal validity threats are ruled out. Though an improvement, the design is still flawed in most contexts where it is used, and its usage can only be recommended when no better design is possible. However, because it is a frequently followed design in evaluation research, the problems associated with it deserve careful consideration.

The most likely internal validity threat in the pretest-posttest control group design is selection-maturation. This, we have seen, is a threat when the observed effect might be due to the different kinds of people in the different groups maturing (i.e., growing stronger, wiser, more experienced, more frustrated, etc.) at different rates. Differential growth rates of this sort are especially common in educational settings, with children from higher socioeconomic classes generally gaining more on tests of cognitive skills than lower-class children in a given time period. In many compensatory education programs, for example, the treatment group is of the most educationally disadvantaged, while the control group consists of individuals whose academic performance and whose rate of increase in achievement is higher than that of the more disadvantaged experimentals. Given this situation, it is difficult to corroborate treatment effects, since any gain by the lower-performing experimentals would have to overcome the naturally occurring greater increase by the controls.

Sometimes, in an effort to control for a selection-maturation threat, an investigator might use matching (performing an analysis using only treatment and control units with similar pretest scores) or multivariate regression techniques (covariance analysis, multiple regression, partial correlation). Each of these approaches is inappropriate for the same reason: The pretest and covariates contain errors in how they are measured, and this unreliability leads to an underadjustment for existing group differences. Subsequently, a pseudo-effect may be obtained. The underadjustment problem in matching and in regression techniques is amply documented elsewhere (Lord, 1960, 1967, 1969; Cronbach and Furby, 1970; Campbell and Erlebacher, 1970; Campbell and Boruch, 1975) and will not be considered further here.

Test and measurement problems also beset the nonequivalent group design with pretest and posttest. For instance, the amount of change that can take place in a group may be restricted because scores are initially very high (the so-called ceiling effect) or very low (the so-called floor effect). This problem is more likely to result in spurious differences in the amount of obtained change when the initial difference between groups is large. It is important, therefore, that the experimental groups and the measurement instruments should be selected so as to minimize ceiling and floor effects. A second type of testing and measurement bias occurs when group pretest means differ and the reliability of tests increases from the pretest to the posttest. This is an especially common occurrence with youngsters, and creates a spurious difference of predictable direction. This is because higher reliability serves to differentiate nonequivalent groups better, so that if the posttest is more reliable, the posttest differences between groups may be sharper than the pretest differences. (See Campbell and Boruch, 1975, for a more complete consideration of these biases.)

Regression will sometimes be a plausible third threat in the pretest-posttest control group design. If we think back to the example of the recreation program designed to reduce fighting in an institution for delinquent youths, suppose that the motivation for the program was that fighting was unusually high the year before the program. If we were to find that fighting decreased by more in the experimental institution during the period of the program than in a control institution, this outcome would strongly suggest regression. It would operate because the pretest fighting mean of the experimental group was unusually high, perhaps due to abnormal factors which would function like measurement error and would usually be followed by a return to the stable pretest level of performance, different from the atypical level that led to the initiation of a remedial program. Regression is, therefore, particularly likely to operate when a treatment is implemented in response to an unexpectedly bad performance, and it is less likely to be a threat when the pretest differences between the nonequivalent groups are stable over time. In this last case, the scores are more likely to reflect a high true score component rather than a high error component.

We have considered three classes of threats to the interpretability of a pretest-posttest control group design. It is a quasi-experimental design which is often interpretable, but it is nonetheless subject to serious internal validity threats and has to be used with considerable caution.

COHORTS AS CONTROLS

The turnover of clients in some organizations, and the advancement of personnel in others, provides a special type of nonequivalent control group, which we call "cohorts." Cohorts are groups of units which move through an organization or institution and can be found at different levels within the organization. Cohorts are useful as controls because they tend to be similar to each other in organizational experience and in background characteristics, thereby minimizing—but not necessarily eliminating—selection problems. (Perhaps the extreme of cohort-ness is provided by identical twins reared in the same home, for they share comparable genetic, social, and historical experiences). Take schools as one example of a setting in which a cohort analysis is possible. Each year a new third grade arrives, and one can use the archives to compare how pre- and post-treatment third-grade classes have been faring. Take the social work profession as another example. The regular advancement of clients through counseling supplies the necessary ingredients for evaluating the effects of counseling by means of a cohort analysis.

The major threat associated with cohort analysis is history, for each group of cohorts has to be measured at a different time or at a different age or stage in the organization. Thus, if one third-grade class is the experimental one receiving a treatment, and the previous third-grade class taught by the same teacher is the control, it is clear that one group could have been subject to different experiences during its third-grade year than the other group during its third-grade year. One of the best ways to control for history is to divide pairs of cohorts according to the length of exposure to the treatment. This controls for history because a treatment effect should be stronger for the experimentals most exposed to the treatment, while there is no reason why history should result in this difference. Dividing according to the length of treatment exposure is easy to do for the experimentals, but how does one do it for control cohorts that preceded the treatments? Sometimes the answer is obvious, as when the cohorts are siblings, for one can classify children by, say, the number of hours spent watching "Sesame Street" and then look to data from each child's older sibling who was of the experimental cohort's age before "Sesame Street" went on the air. The controls are then subdivided depending on how much their siblings later went on to view the show (for extended discussion of this strategy, see Cook et al., 1975).

NONEQUIVALENT DEPENDENT VARIABLES

It is sometimes possible to specify, along with the dependent variables in which we are principally interested, some other dependent variables that (a) should not be affected by the treatment, but (b) would be affected if some plausible alternatives (such as history or maturation) had affected the principal dependent variables. For example, a social work agency might institute a program to increase the amount of information that each social worker records about his or her clients. To rule out the explanation that any obtained effects might be due, not to the program, but to increased supervision, we can examine dependent variables which should not be affected by taking more case notes but would be affected by supervision, such as the number of new cases each social worker processes.

The usefulness of nonequivalent dependent variables depends on selecting a dependent variable that should not be affected by the treatment but should be affected by most plausible alternative causal agents. It therefore requires a strong initial theory. Moreover, it is dependent on accepting the null hypothesis that nothing has happened to the nonequivalent dependent variable, and for logical reasons it is never easy to accept the null hypothesis. Finally, the use of nonequivalent dependent variables presupposes that there will be no generalization from the primary outcome variable one wants to see changed to the secondary control outcome variable. If there is generalization—and remember that the design calls for *similar* dependent variables—then each outcome measure will be affected and no causal inference will be drawn even though a causal change could have occurred. These problems suggest that nonequivalent dependent variables are best used, not as the most basic feature of an evaluation but rather as an adjunct to other features, like pretests, no-treatment control, or cohort groups.

REMOVED TREATMENT

In some cases, it is not feasible to obtain a nonequivalent control group and the design has to be restricted to a single treatment group. Under these conditions, it may still be possible to test for covariation of the presumed treatment and effect by comparing times when the treatment is present with times when it is absent. As an example, consider a token reward system designed to increase the amount of time that problem students sit at their desks. Imagine that we implement the program, and the amount of time students spend at their desks reliably increases from pretest to posttest. Then, removing the treatment and testing whether there is a subsequent decline in the time spent at desks could sometimes rule out the internal validity threats of history, testing, and instrumentation. History is rendered implausible because historical events with effects in opposite directions rarely coincide with the times when a treatment is introduced and then later removed. Maturation is often ruled out because the more plausible forms of *linear* maturation are ruled out by an initial increase and a subsequent decrease, though cyclical maturation patterns are not. Finally, testing is often ruled out because it is simply not plausible to assume that taking a test increases scores at one time and causes them to decline after the treatment has been removed.

Several questions have to be raised about removed treatment designs. First, a construct validity problem arises if the removal of the treatment is frustrating, for any change in the opposite direction to the initial pretest-posttest change may be due to this frustration. Second, if there are only three measurement waves—viz. *pretest*-treatment-*posttest*-removal of the treatment-*second posttest*—then a deviantly high first posttest mean will give the pattern of results that would be interpreted as a treatment effect. It is important, therefore, to control for this possibility. The best control is to add several posttests before the treatment is removed. If this is not possible, then a control should be made for the fact that the first posttest may be deviantly high by chance. This would involve adjusting for the error rate (Ryan, 1959). Finally, it should be obvious that the removed treatment is only applicable when a treatment is expected to have a transient effect that will wear off as soon as the treatment is removed. Any effect that persisted over time would lead to false negative conclusions about the treatment's true impact.

REPEATED TREATMENT

It is sometimes possible not only to introduce the treatment and to remove it, but also to introduce it a second or even a third time. On some occasions, the reintroduction happens spontaneously, but at other times it comes about as policy because removing the treatment suggested that the treatment was initially effective. In any event, reintroducing the treatment is very similar to removing it with respect to both advantages and problems. That is, most threats to internal validity are convincingly ruled out, but the possibility nonetheless remains that apparent treatment effects may be due to cyclical maturation or treatment removal having caused a resentment which disappears as soon as the treatment is reintroduced. Also, the participants in the experiment may notice the change in their treatment status and become suspicious. The design is only suitable when the treatment effect is so transient that it disappears when the treatment is removed and can reappear when it is reintroduced.

INTERRUPTED TIME SERIES

Both removing and repeating the treatment suggest that, under certain conditions, an experimental group can serve as its own control. The collection of multiple pretest and posttest measures over time is also useful in this regard. For example, Baldus (1973) wished to examine the effect of state laws which require that the government be repaid when a recipient of old-age assistance dies and leaves money or property. His concern was that elderly persons would not apply for aid for which they were eligible if that aid jeopardized the estate they hoped to bequeath to their heirs, particularly the homes they hoped to leave. Baldus could simply have examined the number of Old Age Assistance (OAA) caseloads before and after new state laws were passed, but he did not do so since this did not control for all plausible internal validity threats. Any observed decrease in the number of elderly persons applying for aid might for instance be due to statistical regression, as would be the case if state legislatures had enacted such laws when (or because) OAA caseloads were unusually high. The plausibility of this interpretation could be examined by plotting the level of OAA caseloads for an extended time period before and after the law's enactment. If regression to the mean were occurring, the pretreatment point would have a value abnormally high for the time series, or time trend. So a single time series can rule out regression (and, additionally, maturation testing and instrumentation).

History, on the other hand, is the most definite weakness in a single time-series design. In the Baldus case, history would be any event that could have caused caseloads to decrease and that occurred at the same time as the new state laws on reimbursement were passed and enforced. To rule out history as a threat, we have to turn to complex time series that combine the simple interrupted time series with other design features we have previously considered. Combining them gives, for instance, the interrupted time series with nonequivalent dependent measures, or the time series with a nonequivalent control group. These are briefly discussed below.

COMPLEX INTERRUPTED TIME SERIES DESIGNS

Time series with nonequivalent dependent measures. Suppose Baldus believed that a shift in the level of OAA caseloads from before to after enactment of the welfare repayment law was due to a general reduction in the funds being spent on welfare rather than to the specific law being studied. In other words, the new laws may have reflected state effort to reduce welfare spending, and the caseload decrease may have occurred because welfare resources dwindled and elderly people were not served, as opposed to elderly people not even applying for aid. If the reduced level of aid to the elderly was due to a reluctance to spend money on any welfare groups, we would expect to find decreases in the amount spent on other assistance categories at the same time as any decreases in the amount spent on the elderly. This possibility could be easily tested by plotting the time-series for other assistance categories and seeing whether they decreased when the state legislature passed the law which enforced repayment from the estates of elderly persons.

Time series with nonequivalent control group. History effects can also be checked by collecting data on units as comparable to our experimental series as possible. The presumption is that the non-equivalent control units will experience the same historical forces as the experimental units so that any history effects should affect both groups. Clearly, adding the nonequivalent control group series does not control for all history effects—merely for those that the groups share in common. Any unique events that affect one group but not another by virtue of the difference between the groups is not controlled for in the extended design.

Adding a control time-series does not automatically rule out all internal validity threats. For example, a time-series analysis of the effect of the introduction of legalized abortion on the number of live births could encounter the problem of diffusion of treatment, especially if state data were used and adjoining states were used for controls. This is because large numbers of women in the control states could cross state lines to obtain abortions, which would reduce the planned contrast between the experimental and control groups. Nonetheless, the interrupted time series with a nonequivalent control group series is a very powerful design.

A CONCLUDING NOTE

Successful implementation of a true or a strong quasi-experimental design in an evaluation is a difficult task. The use of such a design must be weighed against its alternatives, which are passive correlational techniques such as path analysis, and qualitative methods such as participant-observation. Such qualitative and passive quantitative approaches have properties that can complement well a true or a strong quasi-experimental design. However, it is widely acknowledged that they are not sufficient for drawing causal inferences, and a causal inference about the impact of a program is the primary goal of a summative evaluation. Because they allow more confident causal inferences, use of a true or a strong quasi-experimental design is recommended. In this chapter, we have outlined features which should make such designs both easier to implement and easier to interpret.

Foresight is an essential component for the successful conduct of an evaluation. Possible problems must be identified, and preventive measures taken to avoid their occurrence. Further, methods for the early detection of these and of other unforeseen problems should be included when an evaluation is designed. Achieving the necessary foresight is made more likely by a wide investigation of the literature on evaluations, and by extensive discussion with colleagues on the potential problems that may befall an evaluation.

Although conducting a successful evaluation is not an easy task, it is a challenging and rewarding one, and vital to knowing the impact of a program.

NOTES

1. The reader is referred to Myers (1972), Riecken and Boruch (1974), and Winer (1971) for more detailed considerations of the topics outlined in this section.

2. Substantial debate is ongoing as to the appropriate statistical analysis of the pretest-posttest control group design, which is also known as the (pretest-posttest) nonequivalent control group design. For a consideration of various proposed methods of analysis, see Cook and Reichardt (in press).

REFERENCES

Atkinson, R. C. Computerized instruction and the learning process. *American Psychologist,* 1968, 23: 225-239.

Baldus, D. C. Welfare as a loan: The recovery of public assistance in the United States. *Stanford University Law Review,* 1973, 25: 123-250.

Ball, S. and G. A. Bogatz. *The First Year of "Sesame Street": An Evaluation.* Princeton: Educational Testing Service, 1970.

Bernstein, I. and H. E. Freeman. *Academic and Entrepreneurial Research.* New York: Russell Sage Foundation, 1975.

Bloom, B. J., J. H. Hastings, and G. F. Madaus. *Handbook on Formative and Summative Evaluation of Student Learning.* New York: McGraw-Hill, 1971.

Bogatz, G. A. and S. Ball. *The Second Year of "Sesame Street": A Continuing Evaluation.* Princeton: Educational Testing Service, 1971, two vols.

Boruch, R. F. Bibliography: Illustrative randomized experiments for planning and evaluating social programs. *Evaluation,* 1974, 2: 83-87.

Campbell, D. T. Reforms as experiments. *American Psychologist,* 1969, 14: 409-429.

Campbell, D. T. and R. F. Boruch. Making the case for randomized assignment to treatment by considering the alternatives: Six ways in which quasi-experimental evaluations in compensatory education tend to underestimate effects. In A. Lumsdaine and C. A. Bennett (eds.), *Evaluation of Experience: Some Critical Issues in Assessing Social Programs.* New York: Academic Press, 1975.

Campbell, D. T. and A. E. Erlebacher. How regression artifacts in quasi-experimental evaluations can mistakenly make compensatory education look harmful. In J. Hellmuth (ed.), *Compensatory Education: A National Debate,* Vol. 3, *Disadvantaged Child.* New York: Brunner/Mazel, 1970.

Campbell, D. T. and J. C. Stanley. Experimental and quasi-experimental designs for research on teaching. In N. L. Gage (ed.), *Handbook of Research on Teaching.* Chicago: Rand McNally, 1963. (Also published as *Experimental and Quasi-Experimental Designs for Research.* Chicago: Rand McNally, 1966.)

Cook, T. D. and D. T. Campbell. The design and conduct of quasi-experiments and true experiments in field settings. In M. D. Dunnette (ed.), *Handbook of Industrial and Organizational Psychology.* Chicago: Rand McNally, 1976.

Cook, T. D., H. Appleton, R. Connor, A. Shaffer, G. Tamkin, and S. J. Weber. *"Sesame Street" Revisited: A Case Study in Evaluation Research.* New York: Russell Sage Foundation, 1975.

Cook, T. D. and C. S. Reichardt. Statistical analysis of data from the non-equivalent control groups design: A guide to some current literature. *Evaluation,* in press.

Cronbach, L. J. and L. Furby. How we should measure "change"—or should we? *Psychological Bulletin,* 1970, 74: 68-80.

Fienberg, S. E. Randomization and social affairs: The 1970 draft lottery. *Science,* 1971: 225-261.

Glass, G. V., V. L. Willson, and J. M. Gottman. *Design and Analysis of Time-Series Experiments.* Boulder: Colorado Associated University Press, 1975.

Hudson, W. W. *Project Breakthrough: A Responsive Environment Field Experiment with Preschool Children from Public Assistance Families.* Chicago: Cook County Department of Public Aid, 1969.

Lord, F. M. Large-scale covariance analysis when the control variable is fallible. *Journal of the American Statistical Association,* 1960, 55: 307-321.

Lord, F. M. A paradox in the interpretation of group comparisons. *Psychological Bulletin,* 1967, 68: 304-305.

Lord, F. M. Statistical adjustments when comparing preexisting groups. *Psychological Bulletin,* 1969, 72: 336-337.

McTavish, D. G., E. E. Brent, J. D. Cleary, and D. R. Knudsen. *The Systematic Assessment and Prediction of Research Methodology.* Minneapolis, Minn.: Minnesota Systems Research, Inc., September, 1975, two vols.

Meyer, H. J. and E. F. Borgatta. *An Experiment in Mental Patient Rehabilitation.* New York: Russell Sage Foundation, 1959.

Mullen, E. J., R. M. Chazin, and D. M. Feldstein. Services for the newly dependent: An assessment. *Social Service Review,* 1972, 46: 309-322.

Myers, J. L. *Fundamentals of Experimental Design.* Boston: Allyn & Bacon, 1972.

Notz, W. W., B. M. Staw, and T. D. Cook. Attitude toward troop withdrawal from Indochina as a function of draft number: Dissonance of self-interest? *Journal of Personality and Social Psychology,* 1971, 20: 118-126.

Riecken, H. W. and R. F. Boruch. (eds.) *Social Experimentation: A Method for Planning and Evaluating Social Intervention.* New York: Academic Press, 1974.

Rivlin, A. M. *Systematic Thinking for Social Action.* Washington, D.C.: Brookings Institution, 1971.

Rosenberg, M. *The Pretrial Conference and Effective Justice.* New York: Columbia University Press, 1964.

Rutman, L. and D. deJong. *Federal Level Evaluation.* Ottawa, Ontario: Centre for Social Welfare Studies, Carleton University, 1976.

Ryan, T. A. Multiple comparisons in psychological research. *Psychological Bulletin,* 1959, 56: 26-41.

Saretsky, G. The OEO P.C. experiment and the John Henry effect. *Phi Delta Kappan,* 1972, 53: 579-581.

Scriven, M. *Value Claims in the Social Sciences.* Lafayette, Ind.: Social Science Education Consortium, 1966, Publication No. 123.

Sween, J. A. The experimental regression design: An inquiry into the feasibility of nonrandom treatment allocation. Unpublished doctoral dissertation, Northwestern University, 1971.

Thistlethwaite, D. L. and D. T. Campbell. Regression-discontinuity analysis: An alternative to the ex post facto experiment. *Journal of Educational Psychol-ogy* 1960, 51: 309-317.

Ward, D. H. Evaluation research for corrections. In S. E. Ollin (ed.), *Prisoners in America.* Englewood Cliffs, N.J.: Prentice-Hall, 1973.

Willson, V. L. Concomitant variation in the interrupted time-series experiment. Unpublished doctoral dissertation, University of Colorado, 1973.

Winer, B. J. *Statistical Principles in Experimental Design.* New York: McGraw-Hill, 1971.

Decisions about research design have important implications for the data analysis. The authors identify several data-analytic justifications for randomized experiments. In addition, they show that despite many arguments to the contrary, experiments are feasible, can be sufficiently broad in scope to be useful, and can be conducted in an ethical manner. The authors suggest comparative approaches to determine how well the findings of alternative nonexperimental designs stand against more rigorous evaluations. Common data analysis problems arising from nonexperimental designs are identified, and five analytic categories for handling data produced from such designs are discussed: (1) blocking or matching; (2) standardization; (3) covariance methods; (4) regression approaches; and (5) structural equations.

6

ON RANDOMIZED EXPERIMENTS, APPROXIMATION TO EXPERIMENTS, AND DATA ANALYSIS

Robert F. Boruch and David Rindskopf

1. INTRODUCTION

This chapter concerns the problem of estimating the effects of a new social program on its participants. The first of two principal messages which we try to deliver here is that there is a crucial tie between design of a program evaluation and data analysis. To the extent that the evaluation design is poor, simplistic, or absent, then the data analysis will certainly be difficult and conclusions will, at their worst, be misleading. Randomized experiments are used here as a standard against which other designs for impact evaluation are judged. The second message concerns strategy of data analysis. In particular, one ought to know or have good evidence about the way people behave in the absence of the new program to estimate the program's effect accurately. And where theory or data are equivocal in this respect, competing analyses of the data are warranted.

AUTHORS' NOTE: Background research has been supported in part by a National Institute of Education grant (NIE-C-74-0115).

Because this audience is not especially interested in technical detail, the discussion is nontechnical. Because the audience does include some methodologists, we reference some contemporary statistical work. The illustrations are taken from a variety of programmatic areas—welfare, health, rehabilitation.

2. PRELIMINARY DEFINITIONS AND ORGANIZATION

The need to be explicit about what we mean by evaluation, by experiments, by quasi-experiments, and so on is not trivial, for some contemporary arguments about how to estimate program effects are based on confusion about what the terms mean. To avoid needless ambiguity, we begin with definitions.

2.1 PRELIMINARY DEFINITIONS

The form of evaluation which interests us here focuses on the *relative impact* of the program on the program's target group. One asks whether the program, service, or delivery system works with respect to some alternative condition or program.

It ought to be obvious that impact evaluation, including randomized tests, is not the only legitimate way to assess a social program. Other kinds of evaluation focus on different questions and are often equally important in deciding whether a program should continue. Nor can we ignore the fact that these various kinds of evaluation might be properly combined (along with other types) in a single program evaluation. Process evaluation, monitoring program operations, and so on are crucial, but we do not consider them here.

By randomized experiment, we mean the random allocation of experimental units to two or more program or treatment conditions, so as to permit a fair comparison (unbiased estimate) of program effects on some outcome variable, and to permit a quantification of our confidence in that comparison. So, for example, we might randomly assign some members of a group of elderly persons to a novel day care program and some to conventional (control) services. The objective is to estimate the impact of day care and its costs relative to conventional services. The randomization guarantees long-run equivalence of the participants in the new program and nonparticipants, aside from program effect. And the process permits us to quantify our confidence in the resulting estimate of program effect. Solutions to some of the managerial, institutional, and ethical problems in randomized tests are given by Riecken et al. (1974), and Boruch and Riecken (1975).

A statistical *approximation to an experiment or quasi-experiment* refers to any technique which does not include randomized assignment but which does purport to yield fair comparisons and (possibly) quantification of confidence. There appears to be no easy way to classify the numerous approximations to experiments which have been created. For the sake of concreteness, the relevant methodologists may be split into three camps: adjusters, fitters, and designers. Adjusters dip into conventional statistics texts and use techniques like matching, grouping, and standardization to create comparison groups which are alleged to be equivalent to the program recipient group. Or they use regression and covariance methods to achieve the same end. Some adjusters actually recognize that the adjustments made to the data imply a statistical model and a literal theory of the way people behave in the absence of any special social intervention. If the model is made explicit, we cast them out of the adjuster's camp and into the fitter's camp. This is a promotion to a higher level of technical consciousness.

The fitter's group includes methodologists with an interest in structural equation models. Goldberger (1973) prescribes that the models be developed so that "each equation represents a causal link rather than a mere empirical association." A structural equation expert usually relies on previous research to identify the causal links. Where the structural equations are based on observational (nonrandomized) data, causal links are regarded as potentially testable assumptions in order to develop a better framework for understanding a complex process. To the extent that causal links or models are laid out adequately, the models ought to fit available data. Further, important parameters in the model ought to be estimable, and hypotheses about the size of a program effect will be testable. The state of the art in this area is well represented by Goldberger and Duncan's (1973) volume, covering economic, psychometric, and sociometric views.

The adjuster's group does not differ from the fitter's group in principle, of course. In practice, the adjusters usually assume that the statistical model which underlies their adjustment procedure actually generates the population data. The fitters regard this assumption with much more suspicion, and indeed they make deliberate attempts to recognize explicit alternative models and to assess the tenability of alternative models if the data are sufficient (e.g., Goldberger, 1973).

The designer's group is exemplified by the quasi-experimentalists, notably Campbell (1969) and Cook and Campbell (1976). Its members confront situations in which randomization can*not* be accomplished and deliberately plan data collection efforts which will reduce the level of inferential equivocality and bias to the lowest level possible. Unlike the adjusters or the fitters, this group does have some administrative power to structure the evaluation. The exemplary quasi-experimentalist regards his estimates of program effect as tentative, a matter of examining competing explanations of an estimate of the program's effect.

Of course, these categories are not mutually exclusive. Good methodologists generally pitch their tents in each camp at one time or another. We offer the distinctions here only for convenience, and with the understanding that labels and duties will differ a bit from one substantive research area to another.

2.2 ORGANIZATION OF THE DISCUSSION

The underlying theme is that to obtain unbiased estimates of a program's effect, one ought to have a reasonable basis for establishing the way program participants might have behaved had they not participated in the program. Randomized experimental designs provide such a basis, and the discussion begins below in sections 3.1 and 3.2 with this design and the analytic problems it can help resolve. For the sake of the program developer and research manager, some feasibility issues are summarized in 3.3.

Section 4 covers three ways in which quality of an analytic strategy can be established. The emphasis is empirical rather than mathematical. In particular, section 4.1 covers biases in estimating program effects based on analysis of nonrandomized data. Section 4.2 reviews a general but still imperfect device for establishing the quality of the analysis. In section 4.3, other views of the matter are examined.

Section 5 covers checklist approaches to assessing bias in analysis (5.1), approaches based on stereotypical problems in analysis (5.2), and approaches based on more recent technical work (5.3).

3. THE STANDARD FOR ESTIMATING EFFECT: NULL CONDITIONS

Any good estimate of a new program's effect is based on an explicit standard or reference group. Most often, the standard is how people behave, or would behave, in the absence of the new program. Absence of a new program here does not imply individuals would normally receive no services at all; it does imply normal or control services or some program other than the one under special investigation. For the analyst, the problem of making a fair estimate of a program effect turns around the problem of assuring the accuracy of that standard. That is, we would like to assure that our conception of the way people behave without a program is reasonable. Roughly speaking, three kinds of strategies are used in sustaining the argument for reasonableness—procedural, evidentiary, and rhetorical—and each is considered below. A short litany concerning the benefits of randomized experiments in this area follows in sections 3.4 and 3.5.

3.1 PROCEDURAL STRATEGIES

Consider a setting in which eligible members of a group of elderly persons are randomly assigned to a novel day care program or to conventional, normal services. The random assignment procedure carries a guarantee that in the long run, if the experiment is conducted properly, participants and nonparticipants do not differ. This procedural guarantee is limited, of course: Chance alone will produce differences in the group at hand. But the chance variations can be accommodated with conventional statistical methods. The main point is that, because equivalence of groups is assured, estimates of program effect will be fair and unbiased. A difference in health status or in medical expenditures between groups will be attributable to the new program rather than to preexisting, systematic, and unrecognized differences between groups.

Of course, if randomization is not properly carried out, if attrition from the program degrades the comparability of groups, and so on, the guarantee no longer holds. The management of randomized field tests of social programs is no less important in this regard than the technology. To the degree that the management is poor, the data are also likely to be poor, and the analyst will not be able to rely on the design guarantee.

3.2 EMPIRICAL STRATEGIES

One obvious alternative to procedural guarantees is an empirical approach. Health status of the elderly might, for example, be observed over an extended period of time prior to the program's introduction. Following or during their participation in the program, their health status is again observed periodically. In this instance, preprogram measures provide a basis for predicting the way they would behave without the program. The difference between that estimate and their actual status after the program's introduction would, in the simplest case, reflect the program's impact.

The strategy carries no guarantee analogous to that provided in randomized experiments. Indeed, the frame of reference is different. To the extent that the prediction is accurate, the estimate of program effect will be accurate. To the extent that it is a poor prediction, the estimate will be poor.

The problems in relying on this frame of reference are not difficult to identify. In the crudest cases, the number of points available is too few to make a good estimate. At their nastiest, the problems involve fitting rather complicated models to the data so as to accommodate various cycles, autocorrelated error, the effect of repeated measures per se on the target population, and so on (see Glass et al., 1975).

For *novel* social programs, it is often the case that data are insufficient to sustain a time-series approach. It is partly for this reason that randomized experiments are an attractive option. In part this is why we argue for better if still limited empirical specification of null conditions in section 4.2.

3.3 RHETORICAL APPROACHES: SPECIFYING
THE NULL CONDITION BY ASSUMPTION

In the absence of any opportunity to guarantee the equality of groups by a randomization procedure and in the absence of any good empirical specification, then we might simply assume that our null hypothesis is true and test the observed estimator of treatment effect against the assumed value.

The simplest example is the usual posttest in design: Measurement occurs only after treatment. Here one makes the often implicit assumption that, in the absence of any program effect, the characteristics of the participants which reflect their response to the program will be at a specific level. It might be assumed, for example, that a group of high school students will know virtually nothing about health following the program if the program is ineffective.

Now in this simple case, it is easy to see that if the assumption of zero knowledge, aside from information obtained in class, is incorrect, then any estimate of program effect is also incorrect. Any test of the null hypothesis is incorrect since that null hypothesis, the assumption of stable ignorance, is incorrect. In the absence of any extraordinary intervention, there may be a deterioration or an advancement in knowledge.

This classification scheme is an imperfect one, but it does help anticipate crude problems in analysis. In particular, where there are no procedural guarantees of fairness in estimating the program's effect, then one must rely on projection from data. Where data useful for projection are scanty, then one must rely on assumption, theory, or rhetoric to argue that the standard one chooses is reasonable.

3.4 EXPERIMENTS AS PROPERLY PACKAGED IGNORANCE, AS ASPIRIN, AND AS PROPHYLACTIC

The alternatives to a procedural guarantee of the fairness of comparisons are demanding. They require more substantive knowledge about the social phenomena than randomized tests, more technical sophistication, and more wariness about the invidious effects of unrecognized weaknesses in the analysis.

As properly packaged ignorance. McLuhan and Nevitt (1973) observe that all elementary particles in modern physics are packets of ignorance. So too is error in statistics an elementary particle, a packet of ignorance which consolidates unknown and possibly unknowable causes of human behavior. What is unique about experiments is that they put our ignorance in an explicit form—random error—and more importantly, structure our ignorance so that it does not systematically distort our estimate of a program effect. It is a form that requires the evaluator to know little but distributes his ignorance equitably across treatment and control groups. This is not to say that he cannot or should not capitalize on prior knowledge; he can use randomized block designs or randomized covariance designs to increase the power of his experiment considerably. But with strictly observational data, he can never be sure if his ignorance is working systematically against him, for him, or in a neutral fashion. Randomization guarantees in the long run that the work is neutral in the sense of exerting no systematic impact on the accuracy of an estimate.

As aspirin. A fundamental sense in which planned randomized experiments are ideal is that "randomization relieves the experimenter of the anxiety of considering and estimating the magnitude of the innumerable causes by which his data will be disturbed" (Fisher, 1935: 44). This quote from the scripture does not mean that Sir Ronald was terribly interested in mental health. It does mean that his interest lay in a fair and equitable comparison of (say) two treatments, a comparison of data sets which are not free from innumerable causes but which are affected equally by those causes.

Explicit in Fisher's statement are two sensible but anxiety-provoking activities: identifying and estimating the causes of disturbances in the data. Merely identifying plausible causes of variation in non-experimental data is difficult, of course. But we have had little guidance from the formal statistical community on how to go about doing so. If we look to the econometric curve-fitting tradition for advice, we find numerous pointers on the consequence of misspecification, but virtually nothing about the character (statistical or otherwise) of the missing variables. We might then call on substantive experts to make some judgments about what variables have been ignored. But then we find ourselves relying on idiosyncratic faith in an individual (or an advisory board): Their opinions may or may not be verifiable and to the extent that they are not, the opinions are of less value.

In fact, the only general taxonomy for classifying these causes in evaluative research was produced by Donald T. Campbell (1957) over twenty years after Fisher made his remarks. Campbell's so-called "threats to validity" are an important first step in the direction of systematizing the innumerable causes of disturbances in the data and in speculating about their existence and their effect (see section 5.1). These threats are in fact chronically unrecognized influences on the estimates of program effect obtained on observational studies.

As prophylactic. Experiments can be prophylactic in the sense they can prevent subtle analytic biases from appearing. There will be no specious pessimism to the extent that randomization prevents population differences from occurring and prevents the chronic under-adjustment problem. In particular, a point reiterated consistently by Donald Campbell (Campbell, 1974; Campbell and Erlebacher, 1970) is that conventional methods of analyzing observational data in evaluative research can actually make a social program appear harmful when in fact it has no effect at all, and can make a program appear ineffective when in fact the program impact is large and positive.

Any commonly used technique can result in misleading conclusions. But one such technique appears to be chronically misused in evaluative research: covariance adjustment of differences between preexisting groups. It is easy to prove algebraically that covariance adjustments are inadequate when (a) populations from which experimental and control groups are drawn differ and the differences persist in the absence of extraordinary intervention, and (b) the covariates used to account for those differences are imperfectly measured and/or incomplete. In most nonexperimental studies, condition a will be true for reasons of self-selection and/or voluntarism of program participants, differences in history and development of comparison groups and program participants, and so forth. Condition b is typically true in social and educational research, but exceptions do occur. Imperfectly measured covariates—be they cognitive test scores, demographic characteristics, or other variables—are the rule rather than the exception. We usually know very little about the degree of incompleteness of the covariate set, but this does not seem to prevent many evaluators from making a veritable act of faith that we can define population differences (between participant and nonparticipant groups) in any given evaluation setup with the covariates at hand. When the covariance adjustment is imperfect, as it must be under these conditions, and one computes "adjusted means" for experimental and comparison groups, the magnitude of those statistics can make it appear that the program's effect has been considerably smaller (and even negative) relative to the true effect (see, for example, Director, 1974).

3.5 FEASIBILITY OF RANDOMIZED EXPERIMENTS[1]

We often presume that approximations to experiments are desirable. If experiments themselves are approximations to reality, why do we need further approximations? Are experiments not feasible? Are they unethical and therefore inappropriate? Do they fail to be sufficiently broad in scope to be useful? At least partial answers to these questions are given elsewhere, so we focus very briefly on salient issues here.

Feasibility. Just a little homework reveals that a considerable number of experiments for planning and evaluation have been successfully mounted. Our list of over two hundred field experiments (in Boruch, 1974; and Boruch et al., 1977) illustrates the remarkable variety of novel programs subjected to experimental test. Randomized experiments have been mounted to evaluate new income subsidy and housing subsidy programs, law enforcement strategies and court procedures, training programs for police, military, and industrial workers, health care delivery systems and preventive medical programs, new social service strategies, and a range of others. Not all have been successful in carrying out the evaluation design. But the number and the variety of experiments which have been mounted does suggest that randomized tests are more feasible in the social sector than one might suspect.

Scope and limitations. Nothing in experimental design demands that anthropological and similar narrative information be ignored. The various sorts of information have been combined quite nicely in some studies (e.g., Weikert's, 1972, educational experiments). Similarly, nothing in classical experimental design precludes the use of crude qualitative or ordinal variables, and in fact most experiments capitalize on expert observation of "improvement" versus "no improvement," "change" versus "no change," and the like. In fact, the state of the art in using qualitative variables has expanded considerably over the past few years (see Bishop et al., 1975). That differences in individual's reaction to treatment can be accommodated in experiments is also clear, given our experience with randomized block designs and block-by-treatment interaction (e.g., Molof, 1967; Warren, 1967; and other juvenile corrections experiments). Experiments can also capitalize on important auxiliary data, notably social and archival indicators. We know that such data can be and have been used to optimize designs (in the negative income tax experiments), to improve precision of the experiment (where social indicators serve as covariates), and to accomplish other tasks in randomized field tests (see Boruch, 1973, for more detail). Despite some critics' fears, it is not clear that evaluation of randomized experiments will generally lead to a lack of creativity, or a reluctance to be innovative. Indeed, there are some excellent examples of program developers with sufficient intestinal fortitude to not only be creative and to evaluate their inventions experimentally, but to admit that their program is not especially effective in spite of highly original thinking (e.g., Weikert, 1972). *Creativity and innovation simply do not guarantee goodness of course. Neither does experimental evaluation.* But at least experiments can be used to recognize good, possibly creative, program effects when they appear.

Ethicality. For evaluation design, it is important to discriminate between negative effects attributable to the program itself and those attributable to the conduct of randomized tests. Good practice in evaluation, experimental or otherwise, demands that we anticipate, identify, and try to measure negative program effects. The ethical issues here appear to be no different in experiments and approximations to experiments *except* insofar as experiments permit one to identify and estimate the magnitude of the negative effect less equivocally. In this sense, randomization can be a more ethical approach than others. The experiment itself may also produce some negative effects, however. To accommodate random deprivation of a potentially necessary program, a variety of strategies can be considered: short delays in receipt of the program where these are acceptable; random assignment for the marginally needy to treatment; comparison among levels of program intensity rather than simple comparisons of presence and absence of programs, and so forth. We can also capitalize on the advanced state of the art in sequential experiments designed specifically to reduce the number of individuals deprived of an allegedly good program, the duration and intensity of deprivation, the negative consequences of deprivation, and so on.

Reprise. The main point we should like to make here is that *if we accept bald criticism of experiments without question, we will compromise our goals without ever having tried to reach them.* Randomized field experiments are mounted more frequently than we might suspect, and the feasibility is demonstrable in a variety of settings. Insofar as the usual criticisms of experiments are weak or specious, we cannot and must not justify approximations to experiments on these grounds.

This is not to say that developing alternatives to randomized experiments is unjustified, of course. There will always be situations in which randomization is physically impossible, politically impractical, or ethically unacceptable. The crucial issue is determining whether these conditions actually prevail and uncovering their nature so that high-quality evaluations—including experiments—can be designed around these constraints.

4. METHODS OF ANALYSIS: SIMPLE COMPARATIVE STRATEGIES FOR THEIR APPRAISAL

Some very simple techniques are often advertised as useful in obtaining estimates of a program's effect—before-after approaches, matching or covariance analysis to produce statistically equivalent control and comparison groups, and so forth. Given the variety of competing methods, it is not unreasonable to ask how the estimates of program effect obtained from using each method stand against one another in live evaluations. To answer the question simply, we might choose one of three approaches.

First, we might identify instances in which a randomized test *and* a nonrandomized test have been run on the same program and target population. If quality of each test is similar, and if we use the estimate of effect stemming from the randomized test as a standard, then we might judge the quality of competing estimates by their similarity to the standard. The results of our search for instances and comparisons of estimates stemming from *conventional* quasi-experimental designs are given in section 4.1 below.

A second approach, developed by Steven Director and Donald T. Campbell as dry-run experimentation and by Boruch as multiple pretesting, involves a dummy evaluation with live data and a prescribed analytic technique but no real program. The approach is used to check the biases in estimates likely to occur in identical analysis of live data based on a real program. This technique can be used in both design of new program evaluations and in salvaging a poorly designed evaluation; the first approach can be used similarly.

The final approach is less formal. Articulated by John Gilbert et al. (1975), its main purpose is to consolidate previous evaluations with some similarity, compare them with respect to their equivocality, and reach some judgments about the character of the statistical methods which are most useful under various conditions.

All the approaches point up the linkage between evaluation design and the results of data analysis. More importantly, they illustrate, in a concrete fashion, the way in which estimates of effect based on alternative methods can differ or be biased, sometimes dramatically, relative to a standard.

4.1 COMPARING ESTIMATES FROM RANDOMIZED EXPERIMENTS AND APPROXIMATIONS OF EXPERIMENTS[1]

This approach is geared chiefly toward understanding the limits of statistical manipulation. One locates (or conducts) a randomized experimental test of a program and, in addition, collects sufficient nonrandomized data to support ostensibly appropriate quasi-experimental assessment of the same program. Suppose, for example, that data are obtained on individuals who have been randomly assigned either to a treatment program (T) or to a control condition (C). Similar data are also collected on an additional group (C') whose members, though not randomly assigned, are regarded as similar to members of the C group and T group prior to treatment. The question is then posed: How does the estimate of program effect based on ordinary analysis of variance of the T-C groups compare with an estimate of effect based on the T-C' groups and conventional statistical techniques such as matching, covariance analysis, or change scores analysis? The answer is important insofar as it helps us to understand the nature and direction of bias that may be obtained when using techniques such as covariance analysis which purportedly yield unbiased estimates of effect without randomization.

That estimates of effect will often be biased if we rely solely on nonexperimental evidence becomes obvious with some concrete examples. Consider the simplest form of nonexperimental analysis—comparing the condition of program recipients before the program's introduction to their condition afterward. This before-after (or pretest-posttest) approach is common despite the fact that any increase or decrease in average condition may be entirely attributable to unrecognized growth or development processes.

In the Michigan arthritis studies, for example, severity of condition *increased* after the introduction of an arthritis treatment program. Based on this information alone, we might erroneously conclude that the program's effect was negative, i.e., it actually harmed program participants. In fact, we know from randomized experimental tests that the equivalent control group's condition deteriorated even further, and consequently, the proper inference is that the program did indeed have a beneficial effect [see Deniston and Rosenstock, 1972].

Usually one attempts to find a comparison group against which to gauge the condition of program participants, and also to reduce the equivocality underlying most before-after designs. But this is also hazardous when the comparison group differs systematically and (often) in unknowable ways from the participant group.

For example, one facet of the Salk vaccine trials involved comparing volunteer vaccine recipients to an allegedly equivalent, "natural" comparison group of nonrecipients. The vaccine's effect in this nonrandomized quasi-experiment was positive. But estimates based on a second facet of the trials—randomized tests—gave estimates of effect which were 14% higher than the value based on the nonrandom tests. Given only the evidence from the nonrandom groups then, we would have concluded that the vaccine was notably *less* effective than it actually was in reducing polio incidence [Meier, 1972].

In randomized tests of a retardation rehabilitation program, Heber et al. (1972) collected data on an additional plausibly equivalent comparison group—siblings of children enrolled in the program. The difference in observed IQ between program participants and nonparticipants in the randomized test was about 36 points. A comparison of program recipients against their siblings (an ostensibly equivalent contrast group) yielded a 45-point difference. Had we relied solely on the "natural" comparison group, we would have overestimated the program's impact in this instance.

At this point, the critical reader might observe that there are algebraic techniques which purportedly "adjust out" differences between groups and which equate groups which differ initially, in order to avoid biases such as these. The techniques—matching program participants and nonparticipants with respect to their demographic or other characteristics, covariance or regression analysis—are sophisticated but do require strong assumptions about the underlying nature of the data. More importantly, those assumptions may not be an adequate picture of reality—i.e., of how individuals will behave in the absence of any program intervention. To be specific, when groups differ initially and the difference persists, then these methods will *not* perform adequately if the matching variables or covariates are measured imperfectly or incompletely. Some of the more advanced techniques accommodate the problem of fallible measures reasonably well, provided that reliability of the data is not too low (e.g., Porter, 1967). But none accommodates the specification problem satisfactorily: In many cases, we are very likely to leave out variables which are important but which are unmeasured or unmeasurable. In either case, the adjustment process is imperfect, and estimates of program effect will often be biased. How often will they be biased? It is impossible to say, but a few examples may help to illustrate the problem.

> In the Michigan Arthritis Study cited earlier, a comparison group was identified, differences between this group and program participants were reduced by matching individuals, and estimates of program effect obtained. The estimate of effect based on this comparison is near zero; that is, despite selection of a matched group, the estimate obtained by comparing these individuals to the program participants is biased, relative to the estimate obtained from the completely randomized data [Deniston and Rosenstock, 1972].

> The Middlestart program was designed by Yinger, Ikeda, and Laycock (1970) as a special pre-college program for promising high-school students. In their original evaluation, some students were assigned randomly to participant and control groups. Others were assigned on the basis of post-facto matching. That is, five sets of treatment and comparison groups were constructed; they were not randomized and were equivalent only in the sense that they were matched on the basis of their demographic characteristics. If one examines the pooled data, one finds a significant difference of about six months in grade equivalent achievement test scores between participants and nonparticipants. However, if one examines only the randomized set of students, the estimate is far lower and quite negligible. In this case, the nonrandomized comparisons yield estimates of effect ranging from zero to a two-year difference in achievement test scores [Boruch et al., 1975].

Time-series designs are also a promising approach to estimating program impact. Here one observes some outcome variable over time (e.g., rape rate over the last three years), introduces the program, and then tries to detect subsequent change in the variable (e.g., a drop in incidence of rape). The time-series approach is promising to the extent that there is no good competing explanation for the change in the outcome variable, such as changes in the accuracy of measuring the incidence of rape, and to the extent that the time series is stable, so that a discontinuity will be obvious if it occurs. However, time-series analysis is not always possible and it can yield estimates which differ from those based on experimental evidence.

> In the Cali (Colombia) evaluation of nutrition and education programs, we find that an estimate of program effect based on short time-series projection from the control group is biased downward drastically. The time-series estimate of effect on children's cognitive skills is half the size of the effect based on test scores of randomized recipient and nonrecipient groups. The bias would be smaller if a much longer time-series had been available [see McKay et al., 1973].

> In the Michigan Arthritis Study, time-series estimates of effect were 10% higher than estimates based on randomized experimental tests in the same populations.

Of course, there have been studies employing much less competent methodology than even the imperfect ones we have described which have also led to erroneous conclusions. The more dramatic examples have occurred in medicine, where medical or surgical remedies, adopted on the basis of very weak evidence, have been found to be useless at best or damaging to the patient at worst.

> The so-called frozen stomach approach to surgical treatment of duodenal ulcers, for example, was used by a variety of physicians who simply imitated the technique of an expert surgeon. Later experimental tests showed prognoses were good simply because the originating surgeon was good at surgery and not because his innovation was effective. It provided no benefit over conventional surgery [Ruffin et al., 1969].

> Anticoagulant drug treatment of stroke victims had prior to 1970 received considerable endorsement by physicians who relied solely on informal observational data for their opinions. Subsequent randomized experimental tests showed not only that a class of such drugs had no detectable positive effects but that they could be damaging to the patients' health [see Hill et al., 1960, and other examples described in Rutstein's, 1969, excellent article].

None of this should be taken to mean that estimates of program impact based on experiments will always differ in magnitude from those based on nonrandomized assessments. The estimators will be close, for example, if there is no systematic difference between characteristics of the individuals assigned to one program variation and those assigned to another. If in a particular research project there is no systematic association—i.e., there is a kind of natural randomization process—or if such differences can be removed statistically, then we may expect various types of designs to produce similar results.

We have been able to document few instances of this, however. The first stage of Daniels et al.'s (1968) evaluation of the DANN Mental Health program, for instance, involved allocation of incoming patients to the experimental treatment ward on the basis of number of beds available in each. Controlled (deliberate) randomization was introduced after ward turnover rate had stabilized. Comparisons of the characteristics of ward entrants prior to their treatment in the first nonrandomized stage to the characteristics of entrants admitted in the second (deliberately randomized) stage showed no important measurable differences between the groups. More importantly, separate analyses of the nonrandomized and randomized groups yielded very similar estimates of program effect.

An essential condition for similarity of estimates is that, prior to program introduction, there be no systematic association between characteristics of eligible program candidates and their participation in the program. The association may be slight enough at times to give us some confidence that the program effect is in the proper direction even if we recognize that the magnitude of the estimator is likely to be in error. Holt's (1974) evaluative studies of sentence reduction in prisons is informative in this respect. A number of nonrandomized studies on early versus late release of individuals from prison suggested that length of sentence (within certain limits) had no impact on post-prison behavior. Later randomized experimental tests demonstrated that the magnitude of the early estimates of the effect of early release were reasonable.

In each of these cases, as in others (see Boruch, 1975), randomized tests were needed to verify that unobserved influences were not entirely responsible for the results obtained in nonexperimental studies. More specifically, the Daniels experiment helped to rule out the possibility that program effects estimated from the nonexperimental data of the first stage were attributable to subtle differences in patients assigned to each ward rather than to the ward program itself. In the Holt work, the experiment helped to demonstrate that the success of early releases was not entirely attributable simply to very expert judgments by parole boards about the likelihood of a parolee's returning to prison, but that the length of sentence actually has no discernible effect within certain limits on recidivism.

4.2 DRY-RUN EXPERIMENTS AND MULTIPLE PRETESTING

Recall that one of the main problems in nonrandomized studies is that null conditions—the way people behave in the absence of the program—often cannot be characterized well. One simple vehicle for helping to specify null conditions *and* to establish flaws in analysis based on erroneous assumptions in the nonrandomized studies has been described under the rubrics of "dry-run experimentation" and multiple or dummy pretesting.

To illustrate the dry-run approach, consider an evaluation in which observations are made before (at time T_1) and after (T_2) the program's introduction, and on both program participants and on a control group. Assume, as will usually be the case in nonrandomized designs, that the procedure by which individuals enter the program is ambiguous. The comparability of the groups will then be suspect, and so it is not unreasonable to check for biases in the analysis. Finally, suppose that some conventional method, such as covariance analysis or matching, is used to estimate effects. Under these conditions, it is sometimes possible to retrieve additional data on the same groups, for points earlier in time (say, T_0). If so, an analysis of the data based on the measures over the interval T_0-T_1 should show no program effect, for after all, no program exists during T_0-T_1. Because of errors in the assumptions underlying the analytic method, however, such as a poor projection of null conditions or incomparability of groups, the estimate of effect based on the T_0-T_1 data will not be zero. The dry-run analysis can help to reveal flaws in the analytic strategy proposed for the live T_1-T_2 data, notably by demonstrating sizable program effects when no program exists.

The tactic can sometimes be incorporated formally into evaluation design. One obtains data on individuals who are *likely* to be members of treatment and control groups over at least two time points prior to the program's introduction. After program imposition, actual treatment and control group members are sorted out, and data from the double pretests are analyzed, using exactly the same technique which is planned for the main evaluation. This analysis should show no effect— the data are, after all, collected before the program's introduction. If an effect does show up, then the analytic approach and the model of null conditions which underlies that approach must be reexamined.

Some concrete examples may help to illustrate the approach.

In many evaluations of manpower training programs, the increase in salary levels of trainees based on before-after observations is used to argue that the programs were successful. In fact, we know from other evidence that salary level is quite likely to have increased even in the absence of a special training program. That evidence may include two spaced observations of program participants' salary levels *before* introduction of the program. Or, it may include multiple observations on salary level increases prior to the program's introduction on groups very similar to those actually participating in the program [Director, 1974].

In the evaluation of programs supported by the Manpower Training and Development Act, Borus and Hardin estimated that the program's effect was to *decrease* the income of trainees. They used covariance analysis to "adjust preexisting differences" between program participants and nonparticipants in a nonrandomized study. Director (1974), however, conducted exactly the same analysis on data from similar groups in prior years, before the program's introduction. He found that in the absence of any program at all, the analytic technique yielded nearly the same negative estimate of program "effect." That is, the technique failed in both the original live evaluation and in the dry run to yield unbiased estimate of program effect. Indeed the estimate was biased in a direction which made the program look harmful; the bias is attributable to a seldom-recognized statistical artifact.

More recent examples stem from the evaluation of special compensatory education programs and illustrate that even without elaborate statistics it is possible to appraise the credibility of an analytic approach using the dry-run method.

Wortman and St. Pierre (1975), for example, were concerned with estimating the effect of so-called voucher programs, an educational innovation designed, in part, to increase the achievement level of third-grade students. They used data from the same students, collected during the first and second grades, as a basis for determining which of several different analytic approaches would produce the least biased estimate of program effect. That is, an analysis was run, an estimate obtained and judged as to its size for the dry-run data. The analytic approach finally identified yielded the least biased estimate and so was applied to the live data.

The results of such an analysis may still be very equivocal. And, indeed, Wortman and St. Pierre report that their own analysis is subject to some major threats to validity which are not accommodated by the dry-run approach. Still, the matter of data analysis, especially in the absence of randomized experiments, must be a matter of successive approximation to an unbiased estimate of program effect, and the Wortman-St. Pierre example is admirable in that respect.

Rindskopf (1976) has presented a similar type of analysis. His secondary assessment of data from evaluation of Title I-supported compensatory education programs suggested that a covariance analysis, adjusting out individual differences between nonrandom treatment and control groups, might be useful. However, in order to avoid well-known biases, the analysis would have to be corrected for unreliability in the covariates. Deciding which reliability estimate to use—a measure of internal consistency of the variables, or test-retest correlations, or others—was difficult. To better understand the biases engendered by each correction factor, Rindskopf used background variables to predict the pretest—i.e., used variables like parental income and social status as a surrogate for the measure. A conventional covariance analysis showed that these predictors would yield biased results: Pretest differences using background characteristics as covariates persisted in the form of significant F ratios. When that analysis of pretest and (surrogate) pre-pretest data was corrected for internal inconsistency in the achievement measures, biases still persisted. When on the other hand the correlation between background variables and the pretest was used as an estimator of reliability, the bias (at least as reflected in the test statistics) disappeared.

This multiple pretesting approach is simple, and it can protect the analyst from making faulty assumptions about the way people behave in the absence of a program, about the comparability of comparison and treatment groups, and so on. It is better than a simple before-after approach in this respect. But it is still weaker than a strategy which employs randomized assignment or a long time series for analysis. In fact, it is a kind of weak time series, though it does not deserve the dignity of the phrase.

4.3 RATING INNOVATIONS AND MAJOR THREATS TO VALIDITY

Gilbert et al. (1975) set out to understand evaluative data and methods of analysis by examining rigorous evaluations which have been successfully implemented. The examination gives the analyst some feel for the likelihood of success in well-controlled settings, a frame of reference for judging the realism or credibility of claims of success based on other, less rigorous evaluations. Conducting such an examination of education programs, welfare programs, sociomedical and surgical treatments, all evaluated using randomized experiments, the authors find that success rate is low. Though low, they observe, this is not unexpected, for successes are about as rare in physical sciences and medical research as well.

Having obtained some feel, based on very well-designed evaluations, for the incidence of success, they then examine the evaluations based on poorer design, but which are often advertised as a success. Gilbert and his colleagues reiterate evidence from the medical sector showing that the poorer the evaluation design, the more likely it is that the program director-evaluator is enthusiastic about the program. They argue further that if, in these instances, a major competing explanation is found which might explain away the success, then judgments about the impact of the program ought to be suspended. This suspension of judgment may not be pleasing to the policy maker, but in the absence of any real evidence against a plausible competing explanation it must be regarded as such. In examining a small array of ostensibly successful programs in medicine, education, and welfare, evaluated under less rigorous designs, they do indeed find it easy to explain how "impact" of the programs may be entirely attributable to factors operating outside the direct intervention. "Successful" housing programs, for example, can be made to appear successful simply by choosing residents carefully and by keeping no records on the criteria for selection. Medical or surgical treatments can be guaranteed to show positive impact, as they have in the past, by selecting patients who are improving in any event. And so forth. The only major exceptions to the perspective are so-called "big bang" effects; i.e., the program is so very large, relative to normal variation in the social system and to naturally operating social factors, that it obviously overrides competing explanations. But this event is very rare.

The point is that in examining data from a contemporary program evaluation, precedent can be important. One ought to know something about the incidence and size of effects under rigorous evaluation to reasonably gauge the credibility of claims based on designs which are likely to yield equivocal results. One ought to recognize, as well, the obvious criticisms leveled against previous nonrandom evaluations of programs similar to those of current interest. It is not unreasonable to expect that competing explanations of the past will be the competing explanations for current and future impact studies. By failing to recognize them, we do the public a disservice; the growth of applied social science is no better served.

5. DATA ANALYSIS: MORE GENERAL STRATEGIES

Much of what has already been said, of course, concerns data analysis in one way or another. The following discussion is tied less to evaluation design than to the problem of making sense of the data stemming from nonrandomized studies, including surveys. The review is brief but hopefully not provincial. It ranges from the simpler devices, such as checklist approaches to making inferences about a program's impact, to those statistical methods which yield a better-qualified inference but are technically demanding. None guarantees unbiased estimates of program effect, but all help to establish the plausibility of any given interpretation of the data.

5.1 CHECKLIST APPROACHES

Given some data bearing on a program's impact, the idea behind many checklist approaches is to make some judgment about the existence of an effect, then to enumerate all the competing causes or explanations for the effect *other* than the program itself. The final step is to attach some level of plausibility or import to those competing explanations.

Consider, for example, data on a novel treatment for schizophrenics undertaken in one ward of a hospital and data on schizophrenics treated in another, nonequivalent ward. One might first look at levels of severity following treatment for each group and infer that because severity is higher for the novel treatment group, that treatment harmed rather than helped people. There are a number of competing explanations for a between-group difference, of course. The type of patient normally assigned to the novel ward may, for example, differ from those assigned to the regular ward. And enumerating these explanations is easier if we have at our disposal a checklist of "threats to internal validity" such as the ones enumerated by Campbell (1957), Campbell and Stanley (1966), and Cook and Campbell (1976). Their lists are elaborate, so we provide only a brief description of major themes.

The *maturation* of each group may differ notably. Participants in the novel program, for example, may have been deteriorating over the past few years while the comparison group condition may have been relatively stable. The *selection* process for each ward may be deliberately or accidentally designed to assign those with differing severity to each ward. Even when their history is similar, if initial severity is different in each ward, then their rate of deterioration may differ irrespective of the program's impact. *Testing* patients in the new program may also produce artificial effects—e.g., by heightening patient and staff awareness of their condition. And if the instrumentation changes during the process, if different raters are used at different stages of the evaluation, then the resulting differences in ratings may be mistaken for program effects. So-called *regression artifacts* may also be critical: If individuals are assigned to the new ward on the basis of their high initial severity, in the absence of any program effect and any major trend in the overall population, that subgroup will have a lower severity score at the second testing. The drop is attributable to a regression to the mean which affects any measure with imperfect reliability, rather than to the program. *Dropout rate* or *attrition* may produce artificial differences between groups if, for example, the least severely ill members of the new treatment group reject the new treatment and leave the ward and perhaps even check themselves into the regular ward.

The recent list of threats to validity issued by Cook and Campbell (1976) is complex, and its completion can be very tedious. Nonetheless, in the informal impact evaluation, an approach like this can be enormously helpful in avoiding egregious errors in literal or quantitative analysis of the data.

5.2 APPROACHES BASED ON STEREOTYPICAL ERRORS

Any checklist is inefficient to the extent that the list is long and contains items which are irrelevant for the evaluation at hand. To accommodate the problem, it is sometimes possible to identify stereotypical ways in which inferences about program impact may be wrong and so narrow the list down. The literal stereotypes may apply to only one class of evaluative settings, e.g., in compensatory education, but they can be more useful in developing prescriptions which are quantitative and qualitative, rather than merely qualitative, to deal with the problem of estimating impact.

The basic objective is to recognize chronic problems of data analysis in a given substantive area and to determine their severity for the evaluation at hand. For example, Campbell has identified six such problems, and Campbell and Boruch (1975) furnish some procedures for detecting and accommodating them. Those problems, identified as chronic in the evaluation of compensatory education programs using covariance or matching designs and observational data, are generalizable to other settings. They include regression effects, differential growth rates, differences in reliability of measurement over time and with subgroup, and ceiling and floor effects on measurement.

To make matters concrete, consider an actual cultural enrichment program to which economically deprived preschool children have been exposed. The comparison group, selected after the fact, consists of children from families whose economic condition is better and who are thus ineligible for the program. The specific mathematical character of the setting, given in Campbell and Boruch (1975), is essential to estimating program effects but not essential for understanding the problems and prescriptions which we give next.

The *regression-effects* problem turns on the fact that unreliable measurement in surveys sets the stage for biases in estimation of program effects when covariance, regression, matching, or similar conventional techniques are used. So, for example, a covariance technique might be used by the conventional analyst to adjust out pre-existing differences between a treated group and the control group, without recognizing that imperfections in measurement of the covariates or matching variables often lead to estimates of program effect which are seriously biased. Some conditions, which are common but do not always prevail, can lead to estimates of program effect which are biased downward—i.e., estimated effects are small even where actual effects are large, and estimates are negative, making the program look harmful when actual program effects are negligible. The conditions under which the problem occurs are described mathematically and literally, together with examples, in Campbell and Boruch (1975).

To help assure that the problem is detectable, it is essential that the program evaluator have information on (a) the process underlying assignment of treatment and comparison-group members, (b) statistical data bearing on the character of both groups before the program begins, and (c) reliability of matching variables, covariates. Estimates of reliability can sometimes be used to adjust conventional analyses for the presence of measurement error. The other information is helpful in understanding whether particular approaches can or should be used by the analyst.

Differential growth of the treated and comparison groups appears to be a chronic problem which cannot be remedied without strong theory and good data on growth processes. When tested repeatedly over time, for example, middle-class children's achievement test scores often increase more rapidly than do scores of children from economically deprived settings. The stereotype occasionally identified here is a "fan spread" pattern of mean achievement for economic groups when plotted over time (Kenny, 1975). If the phenomenon goes unrecognized by the conventional analyst, then estimates of program effect will be biased. An analysis which looks only at change scores in the program group relative to the middle-class children will lead to a declaration that because the middle-class group is increasing at a faster rate, the program must have had a negative impact on participants. The declaration will be wrong unless the differential growth rate has been recognized and accommodated.

There is evidence to suggest that the less privileged child is measured with somewhat less reliability, using standard achievement tests, than the middle-class child, and further that the reliability of measurement of each group will (depending on age, grade, and other factors) increase as children and testors become more familiar with the test. One of the stereotypical problems which may crop up in the field setting then is that the differential rate of errors in measurement produces a small difference between groups when in fact the difference is large. That is, the unreliability obscures real differences, especially on initial testing. If children are tested a second time and reliability of measurement of both groups is higher on that testing, the difference between groups will, under certain common conditions, increase. The increase will be attributable to the properties of the test and to practice effects rather than to any real program effect. But if the differentials in reliability of measurement go unrecognized by the conventional analyst, then the post-program differences may be declared (erroneously) as indicating that the program had a negative effect. Again, the exact conditions under which the problem occurs and evidence are given in Campbell and Boruch (1975). The simplest prescription that we can offer to establish the existence and magnitude of the problem is to obtain hard data as a check on its character: pilot tests or side studies in which intergroup differences in reliability or intertime differences are estimated, on-site studies of the test process, post-facto estimates of the internal consistency of test responses estimated by group and by time period. Without the estimates, it is unlikely that adequate corrections can be made to conventional analyses.

Floor effects refer here to the problem of inadequate measurement of children whose ability level is considerably lower than that measured accurately by the achievement test used in the evaluation. That is, children in this range score near the zero or chance level on a test not because they know nothing but because the test is insensitive to ability in the lower range. The consequences can be obvious: Even if the compensatory program has a notable effect, that effect may still be too small to be reflected by an insensitive test—i.e., the effect may not be sufficient to boost children into a measurable range. The problem is not a new one, nor is it confined to education. It is a dangerous one to the extent that conventional analysts who do not recognize it will be tempted to declare that a program estimate which is near zero means the program had no effect, rather than that the measurement was faulty. Worse, the problem can lead, under certain conditions, to estimates of effect which are negative. Again, the only reasonable prescription to follow, especially when the tests' properties are not well documented or are suspect, is to run pilot tests prior to the program evaluation to establish their sensitivity and validity.

To summarize, it is clear from case studies of evaluations that some conventional data analyses are susceptible to stereotypical problems which often go unrecognized. Those problems can be anticipated and documented with side studies and pilot tests. The idea, to identify stereotypes, can be helpful in avoiding serious problems in estimating program effects, especially when unrecognized problems engender estimates which are negatively biased. The hazard, as in any such effort, is that the stereotypes themselves may be irrelevant or misleading in the particular case (see Cronbach, 1976). The approach generally requires expertise of two kinds: Substantive, e.g., in educational program development and applications; and mathematical-statistical, e.g., in establishing presence and character of the stereotype and in accommodating the problem it generates. Similar approaches have been developed around particular evaluation designs, e.g., by Linn and Slinde (1977) in analyzing before-after evaluation designs, by Granger and Newbold (1974) in analyzing time-series data, by Linn (1976) in analysis of the use of standardized test norms, by Glaser (1973) in evaluating criminal offender programs, and by others.

5.3 MULTIPLE ANALYTIC MODELS AND METHODS OF ANALYSIS

Regardless of which broad approach one uses—checklists, stereotypes, comparative assessment—the problem of numerically estimating the impact of a program remains. That is, the literally stated threats to validity, our understanding of how people behave in the absence of a program, and so on, must be translated into mathematical form to uncover the size of the program effect and to attach some level of confidence to the estimate. Having capitalized on substantive experts to learn about qualitative reality, the analyst must then match the mathematical models, which underpin any data analysis, with that reality.

The analyst faced with the prospect of estimating program effects based on nonrandomized data is, with some exceptions, not in an enviable position. There is a wide choice of methods which might be exploited, to be sure. For each, however, there is a set of assumptions which must be met in order for the analysis to be valid—i.e., to produce an unbiased estimate of effect. It is, in many cases, difficult to check assumptions, and for naively designed field surveys checking may be impossible.

The assumptions common to most methods bear on the properties of measurement and of the statistical models which underpin analysis.

Most often, a piecewise approach to verifying their tenability is warranted. Scales of measurement in many analyses are supposed to have interval properties, for example. Roughly speaking, this means that the validity of measurement at any given point in the scale is as good as validity at any other point. Attrition from treatment and comparison groups, if it occurs at all, is usually supposed to be random or at least predictable on the basis of simple statistical models. The fact that a program is in place, and has additive effects rather than (say) multiplicative effects, also must be verifiable both at the structural level and at the level of the individual participant. The structure of variances and covariances for any given analysis must usually have a well-specified form and evidence on the matter can determine which analysis is appropriate.

In some cases, there may not be a method which can be used without violating some assumption. There are two strategies which can then be used. One is to use the results of a sensitivity analysis, which is a test of how much a violation of a particular assumption will affect the outcome of the analysis. Occasionally this can be done through algebraic derivations, but usually it is done using simulation of data in which the assumption is violated. For example, most analysts are aware that violating the assumption of normal distribution of residuals has little effect on the F statistic in analysis of variance. This was established through simulations of data in which various different distributions of data were used.

The other strategy which can be used when assumptions are violated is to try various methods of analysis, each of which involves a different set of assumptions. Under some circumstances, the pattern of results will enable the researcher to deduce not only the probable treatment effect, but also which assumptions were actually violated. Utilization of this method requires that the researcher be able to list every assumption of each analytic method.

Certain methods are suspect because it is unlikely that their assumptions will be met in many evaluation studies, and violation of the assumptions can result in large biases. As indicated earlier, many of these methods are similar in principle, although they look different on the surface: blocking (matching), analysis of covariance, standardization, and multiple regression are all used to adjust for differences in background of the groups being compared. But using these procedures to analyze nonexperimental data is fundamentally different from using the same techniques to analyze data from randomized experiments. When data are gathered from a randomized experiment, the purpose of using various adjustment techniques is to provide a more powerful statistical test. With random assignment, there are fewer problems of bias in the sense of correcting for initial group differences, either in terms of problems caused by errors of measurement or misspecification of the model. With nonexperimental data, on the other hand, the purpose of many adjustments is to correct for these factors, for errors of measurement and misspecification can cause large biases. Statistical power is of typically secondary importance here.

Some applications of *covariance analysis* to nonrandomized data will give unbiased results, but it is not always possible to check the assumptions underlying the application. Cronbach et al. (1976) indicate that if the analyst knows either the complete covariate (one which predicts within-group outcome as fully as possible) or the complete discriminant (which fully represents initial group differences), then unbiased estimation is possible. The problem is that, in practice, the analyst seldom knows whether imperfect prediction is due to errors of measurement or misspecification. A limited subset of cases in which the complete discriminant is known is when the covariates have been used to assign subjects to treatment groups. In this case, covariance and regression estimates will be unbiased (see Rubin, 1975, 1976a; Kenny, 1975; Overall and Woodward, 1977). This is seldom explicitly done, but a discriminant analysis may be useful in detecting the implicit rules for assignment, which can then be used in analysis of covariance or a matching design.

Because assignment on the basis of a covariate (even if imperfectly measured) can provide unbiased estimates of treatment effect without randomization, the regression-discontinuity design advocated by Campbell (1969) is an important tool for evaluators. In the regression-discontinuity design, a continuum of need or merit is established, and subjects scoring above the dividing line are assigned to one group, while those below the dividing line are assigned to the other group. For example, students might be rated on need for compensatory education, and those above a certain point would receive it, while those below would not. In this case, an analysis of covariance would not be biased *if* certain additional assumptions hold. Such clear-cut assignment rules seldom exist, so biases in estimation are probably the rule rather than the exception in present-day research.

If the data satisfy all of the other criteria for ANCOVA (in particular, the slopes of the regression line for each group should be the same), and the covariate set is complete except for random errors of measurement, then it is possible to do an ANCOVA with corrections for unreliability. To ameliorate problems of fallibility in the covariate, for example, Lord (1960) has developed a large sample test statistic (for assessment of treatment effects) which relies on auxiliary data as a vehicle for accommodating the fallibility. The technique, which is restricted to the single covariate situation, yields results similar to Porter's (1967) methods for estimating true covariates for any number of groups, given test-retest reliabilities. Stroud (1972) has derived a large sample test statistic for assessing differences between regression lines when the reliability of the covariate is known for the population; reliability in this case appears to correspond to internal consistency. Implicit in the Cronbach et al. (1976) work is the idea that generalizability coefficients can be used for the adjustment. Still other approaches involve a combination of both blocking and covariance in which matching is conducted on regressed pretest scores (i.e., pretest regressed on posttest and estimates made of pretest scores); the regression might ignore unreliability altogether. There has been no attempt to compare results using these alternative methods or to lay out relations among them. Moreover, the usefulness of these approaches has not been assessed relative to matching and standardization strategies based on fallible qualitative or quantitative variables. At this point, expert statistical help may be necessary (but seldom sufficient), since there is disagreement about what kind of adjustment is appropriate in different situations (see, e.g., Campbell and Erlebacher, 1970; Kenny, 1975; Linn and Werts, 1977; Cronbach et al., 1976).

In doing an analysis of covariance, it is particularly helpful if the covariate is the same as the dependent variable. This is because one of the assumptions which must be made is that the dependent variable and the covariate measure the same traits, and in the same proportions. If not, there is no way to correct for initial differences. For example, suppose that the covariate measures both mathematical ability and verbal ability, in the ratio of 2 to 1; that is, the covariate measures mathematical ability more than verbal ability. Suppose that the dependent variable is just the opposite; it measures the same abilities, but in a ratio of 1 to 2. What we want to do is to correct scores for initial differences between the groups on the dependent variable. But if we correct for differences in mathematical ability, we will overcorrect for differences in verbal ability, while if we correct for differences in verbal ability, we will undercorrect for differences in mathematical ability. We can minimize the chance of this occurring, as well as the probability of the covariate being incomplete, by using the same test (or a parallel test) as the dependent variable for a covariate.

Blocking or *matching* in evaluation studies involves matching each member of the program participant group with a partner in a comparison group. Partners are generally matched on qualitative or quantitative variables such that the absolute difference between their respective scores on matching variables is minimum or zero. A variety of sophisticated strategies for matching samples has been suggested, including individual matching, precision matching, pair matching, and mean matching. Those who want a more complete discussion of matching should consult the work of Rubin (Cochran and Rubin, 1973; Rubin, 1974, 1976a, 1976b, 1976c) which discusses the problems of reducing bias due to initial differences, the effects of unreliability in the matching variables, and techniques for matching. Note, however, that when Rubin discusses reducing bias, he usually means bias due to initial group differences, not bias due to unreliability of matching variables. One instance in which matching can cause problems which may not be correctable is when matching is incorporated into the design of a nonrandomized study. If matched pairs are selected to be studied, and no data are collected on other subjects, then the extent of bias in test statistics may be impossible to estimate or correct for due to these selection biases. Thus, our recommendation is that if matching is used, it should be used after the fact, so that the results can be compared with other analytic methods.

Tactics related to matching, such as *standardization* adjustment, often involve weighting the mean difference between comparison and treatment group means within a given range of scores; the sum of the weighted product is an estimate of the program effect. The weights are chosen to minimize variance of the treatment estimate. Wiley's (1976) direct and indirect standardization methods constitute one related approach; means of subgroups in control and comparison groups are weighted according to the proportion of children (say) in those subgroups in the population. Other related standardization procedures, more commonly applied, include age-grade equivalents and the like, although these do not use a variance criterion for their development. Both matching and these standardization strategies may remove between-cell bias but may do little to remove within-cell biases. In some cases, they will yield results which are similar to covariance adjustment, but predicting the conditions under which they do so is not easy.

There are more complicated methods which allow for errors in measurement, but for the most part they still require many of the assumptions of other methods. For example, *structural equation models* approaches (Joreskog, 1974; Duncan, 1975; Goldberger and

Duncan, 1973) involve translating verbal descriptions of causal relationships between variables into a mathematical description. This mathematical model can then be tested to see if it fits the data.

Work on these methods has been summarized recently in Goldberger and Duncan (1973) and one can rely on papers appearing in that volume and more recent work to guide analyses. The Goldberger and Wiley paper in the volume presents a succinct general approach to the problem of laying out the structural equations to help understand the conditions under which models are overidentified, underidentified, and just-identified, to permit their estimation. A second general theme in the Wiley and other papers is the emphasis on path-analytic framework for the equations, an abstract framework set up to simulate the basic mechanisms generating the data. Various strategies for estimating parameters (associated with, say, treatment effects and individual effects) have been proposed by advocates of the structural equation and path-analytic traditions. For example, a general method for exploring the correlational pattern of (what amount to) structural models has been developed by Karl Joreskog, based on earlier work by Bock and Bargmann. We have been able to apply this factor-analytic approach with some success to observational and experimental studies on rating schemes and college effect studies (Boruch and Wolins, 1970; Creager and Boruch, 1969). The Costner and Schoenberg approaches improve on this early work by introducing a path analytic perspective to guide the search for factor analytic models which fit the data well. Special problems in this context are important insofar as their resolutions are the building blocks for the generalized approaches. Kenny (1973), for example, has cast the problem of discriminating between common instantaneous causation and chain (sequential) causation into a structural model framework. His work improves on and offers alternatives to strategies proposed by Roselle and Campbell (1969) and others in presenting formal strategies for discriminating between models. Other problems such as combining multiple estimates of the same parameters, appraising biases in estimates of the structural parameters and the like are difficult ones, but partial solutions continue to be developed by Goldberger, Griliches, and others.

These models are general enough to allow for measurement error and for omitted variables, although the omitted variables must be uncorrelated with the underlying independent variables. There is still a possibility of bias entering, although less so than with the models previously described. There is a price to pay for using these models, and that is that much more data has to be collected. To get a good measure of errors in variables, underlying independent variables must usually be measured by at least two observed variables (exact rules for prescribing how many observed variables are necessary are usually complicated). Thus, if the researcher feels that socioeconomic status influences test scores, he must usually have at least two, and preferably three or more, measures of socioeconomic status, such as mother's or father's education and family income. Other complications in the particular model will determine exactly how many measures of each underlying variable are necessary, but good planning (or good luck) is necessary in order that all of the plausible causal models can be tested. For this reason, although the structural equation models approach is the most powerful one yet devised to analyze nonexperimental designs, it cannot be used on all data sets because not enough data are always available, nor are the assumptions always plausible.

NOTE

1. Material in this section has been excerpted from Boruch (1975).

REFERENCES

Bishop, Y. M. M., S. E. Fienberg, and P. W. Holland. *Discrete Multivariate Analysis: Theory and Practice.* Cambridge: MIT Press, 1975.

Boruch, R. F. Problems in research utilization: Use of social experiments, experiments, and auxiliary data in experiments. *Annals of the New York Academy of Sciences,* 1973, 218: 56-57.

Boruch, R. F. Bibliography: Illustrative randomized field experiments for program planning and evaluation. *Evaluation,* 1974, 2: 83-87.

Boruch, R. F. On common contentions about randomized field experiments. In R. F. Boruch and H. W. Riecken (eds.), *Experimental Testing of Public Policy.* Boulder, Co.: Westview Press, 1975.

Boruch, R. F., J. Magidson, and S. Davis. *Interim report: Secondary analysis of Project Middlestart.* Paper presented at the annual meetings of the American Psychological Association, September 1975.

Boruch, R. F., A. J. McSweeny, and E. J. Soderstrom. *Randomized field experiments for program development and evaluation: An illustrative bibliography.* Unpublished manuscript, Northwestern University, 1977.

Boruch, R. F. and H. Riecken. *Experimental Testing of Public Policy.* Boulder, Co.: Westview Press, 1975.

Boruch, R. F. and L. Wolins. A procedure for estimating the amount of trait, method, and error variance attributable to a measure. *Educational and Psychological Measurement,* 1970, 30: 547-574.

Campbell, D. T. Factors relevant to the validity of experiments in social settings. *Psychology Bulletin,* 1957, 54: 297-312.

Campbell, D. T. Reforms as experiments. *American Psychologist,* 1969, 24: 409-429.

Campbell, D. T. *Making the case for randomized assignment to treatments by considering the alternatives.* Research memo #Pre 627, Northwestern University, Psychology Department, 1974.

Campbell, D. T. and R. F. Boruch. Making the case for randomized assignment to treatments by considering the alternatives: Six ways in which quasi-experimental evaluations in compensatory education tend to underestimate effects. In C. A. Bennett and A. Lumsdaine (eds.), *Central Issues in Social Program Evaluation.* New York: Academic Press, 1975.

Campbell, D. T. and A. Erlebacher. How regression artifacts in quasi-experimental evaluations can mistakenly make compensatory education look harmful. In J. Hellmuth (ed.), *Compensatory Education: A National Debate.* New York: Brunner/Mazel, 1970.

Campbell, D. T. and J. C. Stanley. *Experimental and Quasi-Experimental Designs for Research.* Chicago: Rand McNally, 1966.

Cochran, W. G. and D. B. Rubin. Controlling bias in observational studies: A review. *Sankhya* (Ser. A), 1973, 35: 417-446.

Cook, T. D. and D. T. Campbell. The design and conduct of quasi-experiments and true experiments in field settings. In M. D. Dunnette (ed.), *Handbook of Industrial and Organizational Psychology.* Chicago: Rand McNally, 1976.

Creager, J. A. and R. F. Boruch. Orthogonal analysis of linear composite variance. *Proceedings, Annual Meeting of the American Psychological Association.* Washington, D.C., 1969.

Cronbach, L. J. *Notes on temptress and Campbell-Boruch.* Unpublished memo. Stanford University, Department of Education, January 18, 1976.

Cronbach, L. J., D. R. Rogosa, R. D. Floden, and G. G. Price. *Analysis of covariance: Angel of salvation, or temptress and deluder?* Occasional paper, Stanford Evaluation Consortium, Stanford University, February 1976.

Daniels, D. N. et al. *DANN services program.* Research report, National Institute of Mental Health, Grant No. 02332, January 1968.

Deniston, O. L. and I. M. Rosenstock. *The validity of designs for evaluating health services.* Research report, University of Michigan, School of Public Health, March 1972.

Director, S. *Evaluating the impact of manpower training programs.* Unpublished Ph.D. dissertation, Northwestern University, 1974.

Duncan, O. D. *Introduction to Structural Equation Models.* New York: Academic Press, 1975.

Fisher, R. A. *Design of Experiments.* New York: Hafner, 1935.

Gilbert, J. P., R. J. Light, and F. Mosteller. Assessing social innovations: An empirical base for policy. In A. Lumsdaine and C. A. Bennett (eds.), *Central Issues in Social Program Evaluation.* New York: Academic Press, 1975.

Glaser, D. *Routinizing Evaluation: Getting Feedback on Effectiveness of Crime and Delinquency Programs.* Rockville, Md.: Center for Studies of Crime and Delinquency, NIMH, 1973.

Glass, G. V, V. L. Willson, and J. M. Gottman. *Design and Analysis of Time-Series Experiments.* Boulder, Co.: Colorado Associated Universities Press, 1975.

Goldberger, A. S. Structural equation models: An overview. In A. S. Goldberger and O. D. Duncan (eds.), *Structural Equation Models in the Social Sciences.* New York: Seminar, 1973.

Goldberger, A. S. and O. E. Duncan, (eds.), *Structural Equation Models in the Social Sciences.* New York: Seminar Press, 1973.

Granger, C. W. J. and P. Newbold. Spurious regressions in econometrics. *Journal of Econometrics,* 1974, 2: 111-120.

Heber, R., H. Garber, S. Harrington, C. Hoffman, and C. Falender. *Rehabilitation of Families at Risk for Mental Retardation.* Madison: University of Wisconsin Rehabilitation Research and Training Center, 1972.

Hill, A. B., J. Marshal, and D. A. Shaw. A controlled clinical trial of long-term anticoagulant therapy in cerebrovascular disease. *Quarterly Journal of Medicine,* 1960, 29: 597-609.

Holt, N. Rational risk taking: Some alternatives to traditional correctional programs. *Proceedings: Second National Workshop on Corrections and Parole Administration.* College Park, Md.: American Correctional Association, 1974.

Joreskog, K. G. Analyzing psychological data by structural analysis of covariance matrices. In R. C. Atkinson, D. H. Krantz, R. D. Luce, and P. Suppes (eds.), *Contemporary Developments in Mathematical Psychology* (Vol. 2). San Francisco: W. H. Freeman, 1974.

Kenny, D. A. Cross-lagged and synchronous common factors in panel data. In A. S. Goldberger and O. D. Duncan (eds.), *Structural Equation Models in the Social Sciences.* New York: Seminar Press, 1973.

Kenny, D. A. A quasi-experimental approach to assessing treatment effects in the nonequivalent control group design. *Psychological Bulletin,* 1975, 83: 345-362.

Linn, R. L. *The Use of Standardized Test Scales To Measure Growth.* Reproduced report, University of Illinois, Psychology Department, 1976.

Linn, R. L. and J. A. Slinde. The determination of the significance of change between pre- and posttesting periods. *Review of Educational Research,* 1977, 47: 121-150.

Linn, R. L. and C. E. Werts. Analysis implications of the choice of a structural model in the nonequivalent control group design. *Psychological Bulletin,* 1977, 84: 229-234.

Lord, F. M. Covariance with fallible covariates. *Journal of the American Statistical Association,* 1960.

McKay, H., A. McKay, and L. Sinesterra. *Stimulation of intellectual and social competence in Colombian preschool-age children affected by the multiple deprivations of depressed urban environments.* Second progress report, Universidad del Valle, Human Ecology Research Station, September 1973.

McLuhan, M. and B. Nevitt. The argument: Causality in the electric world. *Technology and Culture,* 1973, 14: 1-18.

Meier, P. The biggest public health experiment ever: The 1954 field trial of the Salk poliomyelitis vaccine. In J. M. Tanur, F. Mosteller, W. B. Kruskal, R. F. Link, R. S. Pieters, and G. Rising (eds.), *Statistics: A Guide to the Known.* San Francisco: Holden-Day, 1972.

Molof, M. J. *Forestry camp study: Comparison of recidivism rates of camp-eligible boys randomly assigned to camp and to institutional programs.* Research report No. 53, California Department of the Youth Authority, Division of Research, October 1967.

Mosteller, F. Rerandomization. In D. L. Sills (eds.), *International Encyclopedia of the Social Sciences.* New York: Macmillan and the Free Press, 1968.

Overall, J. E. and J. A. Woodward. Nonrandom assignment and the analysis of covariance. *Psychological Bulletin,* 1977, 84: 588-594.

Porter, A. C. *The effects of using fallible variables in the analysis of covariance.* Unpublished Ph.D. dissertation, University of Wisconsin (Madison), 1967.

Riecken, H. W., R. F. Boruch, D. T. Campbell, N. Caplan, T. K. Glennan, J. W. Pratt, A. Rees, and W. Williams. *Social Experimentation: A Method for Planning and Evaluating Social Programs.* New York: Seminar Press, 1974.

Rindskopf, D. M. *A comparison of various regression-correlation methods for evaluating nonexperimental research.* Unpublished Ph.D. dissertation, Iowa State University (Ames), 1976.

Roselle, R. M. and D. T. Campbell. More plausible rival hypotheses in the cross-lagged correlational technique. *Psychological Bulletin,* 1969, 71: 74-80.

Rubin, D. B. Estimating causal effects of treatments in randomized and non-randomized studies. *Journal of Educational Psychology,* 1974, 66: 688-701.

Rubin, D. B. Bayesian inference for causality: The importance of randomization. *Proceedings of the American Statistical Association,* 1975: 233-239.

Rubin, D. B. *Assignment to Treatment on the Basis of a Covariate* (ETS RB 76-9). Princeton, N.J.: Educational Testing Service, 1976a.

Rubin, D. B. Multivariate matching methods that are equal percent bias reducing, I: Some examples. *Biometrics,* 1976b, 32: 109-120.

Rubin, D. B. Multivariate matching methods that are equal percent bias reducing, II: Maximums on bias reduction for fixed sample sizes. *Biometrics,* 1976c, 32: 121-132.

Ruffin, J. N., J. E. Grizzle, N. C. Hightower, G. McHardy, H. Schull, and J. B. Krisher. A cooperative double-blind evaluation of gastric "freezing" in the treatment of duodenal ulcer. *New England Journal of Medicine,* 1969, 281: 16-19.

Rutstein, D. D. The ethical design of human experiments. *Daedalus,* 1969, 98: 523-541.

Stroud, T. W. F. Comparing conditional means and variances in regression model with measurement errors of known variance. *Journal of the American Statistical Association,* 1972, 67: 407-412.

Warren, W. Q. The Community Treatment Project: History and prospects. In S. A. Yefsky (ed.), *Law Enforcement, Science, and Technology.* Washington, D.C.: Thompson Books, 1967.

Weikart, D. P. Relationship of curriculum, teaching and learning in preschool education. In J. C. Stanley (ed.), *Preschool Programs for the Disadvantaged Children.* Baltimore: John Hopkins University, 1972.

Wiley, D. E. Approximations to ceteris paribus: Data adjustment in educational research. In W. H. Sewell, R. M. Hauser, and D. L. Featherman (eds.), *Schooling and Achievement in American Society.* New York: Academic Press, 1976.

Wortman, P. M. and R. G. St. Pierre. *The first year of the Educational Voucher Demonstration: A secondary analysis of student achievement test scores.* Research report, Northwestern University, Psychology Department, Methodology and Evaluation Program, 1975.

Yinger, J. M., K. Ikeda, and F. Laycock. *Middlestart: Supportive intervention for higher education among students of disadvantaged backgrounds.* Report to U.S. Office of Education, Project No. 5-0703, Grant OE 6-10-255, Oberlin College, Sociology Department, November 1970.

There is extensive literature on factors related to the apparent nonutilization of evaluation research findings. Many arguments focus on the research: the poor conceptual and technical quality of the research, the study's lack of relevance, and the lack of cumulative and comparative studies. Others argue that organizations have a built-in resistance to change and the "political" considerations rather than research findings having the major influence on decisions. There are also explanations which focus on the interface—the nature of dissemination procedures and the timing of the report.

Until recently there has been little research on the factors influencing the utilization of evaluation research findings. This chapter describes the development of an effective method for integrating patients released from mental hospitals into the community. Fairweather then discusses a national experiment which tested alternative methods of influencing organizations to adopt this effective program which he developed through his earlier experimentation. From this experiment, factors which are related to adoption of innovations are identified and suggestions are made for increasing the likelihood of utilization of evaluation research findings.

7

A PROCESS OF INNOVATION AND DISSEMINATION EXPERIMENTATION

George W. Fairweather

Before we can seriously begin a discussion about the utilization of research findings, it is important for everyone to recognize that the utilization of research results very often requires social change. When new programs are adopted by social agencies, it usually means that resources will flow to the new programs at a reasonably rapid rate and that old programs aimed at the same social problem will be phased out. This is a particularly difficult transition for social programs because such programs are usually quite complex and often involve changes in social roles and statuses. Because of the centrality of the change process, it is important for us to understand something about the process itself both from an organizational and interpersonal point of view.

There is much agreement among social scientists that there are two basic components to the social change process. They are the creation of a social innovation aimed at problem solution and its implementation throughout a city, region, or nation. Since both social model development and implementation efforts require a theoretical underpinning, I should like to briefly review those elements of a meaningful social change mechanism that are basic to both program development and implementation.

ELEMENTS OF A SOCIAL CHANGE MECHANISM

The first such element is an *active role* for the social scientist. Historically, social scientists have defined their role in society as that mainly concerned with reflective thought. While this has an obvious value for both the individual scientist and society, it is most important that those who are engaged in research realize that the focal point of the research must be the community and the dynamic social processes that are ongoing there. This is particularly important from a scientific perspective because current research shows a lack of relationship between verbal behavior and performance. Thus, the generation of ideas alone, no matter how creative they might be, is not sufficient to create nor to implement actual social programs.

A second aspect of an adequate mechanism is that it must be *innovative.* When old social programs do not meet the needs of society, it is necessary to create new programs that will. The process of innovation requires that an individual free himself or herself from the traditional norms that are inherent in a professional group to which almost all of us belong. Furthermore, it often requires that we question a social policy that has been carried out in the past in order that we can arrive at new programs that can solve contemporary problems. This innovative act requires a good deal of· thought and effort, but most of all a willingness to risk criticism by colleagues who perceive themselves as culture barriers and who are the founders and defenders of the status quo.

A third characteristic of an adequate social change mechanism includes *democratic* participation. While this may not be a necessary consideration in all societies, it most certainly is in all democratic societies. This means that the change process must be a process of persuasion leading to action. Furthermore, if a program is to be developed that in the long run can be implemented on a broader scale, it must involve not only the researcher but the social administrators and the persons who suffer from the pressing social problem. It is, of course, patently ridiculous to assume that simply because a program is developed it will be used. It cannot be used unless the problem population sees it as a program that has meaning to them and unless the social administrators are willing to adopt it and promote it as a social practice. It is, of course, extremely important that any program that is to be disseminated to a broad audience have a known benefit for the social problem for which it is intended as a relief.

The fourth attribute is a *humanitarian* value system as the forcing bed of scientific inquiry. Currently, many natural and social scientists have come to view the future of humans on this planet as contingent upon the manner in which social relations can be made amiable and the integrity of the environment can be maintained. And others have pointed to the lack of concern that social scientists have demonstrated for the humanness of their endeavors. It seems quite clear that in order to avoid the continuing misuse of the social and natural environments, it is necessary to build a social change mechanism on a strong humanitarian base. While this is, of course, related to the democratic process just mentioned, it is a sufficiently independent concept that it is elaborated here as a special characteristic of a meaningful social change mechanism.

The next necessary characteristic for an adequate social change mechanism is *scientific* evaluation. While all of the social science research techniques from observation through survey to experimentation are necessary and can be integrated into the problem-solving approach necessary for an adequate change mechanism, it is most important here to recognize that eventually experiments must be done. That is, eventually it is necessary and important to complete experiments in which persons are randomly assigned to various controlled social conditions. This is because such experiments are necessary for any adequate evaluation from which the necessary inferences can be made. It is, after all, of the utmost importance that pilot programs have generalizability as their eventual goal, since utilization of such experimental programs can only be determined through adequate experimentation and subsequent inferences.

Another characteristic of the social change mechanism is that research done must be *problem-oriented*. Most human problems cut across disciplines and are not affected by the logic or lack of logic of educational institutions which divides subject matter into various disciplinary areas such as psychological, sociological, medical, etc. Real-life problems are affected by a wide variety of variables depending upon the problem and the time at which they are viewed. An example of the problem-oriented focus is the recent man-on-the-moon program. Since the goal of the project was to place a man on the moon, individuals on the research team had to play varying roles. For example, physicians became astronauts and astronauts learned new tasks in order to solve the problem of getting to the moon, exploring it, and returning to earth. It is just such a cross-disciplinary problem-oriented focus that is needed in the last half of the twentieth and in the twenty-first century for the solution to the difficult human problems that are here now and that lie ahead.

Another necessary ingredient of an adequate social change mechanism is that solutions to problems must be *continuously monitored*. It should be obvious to everyone that a solution to a problem at one moment is not necessarily a solution at another. For example, during periods of high unemployment, a social solution that might be extremely valuable would be an attempt to improve the employment picture for those who are unemployed. On the other hand, during periods of high employment a subject of social concern might be more appropriately be addressed to the use of leisure time. It should, therefore, be kept in mind that outcomes of programs must be continuously monitored so that programs that are not valid are exposed quickly and new programs are substituted as the old programs outlive their initial usefulness and are found to be unnecessary.

Finally, the matter about which we will be most concerned involves the *usefulness* of the solutions found. Programs whose outcomes are beneficial but whose cost is so extreme that society cannot bear it are probably not useful solutions. Here we might think of health programs where a private physician is seeing three patients in a continuous program in which all of the physician's time is given to these three individuals. The cost of such a program would be prohibitive. Or we might think of a water pollution program where salt water is converted into fresh water. Again, the cost of such a program might be more than the society could bear. There are other examples where nonuseable solutions are found. For example, the dissolution of the family might very well be a solution to the high divorce rate, but it is quite doubtful that such an approach would be perceived as useable by the majority of the society. It is therefore important to plan solutions that are not only valid but can be used by the society.

The social change mechanism that has been more influential in creating change throughout the centuries in most societies has been this twofold process: The innovation of a new program—social reform, technological device, or the like—and its diffusion throughout the society by interested change agents.

This social change process can actually solve human problems if it is scientific. To accomplish this, models that benefit a society must be identified so that they can then be used by that society. This involves establishing small-scale models as experiments in the naturalistic setting and evaluating them over a period of time and then disseminating those programs found to be beneficial. This process has been called by me elsewhere *Experimental Social Innovation* (1967). I cannot emphasize too strongly that the dissemination of social models—whether they be in mental health, education, the environment, or whatever—is such an extensive and time-consuming process that it is extremely important that the models that are to be disseminated "do what the advocates say they will do." Since we are always dealing with probabilities, it is extremely important that actual experiments where innovative social models are compared for their outcomes be established *prior* to any dissemination effort.

Assume for the moment that we have found a beneficial social model through a longitudinal research effort. The second most important process now is that of implementing the beneficial program in a city, region, nation, or internationally. It is this process—implementation—which is of main concern here.

Simply demonstrating that a given program is beneficial is not sufficient to assure that the program will be implemented. In fact, more social programs have been lost to society than have been accepted because there has been no effort to disseminate them. It is for this reason that social program innovation and evaluation must be linked directly with a dissemination effort or the value to society of the new social program—however beneficial it may have been found to be by adequate scientific comparison—will be of little or no use to that society.

PROCESS OF DISSEMINATION

The general process of dissemination requires social program advocacy. While many scientists believe their job is completed with the publication of an article, monograph, or book, it is patently obvious to those who have been in social program development and dissemination that such written efforts are not productive. It does, of course, usually enhance the scientist's standing with his colleagues, since much attention is paid to scientific writing in professional circles, but it does not aid the society very much even when experimental process involves the development of social programs. This is the case because social program implementation is a different and unrelated process to social program development.

The process of dissemination can be viewed from an experimental and theoretical perspective as involving four stages of successive research. First, there is the *approaching phase,* in which different attempts to approach the target individuals or organizations can be evaluated. This is important because there is a clear lack of knowledge about how to make productive initial contacts with private organizations, people, or other social units who may need to use a particular social model.

Once a number of organizations, individuals, etc., have been approached and have agreed to listen to information about the new, beneficial social model, the process of *persuading* begins. Again, this phase should be established as an experiment so that various types of persuasion can be tried and evaluated for their success with the target population. Here one can explore the persuasive effectiveness of the written word, of demonstrations, of economic reinforcement, and the like. But it is most important to recognize here that this stage needs to proceed as an experimental effort in order that information about the persuasiveness of a particular technique can become known.

The next phase, which may be considered a third experiment, if one views each effort as interconnected but interrelated experiments from a longitudinal point of view, is *activating* the model. Individuals once persuaded to adopt a new innovation must proceed to action. To this process of translating verbal acceptance into the behavioral steps necessary for physical adoption, the title activation has been given. Alternative strategies here need to be evaluated. For example, the disseminators need to discover if such procedures as the use of social change agents is necessary or helps in the process of moving from verbal persuasion to adoption and so on.

Finally, a fourth process is *diffusing.* Once an innovation has been adopted by a group or organization, spontaneous diffusion often occurs. By this I mean that other individuals or groups who come to the organization that has initially adopted the model to see it in action may be persuaded to adopt it themselves. Of course, this process can be subject to experimentation by defining different types of diffusion activity possible and training the adopting units in their use.

While presenting these experimental phases that need to be accomplished in order to not only properly disseminate a beneficial innovation but also to increase our knowledge about the dissemination process, it must be recognized that throughout the four phases—approaching, persuading, activating, and diffusing—a large number of organizations or individuals will refuse to adopt the innovation. In fact, there will probably be a greater number of nonadopters than there are adopters. This sets the stage for yet another round of experiments that can be carried out with that residual population. In such a case, the techniques found to be most beneficial in the preceding four phases can be used on the residual units in order to increase the probability of their adopting the new model. After these experimentally validated techniques have been used, a number of additional groups will have adopted and a subsequent number of what might be called "hard-core" nonadopters will remain. A new experiment then might be designed using different techniques to promote the innovation with this hard-core group. Eventually, the residual group will become smaller, and the experimenters will decide that the cost of further dissemination attempts is no longer warranted in view of the small number of organizations not adopting. Many of them will eventually adopt as they begin to perceive the original innovation as a phenomenon attached, as it usually is, to improved social status and position.

There is another issue about dissemination research that should be mentioned here. It is that the same experimenters who carried out the social model comparison experiments to establish the beneficial model should also conduct the dissemination experiment. In addition to improving our knowledge about the dissemination process, there are some very real reasons why dissemination experiments should be carried out by the same individuals who have helped develop and evaluate the original social models. First, they are the only people who can establish a true replicate of the model since they have been involved in its basic design and know its primary parameters. And second, it ensures that only programs that have been evaluated as beneficial in solving a particular human problem will be disseminated. For these two reasons, it is important that the dissemination of beneficial social models proceed as an experiment carried out or supervised by those who initially completed the social model experiments. Let us now review in considerable detail the manner in which the social science research techniques can be integrated into this social change process.

The usual techniques developed by social scientists who have been interested in social problems may be classified under descriptive- theoretical, survey, participant observation, quasi-experimental, and laboratory experimental. These techniques can be integrated into a problem-solving approach mentioned earlier as experimental social innovation. The manner in which this occurs can be most clearly understood in the context of a number of interrelated researches in the mental health area that span a twenty-year period.

A CASE EXAMPLE–THE LODGE

In 1949, a number of my colleagues and I observed that patients who were defined as cured by mental health professionals very often returned to the mental hospital very quickly. We then conducted a survey which indicated the people who remained in the hospital for ninety days or longer were much more likely to return than those who left within ninety days. The probability of returning increased with the length of stay, so that by the end of two years of continuous hospitalization the probability of return when released was very high. A quasi-experiment was then conducted in which the persons who left before ninety days were contrasted with those who stayed more than ninety days on a number of demographic characteristics available at the time of entry. The notion here was that if we could identify the potential long-stayers at the time of admission, we could intervene with a new kind of program in an attempt to reduce long-term stay. This quasi-experiment showed very clearly that some demographic variables—marital status, diagnosis, legal competence, etc.—were related to return rates. An actual experiment was then conducted to find out if any treatment could be used to reduce the return rate. Four common types of treatment were compared on 120 outcome criteria for three different patient groups. The four treatments were individual therapy, group psychotherapy, a group living situation often called a "psychotherapeutic community," and a work only situation. The latter consisted of a job assignment in the hospital along the lines of the patient's interests and served as a control for the comparison of the three psychotherapy conditions. The three diagnostic groups were neurotics, acute psychotics, and chronic psychotics.

The upshot of this study was that the three treatment programs yielded a higher rate of employment for the psychotherapy conditions for the first six months after hospitalization, but this difference disappeared during the next year. On no other follow-up measure were the treatments differentiated. Therefore, by the end of eighteen months after leaving the hospital, all treatments appeared the same, none yielded lower return rates than the hospital work situation. In addition, the more chronic patients did worse in all treatment programs, the neurotics were next, and the acute psychotics showed the highest rate of recovery. Chronic psychotics returned at the rate of close to 75 percent by the end of eighteen months. The correlations among the various measures showed that measures taken within the treatment context were unrelated to follow-up information—i.e., adaptive behaviors in the hospital were unrelated to adaptive behaviors in the community, and the same was true for perceptions of treatment success and various attitudes and expectancies. Not only was there no relationship between what happened in the hospital and what happened

in the community, but there was also no relationship among perceptions, behaviors, and affective measures within the hospital or within the community. Generally, then, the findings from this experiment
showed that the traditional hospital programs were at the very best not
very helpful to more chronic patients, that acute patients recovered
quite well with a work-only situation, and that the outcome measures
were extremely multivariate, yielding several different dimensions em-
phasizing that test behavior, interpersonal behavior, attitudes, and behaviors were relatively unrelated dimensions of measurement.

Because of these findings, it then seemed essential to approach the
problem from a different point of view. The central question was how
we create a social program that would help retain chronic mental
patients in the community in a meaningful social role. Feedback from
the experiments showed that such persons probably needed some sort
of social organization to which to belong. This seemed all the more
plausible because observations of patients in group situations in the
hospital showed that they formed spontaneous groups in the hospital
which were, of course, destroyed upon their release into the community.

The first question, therefore, that needed answering in this problem-solving approach was whether or not groups of individuals could be
formed from typical mental patients so that they could be moved as a
unit into the community. Thus, the group itself could serve to bridge
the gap between the hospital and the community. Once in the community it could serve as a support system for these ex-patients. A
five-year series of experiments was then completed to explore these
group possibilities. They showed that, indeed, groups of patients could
be formed and they could in fact care for their members in a hospital
situation as long as certain conditions existed. A few of them were that
the group functioned autonomously, without staff members present;
that leadership potential existed in the group; that appropriate communications and rewards were developed, etc. However, upon release
into the community, such individuals returned to the hospital just as
quickly as the control group despite all their previous gains, because of
their loss of group support.

Another five-year experiment was then introduced which created a
self-operated society for the groups in the community. The autonomous society, often called the lodge, was contrasted with the
typical community-type situations. The results of this experiment
showed that those in the community lodge significantly reduced their
return rate to the hospital, improved their employment, and did so at
one-third the cost of traditional community mental health programs. In

fact, the lodge finally became totally self-supporting and throughout this process the ex-patients constantly expressed happiness with their new, more responsible community roles.

What I have just tried to illustrate is a problem-solving approach using theoretical and research information to establish different social models which have been constantly corrected to provide for problem solution. This is essentially a stepwise approach to problem solution. The final social model, the lodge society, did indeed solve the problem of chronic hospitalization.

Of course, those of us cognizant with the experiment believed that an experimentally valid program that reduced cost, improved happiness, and resulted in returning individuals to productive citizen roles would be readily accepted and implemented by mental hospitals. This simply showed our naivete, for few mental health organizations showed any interest in it whatsoever.

It was therefore decided that a dissemination experiment should be carried out to make this beneficial program available to mental health workers and patients across the nation and at the same time to try to discover what were the important parameters in disseminating such innovations.

It is now important to turn our attention to this long-range study in which the implementation process has been the subject of experimental evaluation for the past eight years. Several visits to county, state, and federal authorities, all of whom responded positively toward the new program but did not offer to implement it, convinced the experimentalists that an implementation effort was essential if the lodge was to be made available to a large number of professional people and mental patients who needed it. But how could this be done?

An exploration of the literature in implementation showed a dearth of experimental information comparing different types of implementation efforts. However, there was no dearth of theoretical ideas which fell mainly into the four positions described by Havelock (1969) as (1) the research, development, and diffusion approach, (2) the problem solver, and (3) the social interaction model. The research, development, and diffusion approach essentially presents the prescription that moving in the direction of implementation is an orderly and rational process that essentially flows from a new innovation. The general processes in this model are research, development diffusion, and adoption. Essentially, information is given about new models and leads to their adoption by selected organizations. It is mainly a rational process—i.e., if the organization needs it, the innovation gets adopted.

Needless to say, this change strategy did not fit any of our experiences in attempting to implement the lodge society.

A second approach is the problem solver perspective. Generally this approach is closely linked to issues within the field of organizational theory and emerges from a model of organizational functioning—the human relations school. The literature indicates that interpersonal conflicts affect interorganizational communication and effectiveness, and that irrational facts that impede organizational change need to be resolved before change can occur. Generally, the theory of organizational intervention involves such activities as T-groups and the use of techniques like the managerial grid of Blake and Mouton (1969). From this point of view, organizational problems are solved by self-examination of personal style, communications patterns, and the like, with an emphasis on organizational functioning rather than the context of organizational tasks and goals. Generally, the changes come from within the organization and do not ordinarily require intervention from the outside to get the organization to adopt new programs.

The third point of view is the social interaction model. This model developed mainly from the study of agricultural extension work by sociologists. The original work of Rogers (1962) and the more recent work of Rogers and Shoemaker (1971) are excellent examples of this position. The diffusion of an innovation in this process may be divided into the four phases of knowledge acquisition, persuasion, decision, and confirmation. Communication plays a major role in the entire process.

From this literature and our own experience, an experimental program was established to disseminate the lodge model to 255 mental hospitals throughout the nation. A design was developed which grew out of several questions raised by the literature and our own experiences. First of all, there was considerable question about who should be approached in the hierarchy about entry into the organization. It is frequently assumed that persons highest in the hierarchy can give consent and those lower in the hierarchy cannot. From this point of view, those who need to be approached for an adoption decision are those highest in an organization. However, experience in the mental health field had shown us that sometimes nurses, social workers, and so on have been more influential in creating new programs than have managers, superintendents, and the like. It was, therefore, decided that 255 hospitals would, by random assignment, be approached through the chiefs of services representing the social status structure of the mental hospital—superintendents, chiefs of psychiatry, psychology, social work and nursing.

Another dimension that seemed important was that of the bureau-cratic nature of the organization. Much of the literature indicated that the more bureaucratic an organization, the more task-oriented it is and the less likely it is to receive and make use of new ideas. Accordingly, a plan was outlined to divide the 255 hospitals into yet another dimen-sion, that of federal and state hospitals with the assumption being that federal hospitals had a much larger bureaucracy, where all decisions had to be made at the central level, contrasted with state hospitals where, by definition, the bureaucracy would be smaller.

A third dimension that seemed important was the urban or rural geographic location of the hospitals. Early attempts at disseminating the lodge society had shown that the establishment of the first two lodges showed greater success in the rural hospital, which adopted the lodge while the urban hospital did not. The reasons for this appeared to be a more structured bureaucratic organization in the urban hospitals, featuring many jurisdictional disputes among mental health workers for "their slice of the pie." The rural hospital, by contrast, was perceived as a more problem-oriented hospital with less emphasis on who held the power and more emphasis on how to solve problems. For this reason, the rural-urban variable was considered important.

Another important dimension appeared to be active versus inactive approaches to social change. Many studies showed that the written word was not very influential in creating social change without some sort of demonstration or action program that persons could participate in for them to get a "feel" for the new programs and hence a commit-ment to the change process. Thus, it seemed that more active ap-proaches might yield better results than the less active approaches. Along this dimension, we looked at the written word, the workshop, and an active demonstration which represented three points on an inaction-to-action condition. The persuasion attempts thus involved the written, workshop, and demonstration conditions.

The researchers then entered into the activation phase with those who had volunteered. Randomly assigning matched pairs on back-ground experience to two conditions, one a social change agent and one a written manual, was completed. The attempt here was to discover to what effect a change agent was necessary in helping to activate the lodge innovation once a hospital had been persuaded to implement the new program. This essentially was an attempt to bridge the chasm between verbal behavior and performance.

A third phase to the study involved measuring the diffusion activity—i.e., to what extent had those hospitals who had adopted the model attempted to diffuse it to other hospitals in their area or in the region or nation? This was accomplished with a follow-up telephone survey of all hospitals involved in the experiment two years after the last intervention with a participating hospital.

In addition to the aforementioned experimental variables, a large number of additional variables such as budget, staff size, physical facilities, social climate of the area, staff attitudes toward mental illness, and the like were measured in order to discover if they had any relevance to the change process.

A large number of findings eminated from this study and are reported elsewhere (Fairweather et al., 1974). Let me summarize them briefly in the following form:

(1) Perhaps foremost among the findings was the need for the experimenters to have tolerance of confusion. The change process is not orderly or predictable.

(2) The usual variables of budget size, physical facilities, and staff size have very little to do with the adoption of a new social program. We found no difference between hospitals that were considered poor and those considered to be rich.

(3) Variables such as ruralness and urbanness, federal and state affiliation, also had little to do with the change process.

(4) Attitudes were unrelated to change. That is, organizations which expressed a more positive attitude toward the lodge program did not change any more quickly than those which had a poor attitude. This is not to say that cognitive awareness of the lodge model was not important. It clearly was because without it no movement toward adoption could take place. What it does indicate, however, is that the cognitive process is unrelated to the action or inaction that might follow such an awareness—i.e., whether the change actually takes place or not.

(5) Change does not occur without change agent intervention. All of our information showed that not a single hospital adopted the lodge without a change agent actively intervening from the outside into the organization. This seems most important because, during the course of the experiment, an inside change group developed to which the outside change agent could relate.

(6) Action-oriented intervention is essential. What seems important here is that while more individuals are initially lost in an action-oriented persuasion technique, those who remain are much more likely to go forward and carry out the innovation than those who have participated simply in knowledge acquisition through the written word or workshop discussions.

(7) Another factor is that of participation. The most consistent finding throughout the persuasion and implementation phases was that the degree of implementation achieved was directly related to the number of people throughout the organization involved in the implementation process. Participation in the decision process seemed particularly important.

(8) Finally, there appears to be a principle of group action and implementation. As stated earlier, each hospital that did change developed a social change group. This group was necessary, it appeared, to move the hospital staff toward actual adoption. It was aided throughout by interaction with the social change agent.

These findings, then, have led to yet a new experiment in the social change process. They led to some additional hypotheses that needed to be explored. The first hypothesis had to do with the participation dimension that seemed so important throughout the first five-year experiment. One aspect of such a decision process involved the degree to which people at the different points in the hierarchy are involved in the process aimed at a decision toward adoption. Therefore, in the new study, one dimension being explored is the effect of adoption involving persons from the administration only, persons from the ward only, and a mixture of administration and ward personnel. This is essentially a dimension of individual versus mixed groups in the decision process. Another dimension involves how many persons are involved in the dissemination effort as a whole from the beginning. For example, few persons are contacted in one condition and many in another in an attempt to measure the difference between few versus many. Groups to work directly with the social change agent also seemed extremely important. An attempt to create these groups by forming conditions for group enhancement and contrasting them with those who receive little enhancement is also being employed in the current study. All the aforementioned dimensions are involved in the approach and persuasion phase.

The second phase—the activating phase—concerns the evaluation of organizational development variables in an attempt to discover the effects that organizational development leading toward group cohesiveness might have on a positive decision to adopt. In order to evaluate the effectiveness of organizational development, some hospitals receive developmental training and some do not.

A third phase will consist of training some hospitals who have adopted the lodge in change agentry while not training others. What we are attempting to find out here is whether or not organizations that adopt innovations can also be trained to diffuse them.

SUGGESTIONS FOR INCREASING
THE LIKELIHOOD OF UTILIZATION

There are two basic processes involved in social change. They are the creation of a new social model and its dissemination. Both of these processes can be approached from an experimental point of view which, in fact, makes the probability higher that the innovative model will solve the problem for which it was designed. Whether the process is social model-building or dissemination, there are several methods that need to be completed from the planning of the initial model to the dissemination process itself.

First, it is important to choose a problem for which a solution can be designed that can be implemented throughout the society. For this to happen, the formulation of a solution to the problem is enhanced if it emanates from a democratic process involving social administrators, research scientists, and members of the problem population. It is only by ensuring the cooperation of these three groups of individuals that any solution can be implemented.

It is also important to obtain administrative agreements from the organizations or the community groups who will participate in the model innovation and its dissemination. Such administrative agreements should be in writing so that the longitudinal research processes are not curtailed prematurely.

Large-scale social research of the type just described requires the work of a research team. All members must perceive themselves as interested in the goals of the research and must become identified with the overall project, which requires some willingness to defer personal interests. The research team itself must then define the variables that are important in determining either the innovative social model or its dissemination. These variables come from three sources: They involve, (1) the characteristics of persons who participate in the social model and the administrative staff involved; (2) the internal social processes of the model which concern variables such as organizational components, group dynamics, internal financing, etc.; and (3) the external social variables that might impact upon the social model such as the state of the economy, publicity, etc. After the crucial variables have been defined so that those most important can be manipulated and the others can be controlled, it is important to establish the social model or the dissemination research in such a way that the conditions the experimenters wish to create will continue over a longitudinal time period in order that an adequate comparison can be made. Since both of the social change processes—social model-building and dissemination—are longitudinal processes, it is extremely important to maintain the experimental conditions so that they will be relatively equivalent at different times.

It is equally important to make certain that sampling procedures are properly followed. Random assignments from a representative sample of the population will need to be used in the comparisons. When one is concerned with social models, this means the assignment of persons who volunteer to participate in the experiment to the several different models. When the experiment involves the dissemination process, the sample of organizations or the groups the experimenters are trying to persuade to adopt an innovation must be representative of the organizations or groups as a whole.

When the research processes begin and throughout the duration of the experiment, it is important to use appropriate measurement procedures. As often as possible, these procedures should be unobtrusive, so that the measurements themselves do not affect the functioning of the models or the dissemination process. Finally, it is extremely important to select the most appropriate evaluative techniques. These involve an integration of traditional research methods that have been used independently in the social sciences—observations, surveys, participant-observation, quasi-experimental techniques, and, finally, experiments themselves.

The purpose of planning the social model comparison and dissemination experiments as completely as possible and carrying them out well-controlled is necessary so that the researchers can make valid inferences at the end of the experiment. Since inferences are dependent upon the degree to which the statistics computed from each experiment accurately measure the processes involved and represent unbiased population estimates, the more accurate the research procedures, the more accurate the inferences.

SUMMARY

What I have tried to demonstrate is that implementation involving the adopting, persuading, activating, and diffusing phases can be established as successive experiments where the information from these experiments is used as feedback information to the social change agent so that the possibility of achieving change in various organizations will be enhanced.

Those who are interested in creating new social programs, evaluating them, and disseminating them are engaged primarily in a process of social change. It is now accepted by most authorities in the field that social program development cannot meaningfully proceed without evaluation of the program on a comparative basis so that new programs can be validated by actual experiments.

Because I have tried to devote the core of this presentation to the dissemination process, I have not emphasized repeatedly, as I have elsewhere, that only programs that have been adequately evaluated and, hence, have an extremely high probability of being beneficial to the problem population should be disseminated. From this perspective, it is a misuse of the dissemination process to use scientific implementation procedures to promote programs that have not been demonstrated to yield beneficial results through actual experiments and several replicates. I have explained in great detail in a recent publication (Fairweather and Tornatzky, 1977) the significance of observations, behavioral data, and other outcome knowledge that must be present in order to make generalized inferences that a social program can be viewed as worthy of national implementation. I have also recommended that the individuals who create and evaluate the initial social model also have the responsibility to replicate it until the levels of probability about its beneficial outcome are extremely high. These researchers— those that have developed and evaluated the initial social models—also have the responsibility of carrying out a long-term dissemination effort themselves or arranging for such an effort when their own interests take them elsewhere.

It should also be obvious that implementation must proceed along the same lines. New implementation procedures and knowledge will have to come, it appears to me, through actual experiments in the field situations where the results can be used to increase our knowledge of dissemination and to actually disseminate new beneficial models themselves.

From a more generic point of view, I have also tried here and elsewhere (Fairweather and Tornatzky, 1977) to demonstrate that constructive social change, if it has the appropriate ingredients, can proceed from successive approximations to problem solution through a series of well-defined scientific experiments. Using the knowledge from each experimental phase as feedback to the scientists permits the creation of subsequent experiments aimed at problem solution in both social model-building and implementation efforts.

REFERENCES

Blake, R. R. and J. S. Mouton. *Building a Dynamic Corporation Through Grid Organization Development.* Reading, Mass.: Addison-Wesley, 1969.

Fairweather, G. W. *Methods for Experimental Social Innovation.* New York: John Wiley, 1967.

Fairweather, G. W., D. H. Sanders, and L. G. Tornatzky. *Creating Change in Mental Health Organizations.* New York: Pergamon Press, 1974.

Fairweather, G. W. and L. G. Tornatzky. *Experimental Methods for Social Policy Research.* New York: Pergamon Press, 1977.

Havelock, R. G. *Planning for Innovation for Dissemination and Utilization of Knowledge.* Ann Arbor, Mich.: Institute for Social Research, 1969.

Rogers, E. M. *Diffusion of Innovations.* New York: Free Press, 1962.

Rogers, E. M. and F. F. Shoemaker. *Communication of Innovations: A Cross-Cultural Approach.* New York: Free Press, 1971.

This book has focused on determining whether a program meets the preconditions for an effectiveness evaluation and planning a study which would collect reliable and valid information about the manner and extent to which the program produced the measured effects. A main concern has been the development of an evaluation which allows for making relatively unequivocal causal inferences. These are usually time-limited and highly focused studies.

There is, however, the need for ongoing information systems which serve evaluative and administrative purposes. Information is collected on the clients served, the service offered, and the outcomes achieved. In the absence of design considerations such as randomized experimental and control groups, information systems are usually weak in making causal inferences. Nevertheless, they can provide valuable data on the program's operation, and the feedback of such information serves to make program modifications.

An information system can serve as an important preliminary step toward performance measurement. Moreover, it is the basis upon which intermittent effectiveness evaluations can be built. Directions for developing an information system which serves both clinical and administrative needs are presented in this chapter.

8

INFORMATION SYSTEMS FOR EVALUATION AND FEEDBACK IN MENTAL HEALTH ORGANIZATIONS

Gary H. Miller and Barry Willer

The image of record systems in most human service organizations is one of stacks of files being stored in a basement office. The purpose of these records, beyond taking up space, is quite nebulous. In mental health organizations, once a patient is discharged, these files are consulted rarely and only if the former patient is readmitted or has some difficulty with the courts. In the case of readmission, the patient's file is sent to the ward or treatment unit, but, in at least some instances, the files of readmitted patients are kept in a location which makes them inaccessible to many treatment staff. The important point, however, is that records are completed and stored not for their information value, but rather because it is required by the standards or laws governing the organization, much the same as financial books might be kept for audit and tax purposes.

There are a number of examples from mental health record systems which demonstrate this image of records. Clinicians, for example, often regard record-keeping as a duty—to be completed in order to appease the medical record librarians. They often complete the records long after the patient has been discharged from the program, thereby reducing the chances of influencing treatment or informing others through the records. As well, in many settings, various clinical groups, such as nurses, psychiatrists, social workers, and psychologists have different record procedures and store their records in separate locations often inaccessible to members of the other treatment groups.

Another glaring example of the use of record systems for storage is the lack of any evaluation of new approaches to record-keeping based on their information value. For example, no one to our knowledge has systematically assessed the impact of the problem-oriented record or any of the many computerized mental health information systems in terms of use by clinicians, administrators, or other users.

In the present discussion, criteria for adequate information systems for mental health settings will be presented, with emphasis on the user or informational nature of these systems.

CRITERIA FOR INFORMATION SYSTEMS

Although the exact specifications of an information system will depend on the requirements of the users, there are many criteria that are general to any mental health information system. We will outline below some of these criteria using a clinical information system (CIS) as an example. For a more complete discussion of a CIS system for clinical recording, administrative decision-making, evaluation, and research, see Miller and Willer (in press).

GENERAL CRITERIA FOR A
CLINICAL INFORMATION SYSTEM

The thesis of this chapter is that an adequate information system should meet the needs of several users. The requirements of the system users will be outlined below.

THE CLINICIAN AS USER

Any CIS must consider the needs of the clinician or it will disappear or become irrelevant. If the information is not seen as clinically relevant, clinicians will not collect the information (Wilson, 1970). Also, if available information is not clinically relevant, it will not even be read, let alone used for treatment decisions (Willer and Stasiak, 1973). Basic clinical data should include information such as: (1) why the patient came to the service, (2) what was done to or for the patient, and (3) what was the outcome of the treatment.

Clinical information should also be closely integrated with the on-going activities of the treatment team (Willer and Stasiak, 1973) and with all aspects of the oral reporting system. Thus, information allowing individual patient programming is important. Such information allows the clinician to monitor progress throughout treatment so that procedures can be modified on the basis of results. Monitoring the process of treatment is clearly superior to evaluating progress at termination of treatment when it is usually too late to modify treatment. The CIS, then, should incorporate an objective, reliable method of measuring therapeutic effectiveness during therapy, at discharge, and after discharge.

THE ADMINISTRATOR AS USER

A CIS must also be useful to administration if it is going to get resource support. Administrators usually require aggregate data for several purposes. One data requirement involves relatively simple statistics such as the number of clients seen within a particular time by each program. Information at a higher level of sophistication would include cost-benefit and cost-effectiveness analyses (Levin, 1975). Estimates of the various program costs and impacts are facilitated when accurate data on program usage is available. Thus, the costs of treating a patient can be estimated when the mix of treatments he has received is known. Similarly, the impact of the treatments or programs can be calculated from outcome data. Such information allows the administrator to make rational planning and budgeting decisions (e.g. Binner et al., 1973).

THE RESEARCHER AS USER

A viable CIS should serve the needs of researchers as well as clinicians and administrators. Clinical research can be divided into two basic functions: (1) program evaluation and (2) long-term psychotherapy research. There are at least three different approaches to program evaluation: (1) structure, (2) process, and (3) outcome (Donabedian, 1966). Structure evaluations assess programs on the basis of structural variables such as staff/patient ratios. The assumption is that treatment efficacy is directly related to resource allocation. Process evaluation is based on an examination of the adequacy of the delivery of service. In this case, the assumption is that the delivery of acceptable service can serve as a measure of treatment success. Outcome evaluation, in contrast to structure and process evaluation, directly measures the outcome or results of the treatment. Programs can then be compared on the basis of demonstrated results rather than on variables *assumed* to be related to results.

In our view, a CIS should concentrate on outcome evaluation. Structure and process information alone are of little benefit because the link between them and therapeutic effectiveness has not been adequately demonstrated. When outcome information is available, however, questions about *why* some programs or treatments are more effective than others can be investigated.

The long-term goal of psychotherapy research should be to answer the question, "What kind of patient problem is helped by what kind of treatment for what kind of patients?" (Hayes-Roth et al., 1972). Thus an adequate CIS should be capable of collecting information which can be used to investigate this question.

CONFLICT AMONG USERS

As discussed above, different users have different criteria for a CIS. The needs of clinicians, administrators, and researchers are not necessarily incompatible. The solution to the problem is to maximize the overlap among data needs. This can best be done by utilizing the system analysis principle of upward compatability (Edwards and Schmitt, 1974). Upward compatability suggests that once the information to be collected is carefully defined, it can be combined, integrated, aggregated, and generally "massaged" to fulfill many purposes.

The other general principle applicable here is to integrate the system as closely as possible into the ongoing activities of the user. For example, a CIS should be used at case conferences by clinicians. Routine reports should be generated for administrators, and researchers should routinely receive evaluative data.

SUMMARY OF GENERAL CRITERIA

An adequate CIS must serve the needs of clinicians, administrators, and researchers. This means that the system must be upwardly compatible so that the same data source can serve multiple needs. Finally, the system must be integrated as closely as possible into the ongoing activities of the users.

SPECIFIC REQUIREMENTS OF A
CLINICAL INFORMATION SYSTEM

DESCRIPTION OF THE PATIENT

An adequate description of the patient includes: (1) demographic information, (2) information about social functioning, (3) the events leading to hospitalization or referral, (4) past history of hospitalization, and (5) results of psychological and medical tests. The exact information that should be collected is an empirical question, but the criterion for inclusion is that the variable be empirically related to treatment outcome. For example, research has demonstrated that recidivism is related to past history of hospitalization (Anthony and Buell, 1974; Rosenblatt and Mayer, 1974) and the social adjustment of the patient (Miller and Willer, 1976).

TREATMENT PLAN

The treatment plan should describe the "career" path of the patient with a clear and logical link between treatment and problem. A crucial part of the patient's file, then, is a complete list of his problems with the goals and outcome expectations for each problem clearly stated. The link between problem and treatment is important because patients with the same psychiatric diagnosis often have different presenting problems but are given the same treatment. In a study of utilization review procedures, Richman and Pinsker (1973) found that therapists typically assigned all patients to psychotherapy or milieu therapy regardless of diagnosis or chief complaint.

The treatment plan should specify the goals or purpose of treatment so that therapeutic effectiveness can be assessed. To increase reliability, goal outcomes should be described in behavioral terms (Krumboltz, 1966), with different levels of possible outcome stated (Kiresuk and Sherman, 1968).

ASSESSMENT OF TREATMENT EFFICACY

The CIS should monitor progress toward therapeutic goals during treatment, at termination, and after treatment. Most research designs assess outcome at termination only. We argue that continuous monitoring of therapeutic progress is necessary to maximize treatment effectiveness. New approaches can be substituted for ineffective procedures and justified on the basis of results obtained. Follow-up evaluations are necessary because the ultimate criteria of treatment effectiveness are measures of the patient's adjustment and satisfaction in his own environment (McLean and Miles, 1974). Thus, follow-up evaluations should measure how well the patient is functioning in his own environment (Miller and Willer, 1976; Willer and Biggin, 1976).

SUMMARY OF SPECIFIC REQUIREMENTS

An adequate CIS should describe the patient and clearly state the reasons he or she is seeking treatment. There should be a treatment plan for each problem with a clear obtainable goal of treatment. Treatment effectiveness should be assessed in terms of goal attainment during therapy so that treatment can be based on results. Treatment outcome should be assessed after the patient is back in his own environment as well as at termination of therapy.

SOME PRACTICAL SUGGESTIONS FOR MEETING SYSTEM CRITERIA

IDENTIFY INDIVIDUALS

Each individual person who enters the information system must be uniquely identified; otherwise the system may not be able to distinguish between *events* and *people*. For example, consider the case of the psychiatric hospital with 700 new admissions and 800 readmissions in a one-year period. These statistics give no information about the distribution of readmissions, so that it is impossible to determine if one person was readmitted 800 times or 800 people were readmitted once each. Of course, the most likely distribution will be somewhere between these two extremes.

IDENTIFY EVENTS

Each time something happens to an individual, the event should be uniquely recorded. For example, if an individual is given a specific treatment in a program, identifying the patient, the program, the type of treatment, and the date completely specifies that event. The data can then be rearranged to display in a variety of ways such as: (1) the events for each individual, listed chronologically, (2) the services (events) performed by a program by time units, or (3) services provided by type of patient. Note that uniquely specifying events as discussed above means that information is additive, so that a record of each event is kept. Information should only be replaced in an individual's file when incorrect data are corrected or current status information (e.g., address) is required.

COMPUTERIZATION

Although many people assume that an information system is necessarily computerized, many adequate systems are not. The decision to computerize or not is a very complex one, depending upon many factors such as how the data are to be manipulated, the number of variables to be considered, the number of entries, and the quality of the data.

An important consideration to remember is that an adequate manual system can be readily computerized, but computerization will only exaggerate the deficiencies in an inadequate manual system.

CHOOSING DESIGN TEAM

If the decision to develop a computerized system is made, do not let "computerniks" design it. Technically oriented people tend to concentrate on the technical features of the system while ignoring the social or people component. On the other hand, front-line people will likely be unsophisticated in system design and thus minimize the real practical technical problems. The system design team, then, should be composed of system and people experts.

COMMITMENT

An information system must have commitment and nurturance from different levels of the organization. Administrators must be willing to devote resources to design and implementation, while front-line people must be willing to collect data.

MONITOR DATA

There must be a systematic, easy way to monitor the correctness and completeness of the information collected. Since most information systems overlap with another source of information, they can be used to cross-check each other. For example, an information system in a psychiatric hospital (Larkin and Miller, 1975) validates its input data using medical records data in several ways. First, a simple count of the number of admissions and discharges each month by unit is compared to the medical records department records. Discrepancies are easily and quickly corrected, because only a relatively small amount of data is being considered at any time. Internal consistency checks provide a more complete accuracy assessment. One such check is to order all events for each individual in chronological order so that they can be examined for logical consistency. In this case, the first event must be an admission, the next a discharge, and so on. Another simple check is to generate a list of which patients should be in hospital at any given time. This list is then compared to the list of patients on the books.

FLEXIBILITY

Since most information system users do not have a clear idea of what information will be required in the long run, a useful information system must be flexible. Flexibility here means both input and output. Input data should be periodically reviewed so that information that is redundant or not utilized can be eliminated. Also, some information will probably be added over time. In order to reduce inordinate demands for information-gathering, the system might demand that the user pay for increased information, for example, by collecting it.

An information system should also be flexible in its output feedback because different users need to see information packaged in different ways and any user may also need to see different information packages at different times for different purposes. Thus there must be a well-developed "software" package for data feedback that allows information to be readily cross-indexed. For example, one system user might need to know the number of schizophrenic patients admitted at different age levels during a one-year period, while another user might need to know how many schizophrenic patients were admitted from different geographical areas. The system must be able to handle such requests routinely.

Although we have emphasized the importance of flexibility, it is also important to note that some stability is essential. Key definitions and codes cannot change indiscriminantly or continuity across time will be lost. Paradoxically, one strategy to increase stability is to code information in a way that allows maximum flexibility of usage. For example, coding the census tract where a patient lived before admission is much more useful than coding his borough, city, or town because data at the census tract level can be combined into many different geographical areas such as hospital catchment areas, areas of high-density housing or poor neighborhoods as defined by sociodemographic criteria. Keeping the information collected at as fine a level as possible, then, facilitates both flexibility and stability because definitions can be varied to suit different purposes or held constant to assure valid longitudinal comparisons.

ORGANIZATIONAL LEARNING

An adequate information system should facilitate organizational learning. This implies that appropriate feedback is given to key people in the organization and that the information is used for decision-making.

KISS PRINCIPLE

Probably the single most important consideration is to *Keep it Simple, Stupid.* Many system designers make the mistake of expanding an information system in the belief that bigger is better. Increased complexity is usually accompanied by undesirable side effects such as increased errors and increased feedback delay. A much better approach is to design the system in modules or levels. Using this method, each level would be implemented and thoroughly tested before the next, more complex, stage is introduced.

ADMINISTRATIVE VERSUS CLINICAL INFORMATION SYSTEMS

Although administrative and clinical information systems are often considered to be distinct, the dividing line is actually very fuzzy and in many cases may not even exist. In this chapter, we are arguing that the main difference between clinical and administrative systems is in emphasis or point of view. Some of the differences will be outlined below.

UNIT OF ANALYSIS

The usual unit of analysis of a CIS is the individual. The focus of interest is the events and outcomes pertinent to the individual. In an administrative information system (AIS), *aggregates* of individual data are usually required. For example, an AIS might need information about use or outcome of a program within a hospital or a hospital within a health system.

TYPE OF OUTPUT

There is also a shift in the type or level of output. Where a CIS may produce information about therapeutic processes and outcomes, an AIS may be used to compare alternative programs using cost-benefit or cost-effectiveness analyses.

FEEDBACK

A CIS usually needs feedback on a continuing basis so that ongoing events, such as treatment, can be modified for an individual. Usually, however, it is not feasible to provide feedback for quick adjustments to an AIS. There should still be feedback which may result in changes, but the time frame may be different as an AIS may only provide feedback semiannually or annually instead of daily, weekly, or monthly.

A GENERAL MODEL FOR A SOFT DATA INFORMATION SYSTEM

The model, presented in Figure 1, focuses on mental health data and issues. However, the principles can be applied to other "soft" data systems such as welfare and criminal justice. The boxes (1-5) represent steps in the progression of a person through a system from left to right. An individual from the community (1) enters the system, (2) receives some treatment or services (3) from the system, and then is discharged or released (4) back into the community (5) again. Each of the boxes represents a point in time where data may be collected. Since it is impossible to collect all information about an individual, it is necessary to be selective; hence, "data dips" are made into each pool of information.

The pool of data for box 1 is the client's community. Information about the community can be found from many sources including census and sociological surveys. The information at dip 2 is about the client. It can be gathered in a variety of ways, including asking the client, psychological testing, and records about the client. Program information, box 3, focuses on what was done to or for the individual. Medical records, nursing notes, case conferences, goal-oriented records, or problem-oriented records would all be sources of data. Discharge information, box 4, is about the client with an emphasis on information relevant to discharge status. Finally, box 5, community, focuses on the level of functioning of the client in his own environment as opposed to within the program framework.

The differences in emphasis between clinical and administrative information systems are readily apparent in the model. The focus of interest for most CIS's is on parts 2 through 5, with an emphasis on 3, while 1 is largely ignored. While an AIS might encompass all five parts, the emphasis would probably be on parts 2 and 4, with few resources devoted to gathering information about epidemiological variables (1), treatment processes (3), or ultimate outcome (5).

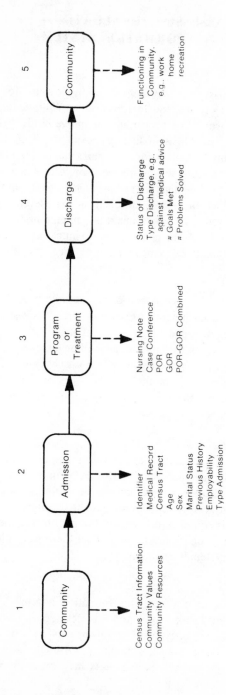

Figure 1: DATA DIP SYSTEM FOR A CLINICAL OR ADMINISTRATIVE INFORMATION SYSTEM

ASSESSING (EVALUATING)
AN INFORMATION SYSTEM

APPROPRIATENESS

An information system may be adequately designed for one application but completely inadequate for another. While we have argued that a good CIS would meet most administrative needs, the reverse is not true. That is, an AIS is of little value to clinicians. However, it should also be pointed out that for some particular and limited administrative data requirements, it may not be feasible to design a complete system. The first (and perhaps last) step would be to set up that part of the system for which there is commitment at some level. For example, some administratively useful data might be gathered using management resources without involving clinicians and clinical data. If and when there is commitment at different levels, the system could be expanded.

DATA COLLECTION

Does the system have an operationally defined procedure for collecting the required information? Collection procedures should specify which data are desirable and which are essential.

Other considerations are more mundane but nonetheless important, such as: (1) whether the forms are clear and easy to use, (2) whether one person is assigned to monitor the accuracy and completeness of data, and (3) whether there is a systematic, simple way to monitor and correct input data.

DATA FEEDBACK

Data feedback is essential if the system is to remain viable. Thus, one should ask questions, such as: (1) Do the people who provide the information get accurate, timely, and relevant information? (2) Is there a systematic routine for feedback or does it require a special request each time? (3) Is someone responsible for monitoring the impact of feedback? If the feedback has no impact on the organization, perhaps the information system is irrelevant.

COST

Can the organization afford the information system? A good information system may take some time to develop and will be fairly expensive. Although money spent on information may be a bargain in the long term, there is such a thing as information overload. The information system as well as the users may suffer from too much information, which may have been gathered for its own sake. Thus, a clear conception of what data are required and the resources that can be allocated to an information system is required.

USING A CLINICAL INFORMATION SYSTEM

The following is an example of the use of the clinical information system by a program management committee made up of clinical staff on a psychiatric unit. This unit had previously introduced a computer-assisted problem-oriented record.

The committee was concerned about the use of certain therapeutic programs offered on the unit. More specifically, it was concerned about the utilization of the primary interventions available: group therapy, individual therapy, family therapy, and occupational therapy. The concern was based upon consideration for the effective use of time and resources on the unit.

The first and most obvious piece of information required was the number of patients being treated through each of the intervention procedures. The committee found that occupational therapy was utilized by 84 percent of the patients on the unit compared with 80 percent for group therapy, 32 percent for individual therapy, and only 12 percent for family therapy. It was quite apparent that most patients in occupational therapy were also receiving group therapy; however, a second run-through of the data revealed that persons receiving individual therapy never received family therapy.

The concerns of the committee shifted to the question of why certain therapies were selected and how successful these therapeutic interventions were.

The record system they had developed subdivided problems into problem areas (relations with family, interpersonal skills, psychopathology, use of leisure time, and occupational readiness). In reviewing which problem areas characterized patients in certain therapies, they found that group therapy patients were most likely to have problems of psychopathology and, secondarily, problems of interpersonal skills. The same was true for individual therapy and occupational therapy. Family therapy dealt primarily with problems of relationships with family, and, secondarily with interpersonal skills. This raised a number of issues for the committee; for example, it was apparent that group therapy and individual therapy were dealing with the same type of patient, while occupational therapy did not seem to be dealing with the patients most in need of occupational therapy (i.e., with problems associated with occupational readiness).

Another concern of the committee was the effectiveness of the various therapeutic interventions. They hoped, for example, that by examining success rates they could develop more systematic procedures for utilization of the various therapy interventions. The committee found that the group therapy was most effective in dealing with interpersonal skills, while individual therapy (especially in combination with psychotropic drugs) was more appropriate in dealing with psychopathology. Family therapy seemed well-established at dealing with relations with family, while occupational therapy was found to be not particularly successful at dealing with any problem areas. (The committee determined that occupational therapy looked less effective than it probably was because the majority of patients had problem areas which were inappropriate to the type of intervention offered in occupational therapy.) As a result of the information produced by the CIS, the committee decided that more rigid guidelines be established for referral to any one of the therapeutic interventions. For example, it was necessary to have specific problems in the occupational readiness category before a patient could be referred to occupational therapy. Similarly, a patient had to have problems in the area of interpersonal skills before referral could be made to group therapy.

As a result of the questions posed by the program committee and the availability of data on individual clients, it was possible to redesign the entire internal referral process. This committee found, like most committees dealing with an automated system, that when you ask one question the answer invariably leads to numerous other questions. This brief example of the use of the clinical information system did not outline all the possible questions and answers raised by the committee. The example, however, does point out the usefulness of readily available information, especially when the information includes some form of evaluation of treatment outcome as is possible in the computerization of the problem-oriented medical record.

USING AN ADMINISTRATIVE
INFORMATION SYSTEM

An example of the use of an AIS as an aid to practical decision-making will be given below. The example is a description of how an administrator actually made use of an AIS in operation at his psychiatric hospital.

The required information concerned a proposed change in catch-ment area between two psychiatric hospitals. The proposed change was that a city borough (borough X) would be transferred from hospital A to hospital B. The administrator at hospital A wanted information from an AIS to help him determine some of the implications of the proposed change.

The first and most obvious piece of information required was the number of patients the proposed change would involve. Since patient records were not coded by borough, the information would be difficult to get from the medical record. However, the census tract of every patient admitted to the hospital was recorded on the AIS. Thus, it was a relatively easy task to determine whether a patient came from the borough in question or not. The number and proportion of admissions from the borough were calculated for a year.

In the one-year period examined, there were 259 (simulated data) admissions from borough X out of a total of 2,519 admissions. Borough X, then, was responsible for about 10 percent (259/2519) of all admissions to hospital A.

The administrator of hospital A now had an accurate assessment of the number of patients that would go to hospital B. With other things being equal, he could also make a rational decision about how many staff should go to hospital B.

However, other things are seldom equal in mental health. The catchment area of hospital A is very diverse, and previous research had shown that there are differences in hospital usage as a function of geographic origin. Thus, it is possible that the patients to be transferred to hospital A were atypical on some important dimension. For example, some patients are more likely to stay for a long time once admitted, while others are likely to stay only long enough to resolve a personal crisis and return to the community. What was required, then, was a reasonable estimate of the staff resources needed to service the patients from borough X.

The practical question is, "Do the patients from borough X require more hospital resources than other patients?" The most direct approach to answering the question is to compare the length of stay and read-mission rates of these patients with other patients. The comparison showed that the patients from borough X were indistinguishable from other patients in terms of length of stay and readmission rates.

In this case, then, other things were equal, so that the proportion of patients from borough X could serve as an estimate of the staff resources required to service these patients.

In summary, the relatively simple analyses of information in the AIS revealed how many patients would be transferred from hospital A to hospital B and gave an estimate of the hospital resources required by these patients. This information then allowed the hospital administrator to decide how many staff should go to hospital B along with the patients from borough X.

The details of the move were negotiated between the two hospital administrators, and the transfer has since been completed.

SUMMARY

We have presented some of the general and specific criteria for information systems in mental health. The user orientation of these systems was emphasized, and criteria were established on the basis of the needs of each of the potential users: clinicians, administrators, and researchers. Some general principles for development and operation were also discussed, including the need to evaluate treatment and provide meaningful feedback to information providers, and the need to keep the system simple. It is suggested that the information system should be evaluated on the degree to which users' needs are met and also on the basis of cost. Finally, some examples of information system applications were presented.

REFERENCES

Anthony, W. A. and G. J. Buell. Predicting psychiatric rehabilitation outcome using demographic characteristics: A replication. *Journal of Counseling Psychology,* 1974, 21: 421-422.

Binner, P. R., J. Halpern, and A. Potter. Patients, programs, and results in a comprehensive mental health center. *Journal of Consulting and Clinical Psychology,* 1973, 41: 148-156.

Donabedian, A. Evaluating the quality of medical care. *Milbank Memorial Fund Quarterly,* 1966, 44: 166-206.

Edwards, C. N. and P. P. Schmitt. Case-oriented information systems: Methodological problems and some simple solutions. *Evaluation,* 1974, 2: 65-67.

Hayes-Roth, F., R. Longabaugh, and R. S. Ryback. The problem-oriented medical record and psychiatry. *British Journal of Psychiatry,* 1972, 121: 27-34.

Guttentag, M. and E. L. Struening. (eds.) *Handbook of Evaluation Research,* Vol. 2. Beverly Hills, Ca.: Sage, 1975.

Kiresuk, T. J. and R. E. Sherman. Goal attainment scaling: A general method for evaluating comprehensive community mental health programs. *Community Mental Health Journal,* 1968, 4: 443-453.

Krumboltz, J. D. Behavioral goals for counseling. *Journal of Counseling Psychology,* 1966, 13: 153-159.

Larkin, J. and G. H. Miller. Automated data system for monitoring psychiatric in-patient services. In B. Willer, G. H. Miller, and L. Cantrell (eds.) *Information and Feedback for Evaluation,* Vol. 1. Toronto: York University, 1975.

Levin, H. M. Cost effectiveness in evaluation research. In M. Guttentag and E. L. Struening (eds.) *Handbook of Evaluation Research,* Volume 2. Beverly Hills: Sage Publications, 1975.

McLean, P. D. and J. E. Miles. Evaluation and the problem-oriented record. *Archives of General Psychiatry,* 1974, 31: 622-627.

Miller, G. H. and B. Willer. Predictors of return to a psychiatric hospital. *Journal of Consulting and Clinical Psychology,* 1976, 44: 898-900.

Miller, G. H. and B. Willer. An information system for clinical recording, administrative decision making, evaluation and research. *Community Mental Health Journal,* in press.

Richman, A. and H. Pinsker. Utilization review of psychiatric inpatient care. *American Journal of Psychiatry,* 1973, 130: 900-903.

Rosenblatt, A. and J. E. Mayer. Patients who return: A consideration of some neglected influences. *Journal of the Bronx State Hospital,* 1974, 2: 71-81.

Willer, B. and P. Biggin. Comparison of rehospitalized and nonrehospitalized psychiatric patients on community adjustment: Self assessment guide. *Psychiatry,* 1976, 39: 239-244.

Willer, B. and E. Stasiak. Automated nursing notes in a psychiatric institution. *Journal of Psychiatric Nursing and Mental Health Services,* 1973, 11: 27-29.

Wilson, N. C. Treatment goal setting and attainment: Staff, patient and community viewpoints. Paper presented at the twenty-second Institute on Hospital and Community Psychiatry, Philadelphia, Pennsylvania, September 21-24, 1970.

It has been repeatedly mentioned that evaluation research aims to account for the manner and extent to which a particular program produced the measured outcomes. Benefit cost analysis attempts to place dollar values on the program (i.e., costs) and the outcomes (i.e., benefits). Using a discount rate which represents the rate-of-return if the funds had been otherwise invested, a measure of efficiency is generated.

This chapter addresses the major tasks in conducting benefit cost analysis. It deals with the issues in computing costs and benefits as well as the implications of using different discount rates. The strengths and weaknesses of using alternative approaches to benefit cost analysis are also discussed.

Benefit cost analysis is often conducted without having a research design which yields relatively unequivocal and unbiased causal inferences about the program's effects. Data from an ongoing information system or one-shot surveys have been used in conjunction with administrative records to yield cost benefit ratios. In other words, in these instances, the computed benefits cannot be assumed to result from the program. Ideally, benefit cost analysis would be based upon a well-designed study which would allow for relatively strong causal inferences about the program's impact on the measured benefits.

9

BENEFIT COST EVALUATION

M. Andrieu

INTRODUCTION

The widespread use of benefit cost analysis for the evaluation of public programs is a relatively recent development. It is closely related to changes which have taken place in the decision-making process in government over the last fifteen years, as well as to the increasing involvement of government in such areas as education, manpower, health, social services, and income maintenance.

Economists usually define economics as the study of the allocation of scarce resources to satisfy human wants within a given time frame. Benefit cost analysis (hereafter referred to as B/C analysis) is an application of economics for determining the efficient use of resources in all sections of the economy. Its main objective is to identify and quantify program effects or "benefits" and compare them with program costs. Overall, if the benefits exceed the costs, the well-being of the community is expected to increase as a result of the program.[1] When alternative programs are compared, the magnitude of the estimates of net benefits obtained for each program provides a criterion for choice.

B/C analysis is suitable for the evaluation of programs for which economic considerations are important and the benefits can be quantified. For instance, B/C analysis has been used in areas as diverse as public works, flood control, manpower training, education, and disease prevention. In all these cases, the problem was to determine if the benefits derived from the program (in terms of increased output or resources saved) have been worth the cost of resources used.

B/C analysis is not a complete approach to program evaluation. It is only one piece of evidence in the evaluation of process which should be complemented by noneconomic considerations to give a more comprehensive assessment of the program under study. In some cases, economic considerations may be insignificant and the use of B/C analysis considered unnecessary.

In many social programs, it is virtually impossible to quantify the expected benefits (e.g., improved mental health, reduced child abuse, or resolved marital crises). In these instances, *cost-effectiveness analysis* can be used to ascertain the most appropriate program alternative for achieving a given nonquantifiable outcome. However, it is worth pointing out that in the last analysis the decision maker must make a *quantitative* choice (i.e., how much resources to allocate to improve mental health as compared to reduced child abuse).

B/C analysis can be carried out either ex ante (i.e., before the operation of the program) or ex post (after the program has been in operation for some time). The purpose of ex ante analysis is usually to provide policy makers with appropriate evidence for choosing between alternative proposals. An important part of the exercise in fact is the formulation of meaningful alternatives. The role of ex post analysis (which can be conducted on a continuing basis) is to determine whether the allocation of resources has indeed been correctly made and to help identify what modifications, if any, are required for improving the program.

Although they serve different purposes, both the ex ante and ex post approaches have many common features and can be discussed simultaneously. The process includes the following steps;

- Definition of objectives (ex ante and ex post)
- Identification of guiding principles (ex ante)
- Identification of alternatives (ex ante)
- Listing of costs (ex ante and ex post)
- Listing of benefits (ex ante and ex post)
- Quantification of costs and benefits (ex ante and ex post)
- Calculation of estimators (ex ante and ex post)

- Listing of assumptions (ex ante and ex post)
- Interpretation of results and recommendations (ex ante and ex post)

As can be seen from the above list, the major difference between the ex ante and ex post approaches is that the identification of guiding principles and alternatives is not part of the ex post analysis. However, this is not always the case. If the program under investigation is found wanting, the mandate of the analyst may be to find alternatives to the existing program. This is rarely done in practice. Instead, the usual concern in this case is to improve the program or reduce its scope.

This chapter gives a general introduction to B/C analysis as a tool for program evaluation using manpower training for illustration purposes. The following two sections deal with the general methodology of estimating costs and benefits. The next section describes three alternative techniques to summarize the results of the B/C analysis, taking into consideration the influence of time. Finally, the conclusion examines some of the criticisms which have been raised against B/C and practical problems faced by the analyst in his work.

ESTIMATES OF COSTS IN BENEFIT COST ANALYSIS

In the estimation of costs, it is important to keep in mind that the purpose of the evaluation is to measure the change, if any, in the well-being of citizens from one particular use of resources (the program under consideration) compared to an alternative use (other programs) of the same resources. This implies that costs will be measured as foregone opportunities rather than in terms of historical outlays of money. However, this is overly simplified because there may be opportunities foregone by using the same budgetary resources in one program rather than another. It is for this reason that both opportunity and budgetary costs are considered in B/C analysis.

In the case of manpower training, for instance, a number of different costs have been identified: course purchase costs, commuting and travel costs, living-away-from-home allowances, trainees' out-of-pocket expenses, departmental overhead, the cost of production foregone, and training allowances (i.e., income maintenance allowances). Among these costs, all those costs which involve pecuniary flows or redistribution of funds from taxpayers to trainees or other parties associated with training (i.e., teachers, administrators, etc.) will be classified as *bud-*

getary costs. Economic costs, on the other hand, will be those costs associated with foregone production.

From the above list, only out-of-pocket expenses and foregone production are purely economic costs. Both of these costs do not represent a transfer or a redistribution of funds from taxpayers to those associated with trainees and, hence, they are not budgetary costs. On the other hand, income, maintenance, commuting, travel, and living-away-from-home allowances all represent flows of funds from taxpayers to those linked to training, without any element of production foregone. They are therefore purely budgetary costs.

A third category which has both economic and budgetary elements associated with it includes course purchase and departmental overhead costs. These are included as budgetary cost because they involve a pecuniary flow from taxpayers to individuals associated with the training. They are also included as economic costs because foregone opportunities are associated with the particular use made of these resources.

In classifying costs as either economic or budgetary, one must be very careful about the implicit assumptions used. For example, suppose one were concerned with examining only the economic costs associated with training. From the discussion above, salaries of civil servants and teachers would be part of economic costs because they are elements of departmental overhead and course purchase costs. However, if the civil servants and teachers would have been unemployed in the absence of the training program, their opportunity cost would be zero rather than the value of their salaries. To use estimates of budgetary costs as a proxy for economic costs in this case would clearly overestimate the economic costs.

ESTIMATION OF BENEFITS

In the previous section, it was pointed out that in estimating costs one should keep in mind that the goal of the evaluation is to measure the marginal contribution of the program to welfare. The same marginal principle applies for the estimation of benefits. The benefits from the program will therefore be equal to the difference between ouput with the program, and output without the program. In most cases, benefits defined in this manner cannot be measured directly. Techniques which can be used to overcome this problem will be discussed. However, at this point attention will be paid to the identification of benefits for manpower training.

Many economic benefits can be conceptually associated with manpower training programs. For example, training can result in a reduction in the mismatching between people and jobs and can contribute to improving the allocation of labor resources. This improved allocation will result in increased potential output. From a dynamic point of view, this should result in higher rates of economic growth, improved price stability, and lower rates of unemployment.

It is important to point out, however, that these benefits will materialize only if the program does in fact contribute to a better allocation of resources, but this is not always the case. The program can be misused by individuals who have no intention of working after training but are attracted by the income maintenance provided through training allowances. In contrast to abuses of income maintenance programs such as welfare or unemployment insurance benefits (which are merely transfer payments), in the case of training, there is the additional misuse of the resources required to conduct the course. Clearly, if it were possible to identify the abuser "a priori," it would have been more efficient to give the income maintenance in an alternative form to the "abuser" (who may have very legitimate needs for income maintenance) and let another person genuinely interested in being retrained take advantage of the training seat purchased under the program.

The program can also be wasteful if trainees are trained for non-demand occupations. If this is the case, there is a strong possibility that they will not be able to find a stable and satisfying job after training, or that they will displace workers already employed. In both cases, there are clearly no benefits from the program, although there is still an economic cost in terms of resources used. This implies that the success of the program depends on an assessment of the training needs of the potential trainees that is based on a correct estimation of future labor market demands. Unfortunately, the prediction of labor demand is not an easy task. It depends on many complex factors, such as the demand for final goods and services at home and abroad, the technical conditions of production and technological change, as well as on labor legislation and regulations.

In addition to its impact on the allocation of resources and on output, the program can also affect the distribution of income. The primary effect is a redistribution from general taxpayers who bear the financial costs to trainees who reap the benefits. To the extent that the geographical distribution of trainees and taxpayers is different, this may also lead to a net redistribution from certain regions of low unemployment to those of high unemployment. This net transfer can be considered as approximately equal to the amount received by the trainees minus the income support (such as welfare or unemployment insurance benefits) they would have received if they had not undertaken training.

The program has a number of additional secondary effects. Some of these effects, however, become rapidly untractable. To the extent that trainees will become gainfully employed after training, the tax burden of other taxpayers will be lightened. If another worker becomes employed as a result of the trainee leaving a job to enter training, then this other worker will indirectly benefit from the program. On the other hand, if workers are displaced by trainees and become unemployed, they will be indirect victims of the program. Furthermore, the impact of training on relative wages will also have distributional effects among workers and other socioeconomic groups. If, for instance, training increases the supply of workers in one particular occupation, this may result in a reduced "real" wage for workers already in the occupation, who will therefore suffer indirectly from the program. On the other hand, employers and possibly consumers will benefit.

As can be seen from the above discussion, the distributional effects are quite complex and difficult to predict. However, it is important to take them into consideration in order to analyze the social impact of the program.

Another important factor in evaluation is to assess the role of the federal government in training. Even if we are able to ascertain from such analysis that manpower training is indeed a successful program, it still remains to be determined *what difference* is made by the program. One could very well argue, for instance, that various mechanisms already exist in the labor market to reduce skill-related mismatchings between jobs and people. The general education system contributes to the upgrading of skills by offering technical courses. Moreover, training is provided in the private sector, where many employers offer some form of training to their staff. A number of private institutions give labor market-related courses. Finally, immigration provides an alternative supply channel for skilled workers and university graduates.

In light of the complex issues raised above, the objective of most B/C models developed for the evaluation of manpower training is relatively modest. In general, the only benefits considered are the increase in the lifetime earnings of trainees as a result of training. In what follows, we shall examine how these benefits are quantified and how benefit-cost estimates are obtained.

The quantification of benefits is probably the most difficult aspect of the B/C analysis. The basic problem is to determine what value should be attached to the "output" of the program.

If the output produced by the program is sold, market prices could be used to estimate the value. Strictly speaking, this should be done only in the case when it can be assumed that the economy approaches a state of perfectly competitive equilibrium. However, this is not very often the case in practice. If the output is sold under some degree of monopolistic conditions, the use of market prices may indeed over-estimate the benefits.

In many cases, however, the output of the program under study is a public good which is not sold in the market. In this case, some imputation must be made to attach some value to the output. The imputed value is what economists call *shadow prices.* These shadow prices are based on the added estimated value resulting from the particular public good. For instance, the value of a dam could be measured in terms of the resulting reduction in flood damage and the increased crop production which can be obtained through irrigation. As well, the value of a new bridge could be measured in the corresponding reduction in transportation costs.

In some cases, an estimate of the value of a public good can be obtained by determining how much users would be willing to pay for an equivalent service. This approach can be used, for instance, to estimate the benefits obtained from the development of recreational areas. The imputation can be estimated on the basis of the fee charged in similar commercial parks. A similar approach could be used for a large number of social services (legal aid, day care centers, and so on).

In some instances, it is not possible to attach a value to the program's output, such as national defense. In this case, the benefit part of the B/C analysis breaks down. However, the analysis can still be valuable to the extent that it informs the decision maker about the social cost that can be attached to a given level of expenditure on military equipment.

Even when a quantification technique has been selected for the benefits, some further adjustments are still required to satisfy the marginal approach of B/C analysis. As pointed out earlier, benefits should be measured as the difference between total output with the program and total output without the program. This with/without approach cannot often be used in practice. Two alternatives are open to the analyst. First, he can use a "before-and-after approach" and base his evaluation on longitudinal data. Second, he can use a control group. In general, this second approach is to be preferred whenever possible. Unfortunately, this is not always the case in practice, as the use of control group can cause serious administrative and ethical problems.

In the case of training, the before-and-after approach is commonly used. The earning differential estimates are based on information on pre and post training earnings and labor force experience. This is usually obtained from administrative forms and follow-up surveys.

In determining earnings, a distinction is made between wage and employability. Employability is defined as the number of weeks an individual has been employed over a given period of time as a percentage of the total number of weeks in the labor force over the same period of time. If, for instance, a particular individual has been employed twenty weeks, unemployed five weeks and out of the labor force for twenty-seven weeks (e.g., going to school) over the last year, his employability would be equal to .80 (20/25). If we call Y yearly earnings, W the weekly wage, E the employability, and P the labor force participation rate, then yearly earnings can be expressed as:

$$Y = P.E.W. 52$$

In our example, the labor force participation rate is equal to .48 (i.e., 25/52). With a weekly wage of $100, for instance, the yearly income is equal to:

$$Y = .48 \times .8 \times 100 \times 52$$
$$= \$1,997$$

It is assumed in the model that training can increase the wage received by the trainee, increase his employability, or increase both. Separate estimates are made for those two effects. Pre-training wage and employability are the basis for estimates of wage and employability without training. Post-training wage and employability obtained from follow-up surveys provide estimates of wage and employability with training.

Wage and employability differential can be computed at a follow-up date, such as three months. The resulting yearly earning differential is assumed to remain constant for the remaining working life of the trainee. It is adjusted, however, for life expectancy and expected labor force participation. In the computation, the pre-training wage should be adjusted for age increment, inflation, and seasonality to make it comparable to any follow-up survey post-training wage. Pre-training employability is projected in a similar manner, adjusting for change in age, in seasonability, and in unemployment rate. The projected figures can then be compared to the post-training data to obtain estimates of wage and employability differentials. The adjustments required for the projections are based on the results of a statistical analysis (multiple regression) on the pre-training data base file. In these regressions, wage and employability are treated as variables to be explained by the personal and labor force characteristics of the trainees.

CALCULATION OF THE BENEFIT-COST ESTIMATORS

The benefit-cost estimator is the key figure which summarizes the results of the analysis and which will be used for decision-making. This estimator is a numerical value generated from one of the alternative B/C techniques. Particular attention must therefore be given in its computation, and its limitations must be clearly pointed out to senior management.

One basic problem in the computation of estimators is the commensurability problem. For example, benefits and costs may not be directly comparable because they occur at different points in time. In the case of training, for instance, costs are borne during training while benefits are assumed to span over the remaining working life of the trainees. Another commensurability problem arises from a fact already pointed out—namely, that public programs often have important income redistribution effects. If the costs are not borne by those individuals receiving the benefits, then they are not strictly speaking comparable unless one is prepared to make interpersonal comparisons of utility or satisfaction. This is precisely what must be done, for instance, in the establishment of an income tax system. In most studies, some attempts are made to cope with the time commensurability problem, but the distributional problem is often left unsolved. This results in the implicit assumption that one dollar to cost bearers has the same value as one dollar to benefit recipients. In what follows, only the time problem will be discussed.

In order to put all costs and benefits on the same time basis, it is necessary to establish a discount rate which will be used to compute the present value of future flows of costs or benefits. The need to compute present values can be illustrated by a simple example. Suppose an individual is given the choice between $1,000 today or $1,000 a year from now. Suppose further that the individual has the possibility of depositing his money in a savings account at 10 percent. Clearly the individual would be better off to choose $1,000 today, since it will be worth $1,100 a year from now. Alternatively, $1,000 a year from now is only worth $909.1 today since $909.1 placed at 10 percent would give $1,000 a year from now.

In comparing different alternative scenarios, it is important to make sure that the same discount rates are used. In what follows, three possible approaches will be given: (1) the present value of net benefit approach; (2) the benefit-cost approach; and (3) the rate of return approach.

In the present value of net benefits approach, net benefits (benefits minus costs) are computed for each year and discounted to the present. The sum of these discounted net benefits over all year reflect the present value of the project. This present value can be positive, negative, or equal to zero. The various projects or alternative scenarios can be ranked according to the magnitude of their present value, and a choice can be made on this basis. It is important to keep in mind, however, that the calculated present value depends on the discount rate chosen. The higher the rate, the lower will be the present value. A change in the rate of discount may not only affect the size of the present value but also in some cases the ranking of the projects. A sensitivity analysis may be required to check the robustness of the obtained ranking. Overall, the present value of net benefits approach is probably the best of the three, especially in ex ante studies, when ranking of alternative scenarios is required.

In the benefit-cost ratio approach, the sum of the discounted benefits is divided by the sum of the discounted cost. The benefit cost ratio gives the average payoff per dollar spent on the program. As the present value of net benefits, the value of the benefit-cost ratio depends on the rate of discount used in the analysis. In addition, the benefit-cost ratio will also depend on how benefits and costs are treated. To illustrate this point, let us consider an example. Suppose that using the methodology described above, an average cost of $2,000 and an average benefit of $6,000 have been obtained for a particular group of trainees. The benefit-cost ratio for the group will therefore be equal to 3. Suppose that the $2,000 of cost includes $200 for the social cost of production foregone. We have chosen in the model to include the net value of this cost (i.e., the production foregone by the trainee while on training minus the contribution of the previously unemployed worker who replaces him in his pre-training job). Another perfectly legitimate approach would have been to count the gross value of the production foregone by the trainee for the full duration of training (say $2,000) among the costs and include the contribution to output during the

training period of the previously unemployed worker among the benefits (say $1,800). In this case, the total benefits would be $7,800
(6,000 + 1,800), while the costs would amount to $3,800 (2,000 +
2,000 - 200). The benefit-cost ratio would now be about 2.1
instead of 3. It is not advisable therefore to use the benefit-cost ratio
approach when one wants to rank projects. It is quite acceptable,
however, in ex post benefit-cost evaluation, where the major concern is
to assess the profitability of a particular use of resources and to
determine if indeed the ratio is larger than one. Another limitation of
the B/C ratio approach is that it does not give any indication of the
total magnitude of the net benefits to be expected.

The third approach is to calculate the rate of return for every project
or alternative scenario, rather than using an arbitrarily chosen rate of
return. This rate of return is defined as being the particular value of the
discount rate which will equate the present value of costs with the
present value of benefits. Since the flow of benefits occurs after the
costs have been borne, it makes sense intuitively that the higher the
benefits relative to the costs, the higher the rate of return will have to
be to equate discounted benefits to discounted costs. The main advantage of this approach is that it does not require the definition of a
rate of discount. Moreover, the value of the rate of return is independent of the way benefits and costs are treated. It appears, therefore, to be a desirable approach for the ranking of projects in ex ante
evaluations. In some cases, however, because of the nature of the
stream of costs and benefits, several discount rates may be found for a
given project which equate the present value of benefits to the present
value of costs. If this occurs, the present value of net benefits approach
is to be recommended. Another drawback of the rate of return approach is that it does not provide any information on the size of the net
benefits.

If the benefit-cost ratio technique is used, a ratio can be computed
for each individual trainee. Its value can be either positive, null, or
negative. However, because of random errors, individual benefit-cost
ratios are usually not very significant. Furthermore, they are not very
useful for policy decision. More important information required by
senior management is the relative payoffs obtained for various training
courses purchased and some indication of what category of trainees
seem to have benefitted most from the program. For this purpose,
overall benefit-cost ratios should be computed for each type of training
course. These results can then be used as an input in deciding which
training courses should be purchased.

Some care must be taken in the computation of aggregate benefit-cost ratios. A relatively common mistake made by inexperienced analysts when trying to estimate the benefit-cost ratio for a group of individuals (e.g., all individuals who have taken the same course) is to take the average of all individual ratios. This approach is incorrect. One should take instead the sum of all benefits over the sum of all costs or, alternatively, the average benefit over all individuals in the group divided by the corresponding average cost.

CONCLUSION

The main objective of this chapter has been to provide an introduction to B/C evaluation and to illustrate the technique with manpower training. In conclusion, I would like to examine some of the criticisms which have been raised over the years by economists and noneconomists alike and discuss some of the practical problems that the analyst may face in his or her work.

Two major criticisms have been made by economists about the B/C approach. The first is related to the quantification problem, and the second to the commensurability problem, discussed earlier. Since the technique is essentially based on a comparison of costs and benefits, the critics argue that the approach will give misleading results, if *all* costs and *all* benefits cannot be quantified. The rebuttal to this kind of argument is that the results of the analysis are misleading only if they are not given a proper interpretation. It is the role of the analyst to clearly spell out the limitations of his evaluation, and it is the responsibility of senior management to use it for what it is worth, having been properly warned of those limitations. The same argument applies to the commensurability problem.

An important decision for the analyst in the evaluation is to determine how far he should carry the quantification of benefits. In all cases, the assumptions used for the quantifications should be clearly spelled out, and some indication on the reliability of the estimate should be provided to senior management. Common sense suggests that if the major benefit of the program cannot be quantified with some reasonable degree of reliability, then the B/C approach is inappropriate for the program at hand.

Another question for the analyst is to ascertain to what extent the benefits he has identified and quantified have indeed been "caused" by the program. In the case of training, for instance, many factors other than training affect the income stream of the trainees. It is questionable that the "before and after" technique used can adequately control for these external factors and isolate the impact of training. Again, common sense suggests that if the causality relationship between the benefits and the program has not been clearly ascertained, then further investigation is required before one can have any faith in the results of the analysis.

Criticisms of the approach have also been voiced by noneconomists. Other social scientists show little interest in the technique because they feel that it does not answer the questions of interest to them. Senior management sometimes feels that B/C analysis is costly in terms of data requirements and computer costs. It is also time-consuming. The need for follow-up information imposes a considerable time lag between the time a decision is made to perform the evaluation and the time the results become available. They may indeed come too late for the decision-making process. In many cases, the evaluator has to face the suspicion (sometimes even the hostility) of program managers who feel threatened by the evaluation and who see the gathering of the necessary data as an additional burden.

In response to these criticism, one can only reiterate that the B/C approach is indeed economic in nature. It is not therefore a complete approach to program evaluation. It must be used only in situations where economic factors are important, and it should be supplemented by other forms of evaluations. B/C analysis is indeed costly, time-consuming, and requires a lot of data. It should only be used for large or ongoing programs for which senior management does not need results too quickly.

The importance of a careful interpretation of the benefit-cost results cannot be overemphasized. It is particularly important to consider the results of the analysis in a wider framework to understand what major socioeconomic forces underlie them. For instance, lower benefit-cost ratios for some groups of trainees may point to underlying social problems such as discrimination and job barriers for certain type of workers (e.g., females). In this case, the policy maker must decide on training within an overall manpower strategy designed to improve the operation of labor markets and provide equal opportunity to all workers.

Perhaps the single most important factor in the evaluation is the creation of a proper data base. This is an area where no compromise can be made. No matter how sophisticated the model or ingenious the analyst in cutting corners, his efforts are doomed to failure if he does not work from a reliable data base. Every effort should be made to have a proper validation of the data collected. Usually two approaches for data collections exist. One approach consists in using administrative documents (e.g., trainee registration forms). The second approach consists of collecting data through surveys (e.g., follow-up surveys). Both approaches have advantages and disadvantages. The use of administrative forms is cheap and provides data on the whole population. However, it increases the workload of program managers. As a consequence, the quality of the data collected may be poor or incomplete, and in general the analyst has no authority to obtain a proper validation of the data. The analyst has more control over surveys and more freedom to ask specific questions which interest him. However, surveys are costly and in general information can only be obtained from a small fraction of the population. In light of my personal experience in this matter, I am inclined to feel that relevant information obtained from surveys of a carefully selected sample may be better (and less costly overall to collect and manipulate) than poor data on the whole population obtained from administrative forms with little or no quality control.

NOTE

1. In many cases those groups who bear the costs of the program will not reap the benefits. To determine whether or not the benefits exceed the costs involves in this case an interpersonal comparison of utility.

INDEX

ABOUT THE EDITOR AND AUTHORS

LEONARD RUTMAN is Associate Professor in the School of Social Work at Carleton University in Ottawa. He received his B.A. and M.S.W. from the University of Manitoba, and his Ph.D. from the University of Minnesota. He has previously worked as a teacher at the University of Winnipeg, and as director of the Windsor Park Information and Resource Center, also in Winnipeg. He is author of *Day Care Services in Manitoba* (1971) and (with Dick De Jong) *Federal Level Evaluation* (1976), and editor of *Drugs: Use and Abuse* (1969).

JOSEPH S. WHOLEY is Senior Research Staff Member of the Urban Institute, and the author of *Federal Evaluation Policy.* He previously served as director of program evaluation for the Office of the Secretary of Health, Education and Welfare, where he was responsible for developing systems and plans for evaluating the costs and benefits of HEW programs and for assisting DHEW agencies in the construction of specific program evaluations. He has had extensive experience in local government and is presently working on a book entitled "Making Government Work: Evaluation and Effective Government."

JOE HUDSON received his Ph.D. from the University of Minnesota in sociology and social work. He is presently Director of the Victim Services Division for the Minnesota Department of Corrections. Previously he worked with the Department as director of comprehensive planning and director of research and planning. He is co-author of *Considering the Victim* (1975); *Community Corrections: Selected Readings* (1976); and *Restitution in Criminal Justice* (1977), and the author of numerous articles in the areas of restitution and evaluation which have appeared in scientific and professional journals.

THOMAS D. COOK is Professor of Psychology at Northwestern University. He is on the editorial boards of the *Journal of Personality and Social Psychology,* the *Journal of Personality,* and *Evaluation Magazine.*

His major research interests are social science methodology, the utilization of social science research, and the effects of unplanned social interventions. In addition to numerous journal articles and book chapters, his books include *"Sesame Street" Revisited* (1975) and *The Design and Conduct of Quasi-Experiments and True Experiments in Field Settings* (forthcoming).

FAY LOMAX COOK is Assistant Professor in the School of Social Work at Loyola University of Chicago. She received her Ph.D. from the University of Chicago in 1977. Her research interests are in the field of aging in the life cycle, differences in public support of various groups on welfare, and policy analysis. She is the author of "Differences in Public Support for Sevel Social Welfare Groups: Description and Explanation," a research report for the National Opinion Research Center, and of articles published in the *Social Service Review* and *The Gerontologist*. She has contributed to Emilio Viano's *Victims and Society* (1976).

MELVIN M. MARK is a Ph.D. candidate in social psychology at Northwestern University. He is currently conducting research on the effects of the economy on social interaction, on the effects of the introduction of television on social and political integration, and on relative deprivation.

ROBERT F. BORUCH is Director of the Methodology and Evaluation Research Division and Professor in the Department of Psychology of Northwestern University. He is also currently President of the Council for Applied Social Research. He is co-author of *Social Experimentation* and an editor of *Experimental Tests of Public Policy*. He has published numerous journal articles dealing with methodological, managerial, and ethical problems in research. He is a member of advisory panels of the National Academy of Sciences, the American Psychological Association, and he consults frequently with federal agencies on research planning and design.

DAVID RINDSKOPF is currently a Postdoctoral Fellow in the Methodology and Evaluation Research Division of the Department of Psychology of Northwestern University. He received his B.S., M.S., and Ph.D. degrees from Iowa State University.

GEORGE W. FAIRWEATHER is Professor of Psychology at Michigan State University. He has had a long-standing interest in mental health, having developed innovative services for patients released from mental hospitals. He has undertaken numerous evaluations of social programs, and a large-scale dissemination experiment. He has published extensively, including such books as *Methods for Experimental Innovation, Community Life for the Mentally Ill,* and *Creating Change in Mental Health Organizations.*

GARY H. MILLER is Assistant Professor in the Department of Psychiatry at McMaster University and a Research Psychologist at the Hamilton Psychiatric Hospital in Hamilton, Ontario. He received his Ph.D. from York University in 1970. He is co-author of *Information and Feedback for Evaluation* and has authored and co-authored numerous articles on evaluation and feedback in people service organizations. His interests are in the teaching of evaluation research methods and in implementation of a management information system for mental health programs.

BARRY WILLER is Assistant Professor of Psychology in the Division of Community Psychiatry at the State University of New York at Buffalo. At present he is directing a study of the impact of deinstitutionalization on the mentally retarded, their families and the community, and a major continuing education program in planning and evaluation for administrators and board members of mental health agencies in western New York. He is co-author of a book entitled *Information* and *Feedback for Evaluation* and has authored numerous articles on evaluation and planning in the human services.

M. ANDRIEU received his Ph. D. in economics from Washington University (St. Louis). He is currently with the Department of Communications of Canada, and his research is in the regulation of common carriers of telecommunication services and the economic problems related to the use of the radio spectrum. He previously taught at the University of Western Ontario and has been employed with the Canadian government since 1972.